mindful
school
communities

♥

The Five Cs of Nurturing
Heart Centered Learning

Christine Mason

Michele M. Rivers Murphy

Yvette Jackson

foreword by Lee Bolman and Terrence E. Deal

Solution Tree | Press

a division of
Solution Tree

555 North Morton Street
Bloomington, IN 47404
800.733.6786 (toll free) / 812.336.7700
FAX: 812.336.7790

email: info@SolutionTree.com
SolutionTree.com

Printed in the United States of America

Library of Congress Cataloging-in-Publication Data

Names: Mason, Christine Y. (Christine Yvonne), 1949- author. | Rivers
    Murphy, Michele M., author. | Jackson, Yvette, author.
Title: Mindful school communities : the five Cs of nurturing heart centered
    learning / Christine Mason, Michele M. Rivers Murphy, Yvette Jackson.
Description: Bloomington, IN : Solution Tree Press, 2020. | Includes
    bibliographical references and index.
Identifiers: LCCN 2019035955 (print) | LCCN 2019035956 (ebook) | ISBN
    9781949539110 (paperback) | ISBN 9781949539127 (ebook)
Subjects: LCSH: Affective education. | School environment. | Behavior
    modification. | Mindfulness (Psychology)
Classification: LCC LB1072 .M369 2020 (print) | LCC LB1072 (ebook) | DDC
    370.15/34--dc23
LC record available at https://lccn.loc.gov/2019035955
LC ebook record available at https://lccn.loc.gov/2019035956

Solution Tree
Jeffrey C. Jones, CEO
Edmund M. Ackerman, President

Solution Tree Press
President and Publisher: Douglas M. Rife
Associate Publisher: Sarah Payne-Mills
Art Director: Rian Anderson
Managing Production Editor: Kendra Slayton
Senior Production Editor: Tonya Maddox Cupp
Content Development Specialist: Amy Rubenstein
Text and Cover Designer: Laura Cox
Editorial Assistant: Sarah Ludwig

Acknowledgments

We each learn about compassion in our own ways. Sometimes it is life's lessons that bring us to our knees. In agony, we may turn to others, or we may turn inward. If we are fortunate, we receive answers that further our own healing, giving us confidence and courage, and helping us open up our own hearts. As humans, no one is immune to suffering, yet we know some have experienced more than their fair share and are more in need and less likely to be resilient. Robert K. Greenleaf (2002) speaks of transforming moments that "may come from anywhere" (p. 341) and be sustained by trust. To those who have aided my healing, helped me learn to trust, and sustained me on my inward journey to understand my heart and theirs, I send my love. To all the children who have been my teachers, to my daughters, my husband, John, and my family: thank you for your patience and guidance as I have learned to value family and to understand that compassion is needed not only for the world and my work, but for those in my inner circle. My love, too, goes to the many students and teachers I have taught over the years for the lessons I learned from your feedback, for the deep heartfelt connections we made, and for those connections that I continue to make. And finally, my thanks to the yogis and philosopher kings and queens, poets, psychologists, and scientists who have deepened my convictions about the need to know our hearts, to speak from our hearts, and to let our hearts be what Greenleaf (2002) calls *servant leaders* from whom we are led on a most remarkable journey to becoming whole. —Chris

There is power to shared emotions like love and compassion. Tragedy and loss can enter our life without notice, expectancy, or invite. The depth and significance of suffering is especially evident in so many of the children, youth, and educators who I have been blessed to know or visit throughout the years. You have all taught me much about compassion and love for others, despite your own hurting. For that, I extend my sincere gratitude for the profoundness of opening your hearts and gifts to others, the power of your unconditional love to change lives for the better, and the remarkableness of your capacity for compassion to transcend all barriers and provide hope.

It is with further gratitude and love that I recognize those who have served as extraordinary examples of love and compassion in my own life: my godson, Jayson, a remarkable teacher and coach, teaching meaningful life lessons on and off the links; Father Peter Gregory, serving as an instrument of compassion, with a capacity to heal; my sister, Audrey Barbarotta, never missing an opportunity to extend her love, supporting heart, and presence; and my mother-in-law, Mary Lou Murphy, opening and emptying her heart tank to anyone in need. With great love and gratefulness to my parents, Dick and Paula Rivers, who willingly and selflessly demonstrate the immense power of compassion and nonjudgmental hearts, opening their doors and selves to comfort, console, and care for others. Most treasurable, endless gratitude, and love for my husband, Tom Murphy, who continues to share an unwavering belief in all our hopes and dreams for a better today, never complaining, always loving and positive, seeing and thinking the best in others, setting an incredible example for our two girls; and to our compassionate and loving daughters, Julia and Abigail Murphy, who continue to surprise us with their goodness every day, and who at a young age, understood the importance of reaching out and being present for those who are suffering, whether in need of a smile, hug, laugh, warm embrace, or conversation, their hearts leaned in to deliver joy and love. Our daughters provide hope and faith that our future todays will be kinder, gentler, and more compassionate. May your heart song always sing! —Michele

The process of education—bringing out the potential of *all* students—is a recip-rocal process. What enables students to thrive and flourish is the same for teachers. But education is also symbiotic—a process in which teachers' joy and fulfillment are bound to those of their students, and vice versa. Together, they form bonds that imprint their hearts and spirits long after their time together has ended and the bond has become unconscious. I want to acknowledge and thank the teachers who give so selflessly to ensure that their students feel that bond, vitalized not only so that their brains are enlightened, but that their hearts are enlivened to appreciate the profound gift they are to others!

I have been fortunate to have had such teachers in my life, with the most impact-ful of my educational career being the eminent cognitive psychologist Dr. Reuven Feuerstein. Dr. Feuerstein taught me the power of belief in the innate propensity of *all* students to be awakened for engagement, high-level intellectual thinking, and the desire to make contributions. It was this belief that encouraged me to affirm in teachers the power of their heart to invigorate in students the belief in their capacity for developing personal strengths for self-determination and contribution!

I am also deeply grateful to my mother, the teacher whose heart guided and fortified my belief in myself! Her spirit is my daily revitalizer! —Yvette Jackson

This book has been a labor of love for many. Our community has been nurtured and sustained by a cadre of educators, editors, and researchers. At Solution Tree, our utmost thanks to Tonya Cupp, who skillfully guided our publishing process. Thanks as well to Meghan Wenzel, Dana Asby, Joanna Marzano, Effie Cummings, Ingrid Padgett, Didi Dunin, Kaela Farrise, Lauren Kiesel, and Lindsey Feltis, who aided our quest to find the best examples for the many practical exercises and historical lessons we have included, and for their questions, critiques, and recommendations. And finally, thanks to our colleagues Jill Flanders, Kate Retzel, Kathleen Sciarappa, Suzan Mullane, Hilary Hodgdon, Paul Liabenow, Jeff Donald, and Matt Bergey for standing beside us, walking with us, and joining with us as we celebrate the joy of being, living, learning, loving, and healing. —Chris, Michele, and Yvette

Solution Tree Press would like to thank the following reviewers:

Jenna Fanshier
Sixth-Grade Teacher
Hesston Middle School
Hesston, Kansas

Gina Isabelli
Principal
Circle Center Grade School
Yorkville, Illinois

Elizabeth Love
Title 1 Elementary Specialist
Spradling Elementary
Fort Smith, Arkansas

Rebecca Marsh
Academic Coach
Bakersfield Elementary/Middle School
Bakersfield, Vermont

Visit **go.SolutionTree.com/behavior** to download the free reproducibles in this book.

Table of Contents

About the Authors

 **Christine Mason, PhD,** an educational psychologist, has over thirty years of experience as a classroom teacher, college professor, educational leader, and researcher, and eighteen years of experience as a yoga, mindfulness, and meditation teacher. She presents experiential workshops for school principals and teachers. Mason is the founder and executive director of the Center for Educational Improvement (CEI), a nonprofit organization whose mission is to uplift schools with teachers and principals who are caring, compassionate, and knowledgeable about learning and teaching. CEI focuses on mindfulness, social-emotional learning, early childhood science, technology, engineering, and mathematics, and collaborated with Yale University staff, educators, psychologists, and social workers to address mental health concerns as a partner with the New England Mental Health Technology Transfer Center, where Mason serves as director of the Childhood-Trauma Learning Collaborative.

An expert in compassionate responses to childhood trauma and organic ways to provide relief to students in stress, Mason has experience teaching and developing teacher-mentor and youth dropout prevention programs in high-poverty urban areas. She is the developer of Heart Beaming®, a meditative practice for classroom mind breaks, and co-developer of the School Compassionate Culture Analytic Tool for Educators (S-CCATE). Her workshops incorporate up-to-date research on brain neuroplasticity, scientific evidence, and practical activities, as well as findings from her work helping educational leaders guide visioning and implementing strategies for transforming school cultures. Mason's experience as a principal at an international boarding school in India has been instrumental in developing the five Cs. While in India, Mason became steeped in the philosophy underlying meditation and its value in alleviating stress and freeing the mind to be more consciously aware and compassionate.

Mason served as executive director of research and professional development for the National Association of Elementary School Principals, a senior scientist in disability education, director of professional development for the Student Support Center in Washington, D.C., and the senior research associate at the Council for Exceptional Children. Mason has authored several books and research reports, including books on teacher mentoring and universal design for learning, and research reports on student self-determination, scenario-based planning, principal mentoring, urban schools, arts integration in schools, and inclusive education. She has presented internationally on mindfulness, trauma, Heart Centered Learning®, visions for 21st century instruction, yoga, meditation, and student self-determination.

Mason is credentialed through the International Kundalini Yoga Teachers Association and Radiant Child Yoga (a Yoga Alliance registered school). She has been a yoga practitioner for over twenty years and a yoga and meditation instructor since 2001, teaching classes at a local recreation center and offering workshops for teachers and students of all ages. She was trained directly by Yogi Bhajan, who brought Kundalini yoga to the West from India in 1968. Early in her career, Mason received an award as researcher of the year from Montana State University. The Robert Wood Johnson Foundation and Ashoka named her a pioneer in children's well-being in 2016. She coauthored *Mindfulness Practices: Cultivating Heart Centered Communities Where Students Focus and Flourish* (2019) with Michele M. Rivers Murphy and Yvette Jackson and coauthored *Visioning Onward: A Guide for All Schools* with Paul Liabenow and Melissa Patschke (2020).

Mason received her doctorate in educational psychology at The Ohio State University, with post-doctoral research at the University of Washington and a fellowship to further inclusive education practices in India.

To learn more about Mason's work, visit www.edimprovement.org or follow @Edimprove on Twitter or CEI on Facebook and LinkedIn.

Michele M. Rivers Murphy, EdD, is the associate director of Heart Centered Learning for the Center for Educational Improvement (CEI) and an independent educational consultant at KIDS FIRST! Rivers Murphy is a seasoned consultant, presenter, and educational leader for both regular and special education. She has served as a change agent for over two decades, helping transform some of the highest-needs neighborhoods and districts by improving student engagement, school culture, and academic success.

Rivers Murphy's work is based on the most current neuroscience and organizational research and specifically addresses the challenges associated with childhood trauma and stress that compromise learning and teaching. Rivers Murphy is also a program associate for the New England Mental Health Technology Transfer Center Network (MHTTC), where she delivers presentations and webinars on mindfulness practices to promote healing and healthy school communities and on encouraging self-care for students and teachers suffering from trauma and stress.

Rivers Murphy coauthored the School Compassionate Culture Analytic Tool for Educators (S-CCATE) and created a full-service innovative 21st century school community model, supported by an equity framework and driven by the pedagogy principles of confidence, to inspire high intellectual performance. She presented her 21st century high-performing public school solution for high-needs neighborhoods and districts to the Massachusetts secretary of education and facilitated a pilot study using S-CCATE as an envisioning tool and guide for transformational school culture change. She is also facilitating CEI research regarding Heart Centered Learning, with the foundational practices of mindfulness and mindful leadership.

Rivers Murphy believes that a holistic approach is critical for the development, growth, and success of every child and that children's lives cannot be compartmentalized; all parts must be key to the big picture of educating the child. Rivers Murphy's passion is to help facilitate mindful leadership and mindfulness practices in school communities, cultivating heart centered, compassionate, supportive school environments so that educators and students alike can thrive from a more balanced social-emotional health and well-being *and* academic achievement focus. She coauthored *Mindfulness Practices: Cultivating Heart Centered Communities Where Students Focus and Flourish* with Mason and Jackson.

Rivers Murphy obtained a doctorate in educational leadership (K–12) from Northeastern University. Her doctoral thesis specifically addresses the gap between what students are learning in school and what they need to know to prepare for college, career, and life in the 21st century.

To learn more about Rivers Murphy's work, follow @RiversMurphy on Twitter.

Yvette Jackson, EdD, winner of the 2019 GlobalMindED Inclusive Leader Award, is adjunct professor at Teachers College, Columbia University, in New York and senior scholar for the National Urban Alliance for Effective Education. Jackson's passion is assisting educators in cultivating their confidence and competence to unlock the giftedness in all students. She is driven to provide and promote pedagogy that enables students who are disenfranchised and marginalized to demonstrate their strengths and innate intellectual potential. Jackson's approach, called Pedagogy of

Confidence, helps educators believe in and value these students and optimize student success, which for Jackson is the basis of equity consciousness.

Jackson is a former teacher and has served New York City Public Schools as director of gifted programs and executive director of instruction and professional development. She continues to work with school districts to customize and systemically deliver the collegial, strengths-based High Operational Practices of the Pedagogy of Confidence that integrate culture, language, and cognition to engage and elicit the innate potential of all students for self-actualization and contributions to our world. Jackson has been a visiting lecturer at Harvard University's Urban Superintendents Program, the Stanford Center for Opportunity Policy in Education at Stanford University, the Feuerstein Institute, and Thinking Schools International. In 2012, the Academy of Education Arts and Sciences honored Jackson with its Educators' Voice Award for education policy/researcher of the year. She has applied her research in neuroscience, gifted education, literacy, and the cognitive mediation theory of the eminent cognitive psychologist Dr. Reuven Feuerstein to develop integrated processes that engage and elicit high intellectual performances from students who are underachieving. This work is the basis for her award-winning book, *The Pedagogy of Confidence: Inspiring High Intellectual Performance in Urban Schools*. Jackson also coauthored *Aim High, Achieve More: How to Transform Urban Schools Through Fearless Leadership* and *Unlocking Student Potential: How Do I Identify and Activate Student Strengths?* with Veronica McDermott, and *Mindfulness Practices: Cultivating Heart Centered Communities Where Students Focus and Flourish* with Mason and Rivers Murphy.

Jackson received a bachelor of arts from Queens College, City University of New York with a double major in French and education, and a master's degree in curriculum design, master of education, and doctor of education in educational administration all from Teachers College, Columbia University.

To book Christine Mason, Michele M. Rivers Murphy, or Yvette Jackson for professional development, contact pd@SolutionTree.com.

Foreword

By Lee Bolman and Terrence E. Deal

Public schools once had heart and soul. Writing in 1932, Willard Waller captured the zeitgeist:

> Schools have a culture that is definitely their own. There are, in the school, complex rituals of personal relationships, a set of folkways, mores, and irrational sanctions, a moral code based upon them. There are games, which are sublimated wars, teams, and an elaborate set of ceremonies concerning them. There are traditions, and traditionalists waging their world-old battle against innovators. (p. 96)

Beneath the veneer of rationality, these age-old dynamics still prevail, though in a more muted sense. But what has been lost is the vital spirit that once made schools special, and the notion that teachers make a difference. That is something Tracy Kidder (1989) observed after spending a year in a teacher's classroom by saying that "good teachers put snags in the river of children passing by, and over the years they redirect hundreds of lives" (pp. 312–313).

Somehow, these warm sentiments have been challenged or replaced by the cold logic that casts schools in a factory motif where results, as measured by tangible outcomes, prevail. As one government official reportedly pronounced, "If it can't be measured, we aren't interested." This sentiment flies in the face of sociologist William Bruce Cameron's contrary observation: "not everything that can be counted counts, and not everything that counts can be counted."

The message of Heart Centered Learning in mindful school communities could not be more timely and vital. When many would-be school reformers push for testing, policy prescriptions, and other failed remedies, Christine Mason, Michele M. Rivers Murphy, and Yvette Jackson rightly focus on a much more humane and holistic approach. They recognize that the heart of teaching lies in the hearts of teachers—and in their students.

Almost everyone argues for educating the whole child, but too often it is only empty rhetoric. Mason, Rivers Murphy, and Jackson take that idea seriously and develop intellectual, emotional, and psychological qualities for modern classrooms. Their five Cs—(1) consciousness, (2) compassion, (3) confidence, (4) courage, and (5) community—are just what classrooms need to nurture the whole child. For each factor, the authors explain why it is powerful and vital for student development and offer specific activities and strategies that teachers can use in their classrooms.

The authors' message is rooted in educational and neurobiological research, but even more importantly, it embodies the wisdom of experience these educators have attained from devoting their professional lives to understanding how schools work and what it takes to make them work better.

Mason, Rivers Murphy, and Jackson provide a varied and stimulating compendium of ideas, techniques, and strategies. Read straight through, or dive in at random, and you will keep finding insights or pearls of wisdom. They note, for example, that when teachers hover, micromanage, or overcontrol, the paradoxical result is an increase in chaos and unrest. The result is mindlessness rather than mindfulness. When teachers see the big picture and model compassion and courage, they inspire students to new levels of achievement and self-confidence.

Test scores dominate school performance assessment, despite the fact that standardized test scores capture a small part of what education offers to young people. In our book, *Reframing the Path to School Leadership*, we write:

> Too often, outside pressures have sapped the spirit of principals and teachers. Most external reform initiatives unfortunately are based on narrowly rational assumptions. With few exceptions, teachers are pressured to raise test scores, particularly in the STEM skills of math, science, and the other technical skills often assumed to be the keys to future success. . . . [M]ore and more businesses and other places of employment are coming to realize that this mythical assumption does not hold up to reality. The "soft skills" that are often undervalued contribute at least as much as technical skills to career and life success. (Bolman & Deal, 2014, p. 153)

We add that preparing the next generation for the future they will inherit is sacred work—nothing is more important. Mason, Rivers Murphy, and Jackson echo that message. They call on teachers to embark on a soulful journey of joy and reverence with the confidence that educators can make a real difference in their students' lives.

As we emphasize in our own work, schools succeed when they develop a culture that is rooted in the local community and its deepest values. For too long, educational critics with little real experience in contemporary classrooms have brought a bird's-eye view that obscures the authentic and grounded knowledge that is offered by people who serve in the schools on a daily basis. Views from ten thousand feet almost invariably miss the fine-grained details that make schools special. Schools are filled with heartwarming stories of students who suddenly manifest new insights or surprising capacities. The abstract perspectives of policy-makers bring a bloodless and distorted picture of what schools are all about. *Mindful School Communities* offers a much-needed alternative that enriches the possibilities in schools.

Kudos to this timely trio, who have courageously offered new ways to think about the challenges of education!

Introduction

A good head and a good heart are always a formidable combination.
—Nelson Mandela

Imagine schools filled with joy, where learning is fun and engaging, where excitement fills the air, and where the vibrations of love are palpable and students step forth with confidence to tackle difficult problems. Imagine schools where students and educators gain a sense of *equanimity*—calm and balance—and where academic learning and social-emotional health are equally recognized and considered crucial to success in school, career, and life. Most important, imagine that compassion, love, and heart are at the core of everything we do and become in school communities.

And yet, the reality we face is far removed from this vision. Varying levels of stress and trauma accompany hundreds of thousands of students as they struggle to complete everyday tasks, learn new skills, and meet parents' and teachers' expectations—and their own expectations. The prevalence of the most severe forms of childhood trauma is staggering. According to a U.S. Department of Health and Human Services (2019) report, in 2017 child protective services (CPS) "received a national estimate of 4.1 million referrals involving approximately 7.5 million children," mostly for neglect (74.9 percent) and physical abuse (18.3 percent; p. ix). While it's difficult to measure childhood abuse and neglect rates on a global scale because of differences in reporting methods, measures, and cultural norms, we know this issue influences the lives of children worldwide. For example, neglect happens to around 14 percent of children in Europe; in Asia, the statistics are around 25 percent (Moody, Cannings-John, Hood, Kemp, & Robling, 2018).

Stress and trauma invade the lives of many students regardless of their race, culture, gender, location, or socioeconomic status. Whether it is poverty, violence, abuse, neglect, bullying, rejection, or feelings of inadequacy, trauma and stress compromise students' well-being and futures (Shonkoff, 2012). Stress, whether short term or pervasive, presents a huge barrier to learning, undermining people's "ability to concentrate, remember things, and control and focus their own thinking" (Thompson, 2014, p. 45). Under stress, people's minds may even shut down or slow down, their attention may wander, and they may suffer from low self-esteem (Breslau, Peterson, Poisson, Schultz, & Lucia, 2004; Scibberas et al., 2014; U.S. Department of Health and Human Services, 2016).

Thankfully, there are strategies and techniques that teachers and administrators can use to improve all of these learning barriers. Our experience is that these strategies and techniques can make a difference for individual lives even in the midst of global anxiety, terrorism, and trauma. Somewhat surprisingly, it is almost like being in the middle of a blue sky in the eye of a hurricane—trauma whirling around us as we feel centered, calm, happy, and successful. We believe one viable and sustainable solution is what we call *Heart Centered Learning*®. Supported by neuroscience and neurobiology, Heart Centered Learning is where emotions, consciousness, and student interests and needs are central parts of curriculum and instruction and the essence of creating a compassionate learning community (Davidson & Begley, 2013; Kaunhoven & Dorjee, 2017; Lazar et al., 2005). We believe that Heart Centered Learning is the necessary ingredient to build strong, supportive school communities for students, teachers, and school leaders. While Heart Centered Learning may, at first blush, sound like it is all about being kind (which is important), it is based on years of rigorous scientific investigations documenting how to help children thrive. You will see that research cited throughout this book.

If you are like many educators, you think about how to help your students improve not only their academic achievement but also their self-esteem, self-regulation, and likelihood for lifelong success. You may come back to questions about what to do. If it isn't foremost in your mind, you may reflect on it when contemplating your successes and the barriers that stand between the students you serve and the dreams you have for them.

The education that we envision for the future will have heart—a true connectedness. Schools with a solely academic focus are not addressing these urgent issues, yet they could be a critical part of the solution (Blankstein, Noguera, & Kelly, 2015; Noddings, 2016; Wright & Ford, 2016). As sociologist and author Parker Palmer (2007) explains, the teachers who will help students thrive "possess a capacity for connectedness. They are able to weave a complex web of connections among themselves, their subjects, and their students so that students can learn to weave a world for themselves" (p. 11). This book ultimately answers how to create this connectedness. This introduction answers questions such as, What is connectedness? What is Heart Centered Learning? What are heart centered school communities? What will you learn in, and how might you approach, this book?

What Is Connectedness?

Connectedness is a sense of belonging, or *relatedness*, which is important for teachers and students alike (Marshik, Ashton, & Algina, 2017; Reis, Sheldon, Gable, Roscoe, & Ryan, 2000). It is crucial to psychological health, as well as to motivation (Marshik et al., 2017). Connectedness—belonging—is critical to healthy growth and development. Alienation, isolation, trauma, and stress mean there is a need for conscious development of connectedness. The repercussions from these experiences vary from individual to individual, but their effect on overall well-being and the capacity to learn is damaging (Shonkoff et al., 2012).

Teacher-student connectedness is not often part of preservice teacher education or in-service professional development. However, to nurture and support the complex web of connectedness that Palmer (2007) describes, school leaders and teachers consciously weave webs of relationships with everyone in the school community. Connectedness is important to Heart Centered Learning.

What Is Heart Centered Learning?

Heart Centered Learning is "education that is not overly dependent upon a focus on rigid academic scheduling or expectations for academic growth—instead taking a holistic approach" (Center for Educational Improvement [CEI], n.d.). This approach encourages and fosters the five Cs of social-emotional learning (external) and mindfulness (internal):

1. Consciousness
2. Compassion
3. Confidence
4. Courage
5. Community

Heart Centered Learning reflects recent neurobiological information that provides strong evidence of neuroplasticity—the brain's ability to recover from stress (Davidson & Begley, 2013; Kaunhoven, & Dorjee, 2017; Lazar et al., 2005). Mindfulness, or conscious awareness, can help individuals who are experiencing trauma or stress by providing relief that calms hyper-alert neuropathways (Mason, Rivers Murphy, & Jackson, 2019). When we are conscious of our breath, of our emotions, and of those around us, we are more likely to act in compassionate ways and reinforce neuropathways that provide positive feedback about our lives (Singer & Klimecki, 2014). As we feel a sense of calm and goodwill, we are more likely to feel confident about our abilities. Over time, this sense of confidence can strengthen executive functions (including memory, attention, and organization; Diamond & Lee, 2011; Zelazo &

Lyons, 2012) and our potential to be courageous—standing up to bullies, helping others in need, and considering someone else's feelings—thus strengthening a sense of community. Heart Centered Learning intentionally provides a new lens for the neurobiological challenges of youth who struggle with impulse control, de-escalation, anger management, and self-regulation as a whole. Through this new lens we are less likely to blame students for acting out and more likely to seek ways to alleviate their stress and nurture their well-being.

Put simply, when teachers and administrators strive for Heart Centered Learning, they place the learners' social-emotional needs at the forefront of their instruction and policies while cultivating a natural safety net within the learning community. When their teaching is heart centered, educators' conscious understanding of neuroscience (including neurobiology and also a conscious understanding of learning, perception, and behavior) and stress informs their attitudes, practices, communication, and instruction with learners. This effort can lead to a heart centered school community.

What Are Heart Centered School Communities?

In heart centered school communities, there is a shared belief that it is not enough to only *educate with our minds*, nor is it enough to only *educate our minds*. If we are to help mediate the inattention and inaction that so many decades of ignoring social-emotional factors have created, and if we are to teach students strategies to ameliorate trauma and stress, then new ways of being, learning, and leading together are necessary. In heart centered school communities, caring and compassionate action are embedded into practices, policies, and protocols. Further, as they implement Heart Centered Learning, educators also use the principles during interactions with families and the surrounding local community. Such a practice shows care for the whole heart centered school community. See figure I.1.

INTRODUCTION EXERCISE: Reaching for the Stars

To consider the benefits of adding heart, we would like you to pause, consider someone you love (it could be a family member or friend), and check to see how you feel. Now, participate in the following exercise (Mason & Banks, 2014). Read through the steps and then close your eyes and follow them.

1. Close your eyes, put your hands on your heart, and take a few deep breaths.
2. Focus on the warmth at your heart center and imagine stars twinkling in a night sky.
3. As you continue to look, notice that one star seems to shine a bit brighter. Focus on that star.
4. Visualize the face of a loved one on that star.

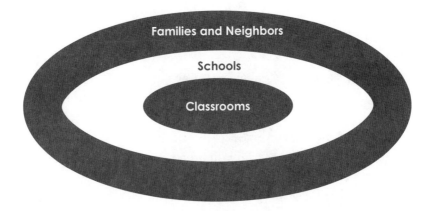

Figure I.1: Heart centered school communities.

5. Feel the love bond, take a few deep breaths, and reach up with one of your hands and pull that star into your heart.

6. Take a few more deep breaths, feeling the love bond and a sense of peace, and open your eyes.

When you do the exercise, remember to take a few deep breaths at the beginning and at the end. How did you feel? Did you notice a difference in how you felt between simply thinking about someone you love and after doing the Reaching for the Stars exercise? You have activated a connection between your feelings, your mind, and your heart. A positive physiological change in your heart actually occurred (Childre & Martin, 1999).

What Will You Learn in This Book?

In *Mindful School Communities: The Five Cs of Nurturing Heart Centered Learning*, teachers of grades K–12, school counselors, social workers, and administrators get the research-based essentials to creating mindful classrooms and school communities that better prepare students to be more responsive to their individual, collective, and societal needs. We also provide the following.

- Insights into research
- Examples of how other educators have implemented the practices
- Guidance for thoughtful and conscious decision making
- Exercises to improve students' and educators' lives (Visit **go.SolutionTree .com/behavior** to access free reproducible versions of these exercises.)
- Activities and tools to infuse heart centered factors naturally into curriculum in the context of academic subjects and across grade levels

Readers who have little knowledge about mindfulness, or "paying attention on purpose, in the present moment, and nonjudgmentally" (Kabat-Zinn, 2003, p. 143), will find that *Mindful School Communities: The Five Cs of Nurturing Heart Centered Learning* gives them food for thought regarding consciousness, compassion, confidence, courage, and community—the five factors that compose Heart Centered Learning. Each of these topics is covered in an individual chapter, with examples of activities that can be used across grade levels and academic subjects. Each chapter also has examples of how teachers can build their capacity for awareness and heart centeredness in their interactions with students (and how administrators can do so in their interactions with teachers) and establish mindful school communities that are more caring and compassionate.

Will readers who are already implementing mindfulness also be interested in what we have to say in *Mindful School Communities: The Five Cs of Nurturing Heart Centered Learning*? Jeffrey Donald, a teacher and mindfulness coordinator in Maryland's Montgomery County Public Schools, is implementing mindfulness across his district, and he thinks they will be interested:

> Developing and sustaining compassionate classrooms is not a short-term investment. We are in such need of a curriculum that will help integrate compassionate practices, including the five Cs, across academic areas. Teachers need guidance and advice about how to incorporate these important practices while continuing to focus on academic development. (J. Donald, personal communication, June 5, 2019)

Mindful School Communities: The Five Cs of Nurturing Heart Centered Learning is divided into two parts.

Part I: Scientific Basis and Overview

Chapters 1 and 2, in part I, provide an overview of the theoretical, scientific, historical, and contextual information that is the rationale for Heart Centered Learning. Chapter 1 provides a brief overview of Heart Centered Learning. Chapter 2 describes the physiology of the heart and why it's important to help students understand their emotions (our bodies' responses to external stimuli) and feelings (our mental reactions and associations to these emotions).

Part II: Heart Centered Components

In part II, chapters 3–7 each cover one of the five Cs that being a heart centered community requires. Chapter 8 centers on conscious leadership, and the epilogue reflects on the implications for schools, communities, and nations, and looks to the future. The appendix introduces the School Compassionate Culture Analytic Tool for Educators (S-CCATE), a data-analysis and envisioning tool that ties directly to the five Cs. Visit **go.SolutionTree.com/behavior** for free reproducibles of planning tools for each of the five Cs, heart centered leadership, and heart physiology and heart-mind connections. Figure I.2 (page 8) is an example of a completed planning tool.

Throughout the book, you will see the following.

- **Key principles:** Each chapter begins with an underlying principle that summarizes that chapter's main concept or theme.
- **Exercises and activities:** These are interspersed throughout the chapters in a purposeful order. The exercises are examples of how to implement Heart Centered Learning in classrooms and schools. Some are mindful breathing, yogic, meditation, or mindfulness exercises; some are discussion- or project-based activities. We recommend practicing the exercises first before implementing them with students.
- **Professional development opportunities:** We make references to resources and activities across a variety of subjects and grade levels for introducing each of the five Cs.
- **Reflections:** Each chapter ends with a few questions that may help you understand the relationship of the material to your own situation, including your students, your classrooms, and your schools.

In chapters 3–8, you will see the following organizing structures, where *It* stands for consciousness, compassion, confidence, courage, community, or conscious leadership.

- **What Is It?** This is a definition and explanation of the factor and how it relates to education. We also talk about issues you might have to take into consideration when planning to practice or teach the factor.
- **Why Does It Matter in School?** Here are the rationale and research for teaching this factor to students.
- **How Do We Teach It?** You get examples of how to infuse the factor into academic curricula.
- **What Does It Look Like Historically?** We discuss historic leaders who personify or who have advanced one of the factors. This topic can work as another way to introduce the factor into the curricula. Additionally, you can tap into current events or visit websites such as the Smithsonian Institutions (http://americanhistory.si.edu) for inspiration. Look for examples of these factors in the news or on social media, consider other gifted adults, and compare some of the traits they share.
- **How Do We Measure It?** We share several ways to assess how thoroughly or well each of the five Cs, plus conscious leadership, is incorporated into a

Date and Time or Sequence Period	Exercise	Grade Level	Plans for Infusing in Academics	Adaptations	Plans for Future Use
One day each week	Reflect on Your and Your Students' Confidence (page 84)	n/a	See strategies listed in this form.	n/a	n/a
October 10 One plan period	Strategies (page 85)	Grade 5	During teacher planning, complete the strategies chart, decide one focus, and choose two or three strategies.	• Decide how to apply conclusions in classrooms and how to monitor results. • Determine if we need to focus on helping specific students or specific situations. • Commit to monitor impact.	We'll complete twice annually.
October 15 Art class (1:00 p.m.; extension activity: three days)	Confidence Superhero Capes (page 86)	Grade 2	Talk with students about their successes, academic and otherwise, before we begin making capes.	• Parents or other volunteers might be able to help students with preparing their capes, and we will consider recruiting their help. • We will determine a time during academics when students can wear their capes. • Do this for one week.	• We'll do an extension activity after students have worn their capes for one week. • Extension: Class develops a superhero drama, developing vignettes where a good reader helps another student with a library book. The extension ends in a superhero celebration at the end of the week. Take a class picture with the capes. • We will repeat annually.

Date and Time or Sequence Period	Exercise	Grade Level	Plans for Infusing in Academics	Adaptations	Plans for Future Use
Every day	Acknowledging Negative Emotions and Supporting Positive Emotions (page 88)	n/a	*Focus on praise during tough self-controlled times and boosting celebrations, informal and formal.*		
October 12 8:30 a.m.	Strengthen Your Core (page 90)	K–grade 12	*Consider as a transition movement—perhaps as students prepare to leave a circle area.*	*Bring knees to chest and rock back and forth.*	*Consider making this a part of movement brain breaks to be used regularly.*
	Affirmation Meditation (page 92)	Grades 4–12	*Will wait until second semester to infuse.*		
	Following Talent (page 95)	Grades 4–12	*Will wait until world history unit to infuse.*		

Figure I.2: Confidence Planner reproducible—example.

school or district. Examples of three S-CCATE items for measuring each of the Cs are included as well.

How Might You Approach This Book?

How can you put more heart into your life? We expect that each of you has your own special interests and needs. You may be most interested in building students' confidence or courage, for example. Before jumping to that chapter, please consider the advantages of reading this book cover to cover, starting with this introduction, and following the chapters in sequence. There is a rationale for the sequence, and our discussion of each factor will help you gain knowledge and skills that form the basis for the factors that follow. Also, you will gain the most if you savor the experiences of the exercises. Unlike in many other books with academic content, we have woven mindfulness exercises throughout the chapters. These exercises will enhance your preparation and understanding.

As you proceed through this book, *we urge you to practice the exercises* before *implementing them in class with students.* You will be better prepared, with a more thorough understanding of the material, if you practice the exercises individually first. You may want to take notes, recording how long it takes to go through the recommended steps and comparing how you feel before and after the exercises. This individual practice is particularly important for any of the exercises that have a breathing, yoga, or meditative component. We also recommend that you consider the following.

- **How to embed the exercises and activities into your routines and procedures:** We provide some suggestions, but some might work well at specific times of day, during transition times, or even as a routine part of opening or closing your lessons.
- **When you may need to discuss the process and implications with administrators or parents:** We provide examples of educators and school leaders introducing Heart Centered Learning into their classrooms or schools and how they encouraged buy-in from key stakeholders.
- **How you can benefit by reading and applying this in a book study group:** The reflection questions at the end of each chapter are helpful for this. The authors have successfully used this approach for virtual study groups for the 2019 companion book, *Mindfulness Practices.*
- **If, and with whom, you will share results from any assessments measuring a five Cs component:**
  - Teachers may or may not want to share individual student outcomes with students. In some cases, it may be wisest to share some general findings with the class and use the information primarily to help make instructional decisions about the types of activities to pursue.

- We recommend that teachers use care in sharing results so students are not embarrassed, but rather empowered to share only what *they* choose to share with others. Err on the side of maintaining confidentiality. For example, a teacher could conference individually with a student or students, discussing strengths and needs, or could walk through an example of hypothetical results with students and suggest the implications of the results. For example, the teacher might say, "These hypothetical results show us that this student . . ."

- Depending on the class, students' ages or grade, and circumstances, teachers might walk the class through how to interpret and use the results for a hypothetical student, and demonstrate how the hypothetical student uses the results in a metacognitive way—that is, in a way to gain a greater understanding of him- or herself. The class could discuss the implications of the results and decide on one goal that this student might develop. The teacher could then circulate results to individual students, giving each the opportunity to develop one goal.

This book has been designed as a resource. It is not a step-by-step curriculum with rigid expectations. Rather, we encourage readers to approach a chapter with a sense of curiosity and wonder, being open to what it might reveal. You might even review an exercise for, say, preschoolers and think, "Ah, I can modify this for my middle school students." Or you might find two exercises in a chapter that most appeal to you and start with these. While we have sequenced exercises within a chapter, it might be, for instance, that you are quite interested in the area of self-confidence and will consider how to introduce that topic, rather than starting with the first exercise in the confidence chapter. In other words, let your intuition, your heart, and your expertise guide you through the selection of what to present in your class or school.

Also, please keep the following in mind.

- Some of the background material may work well as a way to introduce or explore specific aspects of the five Cs. The historical background information we provide might make good introductory lessons, providing exemplars and inspiration. For example, you can introduce or reinforce multiple C factors by explaining Mary Wollstonecraft's confidence in speaking out in support of women's rights to strengthen her community.

- We encourage you to build community, which is covered in chapter 7, as you work through the other Cs. Creating community begins with consciousness and is essential to establishing compassion, confidence, and courage.

Whatever approach you take, we believe you will grow in your understanding and appreciation of the compassionate side of learning. Now, we invite you to sit back, open your heart and mind, and begin what can be a transformational journey into your future and your classroom, school, and community's future.

PART I

SCIENTIFIC BASIS AND OVERVIEW

Authors and educators Lee G. Bolman and Terrence E. Deal (2011) start their book *Leading With Soul* with a chapter titled "The Heart of Leadership Lives in the Hearts of Leaders" (p. 15). What an insightful phrase! Consider the leader without heart. Consider morale. Later in that chapter they write, "Wisdom will come. First you have to look into your heart" (p. 22).

Chapter 1 explains the concept of Heart Centered Learning and why it's important for schools to cultivate heart centered school communities. Chapter 2 looks at the heart's physiology, how our bodies' responses to stress and trauma affect our emotions, and how we can use mindfulness to regulate this system. Throughout these chapters, we explore the idea of heart coherence—finding a sense of harmony where brain, body, and emotion are in sync, individually and as a community.

CHAPTER 1

Heart Centered Learning

A loving heart was better and stronger than wisdom.

—Charles Dickens

key principle

Educators can infuse Heart Centered Learning in an organic yet systematic way in classrooms and school communities.

Consider a time in your life when you were in emotional turmoil. You may have experienced a significant loss, found yourself living with anxiety, or been stressed out by expectations that magnified your sense of vulnerability. In these circumstances, it may have been difficult to continue your daily routine. You might have had trouble concentrating, found yourself frequently reflecting on the circumstances that were so upsetting for you, or even become aware of a prolonged sense of sadness or a rising sense of anger. In a word, at these times, your emotional pain was *foremost* in your mind.

Now consider your students and perhaps a student who has experienced trauma, a significant loss, or overwhelming stress. Caring and compassion are critical. John Hattie's (2012) expansive research on positive learning outcomes finds that teachers have the most impact when they are "directive, influential, *caring*, and actively and passionately engaged in the process of teaching and learning" (p. 19; italics added for emphasis). What does it mean to care? Why does caring matter? How can teachers demonstrate their care? Importantly, how can educators take their innate ability to care one step further to compassionate action?

When we give care and compassionate action, we recognize the need for positive support and take steps to provide it. In schools, this support may begin with a hug, a thoughtful accommodation, a listening ear, or a smile. It is not sufficient to only show compassion in a single moment, however. It is not enough to have a social-emotional learning program delivered once or twice a week. And the antithesis of caring is to put our response to trauma on the back burner. Toxic stress and trauma require a response like compassionate action. Compassionate action is more than caring or empathy. It is an authentic desire to help others, to have a positive effect on them, and to act on that desire.

How do we implement Heart Centered Learning that leads to compassionate action? How can administrators and teachers become mediators for compassion development? What more should we know about why Heart Centered Learning matters in school?

How Do We Implement Heart Centered Learning?

One version of a Heart Centered Learning community is a school embedded with the five Cs, which are factors essential to compassionate action: (1) consciousness, (2) compassion, (3) confidence, (4) courage, and (5) community. See figure 1.1.

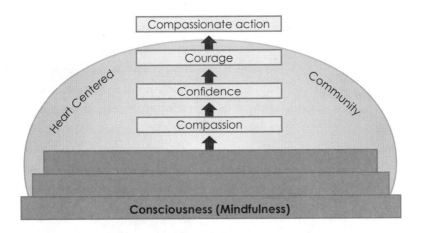

Figure 1.1: Five Cs of Heart Centered Learning, and the result—compassionate action.

In the context of heart centered communities, these steps begin with consciousness, or mindfulness, which leads to the rest of the factors. Consciousness improves classroom interactions by increasing the coherence between our emotional experience and our individual understanding (mindful awareness) of that experience. This enhances our sensitivity to what is happening and how students are responding, which leads to compassion and then to confidence. In a series of purposeful choices, each factor builds on the other so that, after establishing confidence, teachers can help students develop courage and, finally, a community that takes compassionate action. Throughout this process, conscious leadership is a driving force. With it, teachers and other school staff are supported by school administrators who seek to further understand ways to improve teaching and learning and to consolidate positive steps that lead to improved overall morale, well-being, and achievement.

In heart centered mindful school communities, students are given exercises and opportunities to increase their consciousness, demonstrate compassion, build their confidence, and show courage. In these communities, administrators and teachers become mediating models, demonstrating these virtues in their daily interactions with staff, students, and families. Heart centered school policies and protocols reflect compassionate understanding of students', families', and the community's needs. In school environments where compassion is demonstrated in multiple ways, as their confidence increases over time, students build their courage or ability to stand up for themselves and others—courage to address a bully, the moral strength to do the right thing, and the grit to persevere. All of these building actions take place within the context of the larger school community, even as the senses of community and belonging also evolve.

- *Consciousness* is the foundation. It is the awareness of others and ourselves, including awareness of what we are feeling and what is happening around us (environment). This conscious awareness takes time to develop; it does not happen overnight. As teachers provide opportunities for students to learn about themselves, their perceptions, and their emotions, their consciousness grows. Consciousness provides a natural foundation for the heart centered steps that follow.

- *Conscious* or *heart centered leadership* amplifies Heart Centered Learning by establishing schoolwide initiatives and creating and applying consistent policies and protocols across classrooms and grade levels. School principals are called on to understand the elements of Heart Centered Learning to inspire teachers and other school staff and to guide its implementation.

- *Compassion* is more likely after consciousness is raised; teachers increase individual compassion for self and others by embedding compassion as a primary value in classrooms. Modeling compassion and helping students reframe situations increases the understanding of trauma and leads to ways to reduce stress and increase kindness and caring.

- *Confidence* propels the transformational change necessary to remediate trauma and build self-esteem, leading to success on many levels. Without confidence, students may not master essential skills. Without confidence in the emotional realm, they may feel empathy but fail to act in ways that support a compassionate community.

- *Courage* is another critical component for developing compassionate responses to the multitude of issues that we all experience on a far-too-frequent basis. Leaders and citizens need courage—to speak out, to further their growth, to take the road less traveled, or to make decisions that do not directly support their own self-interest. While courage develops in a natural way for some individuals, schools can help systematically nurture courageous mindsets, supporting resilience and courageous actions for many.

- *Community*, whether it is a neighborhood, town, classroom, or school, is where people come together around a shared purpose or belief, supporting each other and often accomplishing a goal together. So much of the western world focuses on getting ahead at an individual level. Yet, we all live in communities. There are strategies for systematically magnifying the benefits of our compassionate thinking and actions and growing compassionate attitudes, values, and practices, all within mindful school communities that are intentionally designed to support kindness and caring.

- *Compassionate action* arises when individuals recognize their own compassion and also have the confidence and courage to act compassionately. Opportunities to practice compassionate behavior to gain confidence and courage will facilitate treating themselves and others compassionately. Compassion alone is like a road that is not yet finished. Although we may start out on the road, it will not get us to our destination. To achieve our intent—treating ourselves and others compassionately— compassionate action is needed.

Here is an example that clarifies how instruction about compassion, and practicing compassion, can lead to compassionate action. Tony is a thirteen-year-old gang member who has experienced significant trauma. As we describe the steps to compassionate action for Tony, note the coordination with figure 1.1 (page 16). Tony has learned to be tough and to exude apathy. Tony is used to showing bravado, and before he can do otherwise, the barriers to his compassionate action need to be torn down. For Tony, any sign of weakness or vulnerability can mean trouble—that he is losing status and power. Living by the gang's code, Tony is ruthless.

For Tony to understand and demonstrate compassion will take time. It begins with a series of exercises and conversations where Tony learns more about himself, his perceptions and emotions, and how others feel under a variety of circumstances. Tony will learn about his anger, frustration, and anxiety, as well as how he feels when he is calm and his life seems to be going better. As teachers show compassion and teach about compassion, Tony will learn how to control his impulsivity and to consider himself and others before he acts. Once consciousness and the compassionate foundation exist, teachers work on helping Tony gain confidence. In safe, secure environments with trusted adults, Tony gradually gains enough confidence to demonstrate compassion through repeated practice. Courage, again, takes time. Only after significant practice and success will Tony have the courage to stand up for a classmate by showing compassionate action, rather than reverting to the code of the streets.

In the following chapters, we show you how to naturally infuse Heart Centered Learning into your classroom instruction and school so that preparing for and implementing the exercises and activities is not a burden. Rather, it will become an automatic way to permeate your school with a sense of wholeness and well-being *and* increase instruction efficacy. This is not one more thing for your to-do list. Instead, it is a way to rediscover a sense of purpose as an educator; it helps you leave the building at the end of the day feeling as if you have reached a student and connected in meaningful ways.

Please know that heart centered community building is not only for students like Tony. Community building affects both the givers and the receivers, and *every* student needs the loving support we are recommending.

Reflecting on Heart Centered Communities

Heather Lucy, the school adjustment counselor at Lee Elementary in Lee, Massachusetts, reflects on her school community's participation and its continued heart centered focus, which has impacted her school community as a whole. Heart Centered Learning was implemented during the 2016–2017 school year at her school. After six months of implementation, Heather, the pilot coordinator, said:

> This experience has been a call to action of sorts to create a shared vision and sense of community filled with love, light, and healing for both students and staff, creating shared time together, and more meaningful and supportive experiences. . . . Common practice, vocabulary, expectations, and permissions of expression have opened doors and minds in a loving way. (H. Lucy, personal communication, May 16, 2017)

Why Does Heart Centered Learning Matter in School?

Some of you may be feeling that all of this sounds well and good but you can just do it without having to read further, learn more, or practice whatever we recommend. We know the obstacles are huge and that quick fixes have already been tried. After many discussions and much work with districts, we recognize the enormity of this challenge. With this in mind, we—Chris, Michele, and Yvette—made a conscious decision with a moral imperative to find a solution, infusing love, kindness, and compassion in every heart in every class, in every grade, in every school community to help and to heal.

Heart Centered Learning matters because the students in your class who have experienced or who are experiencing abuse, neglect, poverty, racism, bullying, or discrimination benefit from your efforts to make them feel safe at school. For elementary students, this may include a principal greeting them with a smile and a kind word as they walk into the school building. Also, it is beneficial to make sure that bus drivers, cafeteria workers, and janitors are clued into the special needs of these students and able to offer a friendly smile, support, and, if necessary, adult intervention. Feeling that there are many adult allies throughout the building can be a huge relief to a student who is carrying a burden of fear. For middle or high school students, it is helpful to have mentoring and peer mediation programs (Peterson & Skiba, 2000).

An analysis of over three-hundred-thousand responses from students in grades 6, 9, and 12 finds that students who are bullied are at higher risk for emotional distress, self-injury, depression, suicide, sexual acting out, and alcohol and drug abuse (Borowsky, Taliaferro, & McMorris, 2013). For these students, particularly important *protective factors* (which help mitigate negative effects and improve health) include increasing connectedness—participating in sports or arts, talking with a teacher or parent about things that matter—and increasing feelings of school and neighborhood safety.

Adults are frequently the ones who traumatize young people, but students may also inflict harm on others or themselves. According to a survey, one in ten high school students experiences physical violence from a dating partner each year (Vagi, Olsen, Basile, & Vivolo-Kantor, 2015). Other research confirms that 40 percent of youth have reported a dating partner has been violent or performed a nonconsensual sexual act (East & Hokoda, 2015). When we consider classroom bullies, gang members, murderers, and rapists, we must realize the huge societal need to address these issues with youth. Research suggests that awareness of one's emotions, combined with self-talk, metacognition, moral reasoning, impulse control, and emotional self-regulation, can help prevent such violence (Frazier & Vela, 2014; Hornsveld, Kraaimaat, Muris, Zwets, & Kanters, 2015; Parkhill & Pickett, 2015; Porter & Critelli, 1992).

Trauma takes many forms, and schools can help in many ways. For example, students who have been traumatized have good reasons for not trusting certain people. Teachers, perhaps with assistance from a school counselor or social worker, or as part of a social skills, sexuality, or mindfulness curriculum, may be able to help guide discussions that will help students better understand their own feelings. School leaders are tasked with ensuring teachers have the training and other resources to prepare for such discussions. When teachers talk with students about who they trust and who causes discomfort and uneasiness, teachers can help students process their feelings, including possibly conflicting emotions. When teachers discuss personal space, boundaries, rights to privacy, and inappropriate touching, students who might be sexually abused, for example, are more likely to acknowledge their discomfort and tell a parent or another adult about their uneasiness. So, one of the ways that heart centered practices can help students is by helping them know more about their feelings and emotions and what important information they might glean from feelings such as distrust. It's important that before educators begin these conversations, they receive training about appropriate language to use and how to respond when a student discloses abuse.

Figure 1.2 further clarifies the relationship between trauma and stress and Heart Centered Learning, showing how the five Cs can serve as mediating factors between various types of trauma and individual healing and well-being.

Trauma or Stress
- Minor disappointments
- Academic struggles
- Performance anxiety
- Minor illness or injury
- Death of a parent or significant person in their lives
- Parents' divorce or separation
- Bullying, including cyberbullying
- Physical, mental, or sexual abuse or neglect
- Discrimination, injustice, and inequity
- Domestic abuse or violence
- Peer-inflicted violence (rape, sexual abuse, gang violence)

Consciousness
Compassion
Confidence
Courage
Community

Impact
- Increased understanding of self and others
- Improved executive function
- Improved self-regulation
- Improved social skills

Resilience
- Better adaptability
- Improved sense of well-being
- Better readiness to learn
- Improved academic achievement
- Better lifelong health

Figure 1.2: Relationship between trauma and stress and Heart Centered Learning.

Professional Development

To implement Heart Centered Learning, professional development might include some information on related educational, psychological, and neuroscientific research that supports the purpose of the book. During one of the early sessions, after a brief presentation on this research, teachers and others who will be implementing Heart Centered Learning might meet in small groups to discuss the five Cs. You will share why each is included and will relate the five elements to existing methods and procedures that may be used in your school. For example, you might discuss the five Cs in relationship to existing social-emotional (SEL) programs or exercises used for certain grade levels.

After an introductory session, priority decisions about professional development can be made from recommendations that accompany the School Compassionate Culture Analytic Tool for Educators (S-CCATE). Schools and districts can use S-CCATE action guides to go through planning and implementation. Specific recommendations for interventions, professional development sessions, and policy changes are provided to target S-CCATE factors that show room for growth.

For a holistic approach to becoming a compassionate school community, we recommend at least one professional development session for each of the five Cs. During each session, a facilitator can lead teachers through at least three of the exercises presented in the chapter about the specific element. Additionally, there is background information in the chapter that could be considered for incorporating into lessons in classrooms. For example, for the chapter on courage, the facilitator could talk about courageous leaders and lead teachers through a brainstorming session about their personal courageous heroes. In these sessions, teachers could also discuss potential modifications for various grade levels, academic subjects, or circumstances, such as current events.

Another way to provide professional development is to consider a jigsaw approach, where groups of teachers are assigned various exercises in the chapters. The groups prepare presentations with each group leading the others in a simulation of how that exercise could be presented to their classes.

Reflection

To get the most out of this chapter, reflect on these questions after reading it.

- How do you exhibit care in your day-to-day interactions in your classroom?
- What does the term *heart centered* suggest to you?

- What do you know about the importance of the five Cs—(1) consciousness, (2) compassion, (3) confidence, (4) courage, and (5) community—for social-emotional and academic learning?
- Are you already implementing SEL curricula that address the five Cs? If so, are most teachers in your school implementing the curricula? How is it influencing student learning and well-being?
- What do you hope to gain from this book?

— Notes —

CHAPTER 2

Heart Physiology and Heart-Mind Connections

The heart is more than just a physical organ. It is the essence
of life, providing us with bottomless enrichment and giving
meaning, emotion, and spirit to our existence.

—Cynthia Thaik

key principle

By focusing on our hearts through mindfulness, meditation, and yoga practice, we gain greater heart coherence, reduce stress, and increase happiness.

We are intentional in our use of the words *Heart Centered Learning.* Just as mindfulness, or tuning into our thoughts in the current moment without judgment, is gaining popular acceptance, we predict that educators will realize the importance of heart-mind connections. We are more than our intellect. As Timothy Kanold (2017), recipient of the Presidential Award for Excellence in Mathematics Teaching and former president of the National Council of Supervisors of Mathematics, says, "Great teaching is always a form of love" (p. 19). Psychologist Daniel Goleman (n.d.), author of *Emotional Intelligence: Why It Can Matter More Than Intelligence*, underscores the importance of understanding our emotions in an academic context:

Most of us have assumed that the kind of academic learning that goes on in school has little or nothing to do with one's emotions or social environment. Now neuroscience is telling us exactly the opposite. The emotional centers of the brain are intricately interwoven with the neurocortical areas involved in cognitive learning.

Yet, people process emotions in different ways. It is one thing to calmly discuss our feelings and emotions, and it is another to focus on *how we are feeling.* Consider the following scenario: You are sad because one of your parents has died. You may find, especially as time passes, that you can calmly discuss what happened and the significance of your loss. However, this may take some effort, and perhaps after some time has passed, you will have responded to so many inquiries that you are able to describe the circumstances surrounding the loss without triggering much of an emotional response. Sometimes, in the case of particularly painful situations, we intentionally suppress our feelings. If you allow yourself to genuinely feel your emotions in moments such as when you are talking to a friend about losing your parent, you may break down with inconsolable crying. That release of emotion may cause discomfort because of the vulnerability it requires, especially if it is in the presence of someone you don't know well. However, you may find that with a particular friend, you are more at ease letting down your guard and grieving.

The Origins of the Focus on Heart Centeredness

As a teacher, administrator, or other school staff member, you may find yourself being strongly pulled to act on behalf of a student or family. It is almost as if a current is pulling you to action. It is. According to researcher Rollin McCraty (2003), "it is possible for the magnetic signals radiated by the heart of one individual to influence the brain rhythms of another" (p. 12). So, your heart may help you process not only your feelings but also other people's pain as you empathize and attune to their angst and needs. It is almost as if we are drawn to consider others' needs.

You may also find that when you act on these urgings, you feel more fulfilled. Sometimes despite all the logical reasons for not acting—for not helping a hurricane victim, for not giving a student one more chance to complete an assignment—the most satisfying thing we can do is the very thing that flies in the face of logic. That is a matter of listening to the wisdom of your heart.

But the rationale for taking a heart centered approach does not rest solely on supporting neuroscientific and educational research. It is also based on the heart's physiology and influence in decision making. Many reasons for tuning into our hearts go beyond the neuroscientific and educational research and the typical association of heart with feelings of love and positive caring. Here, you read about the origins of the focus on heart centeredness, your heart's influence, heart-versus-head decisions, physiology, and awareness of heartbeat.

Our use of the term *heart centered* stems not only from research demonstrating how the heart is involved in processing events, thoughts, emotions, and actions, but also from ancient yogic teachings (Carrera, 2005; Tigunait, n.d.). The philosophical and theoretical grounds for our heart centered approach are influenced by our mindfulness practices. In fact, practitioners may describe acting with *an enlightened heart*, using mindfulness to *balance head and heart*, or transforming thinking and being when we *journey from head to heart*.

Your Heart's Influence

Consider the following scenario.

> *You're on your way to an important school event. Perhaps you will be introducing the key speaker at a parent meeting. Along the way you see a horrible accident—two cars are involved, one flipped over, and an ambulance is there on the side of the road, lights flashing. As you approach the accident, you even hear a siren, and in your rearview mirror, you see a police car speeding to the accident scene. Can you picture this? How does it make you feel? Does your heart start to race even thinking of this scene? Do you feel a sickness in your stomach? Do you feel concern for the drivers and passengers of the vehicles?*
>
> *Imagine, now, that as you pass the accident, you feel some relief that medics are there, and so you try to compose yourself, to shift back to practicing your speech, so that you will not let your emotions interfere with the job you have at hand. Perhaps you even find yourself taking a few deep breaths to reset.*

In that scenario, most likely your heart was engaged, and your reaction was influenced by your heart.

Now let's approach this a bit differently.

> *You are on your way to introduce someone at a parent meeting. You are listening to a traffic update. The speaker announces three incidents that might influence the route you take: there is a traffic tie-up on Route 3, there has been a head-on collision on Route 5 and medics are on the scene, and a traffic light is out on Route 6. As you hear the update, you consciously make a decision to avoid these three routes and instead to take a few side streets. You glance at your watch and realize that, even with this detour, you will likely arrive twenty minutes early and have plenty of time to rehearse your speech.*

During this scenario, how did you feel? Most likely your heart was not as engaged in your decision making and reactions.

HEART PHYSIOLOGY AND HEART-MIND CONNECTION EXERCISE:
Heart Meditation

Try the following meditation to gain some sense of how a heart meditation can bring you a sense of well-being. Read through it one time, then close your eyes, take a few deep breaths, and follow the meditation.

1. Bring your attention to your heart center.
2. Imagine a bright, glowing light in your heart space. This light is so bright that it is free of all pain and it is beyond any fear, worry, or anxiety.
3. See the light growing beyond your heart space to form a protective halo around your entire body.
4. Feel the light moving into your arms, legs, and head, bringing a sense of ease and comfort to your entire body and mind.
5. Open your eyes and check in with your heart, mind, and body. Note any differences from how you felt before you began this exercise.

Whenever you feel incomplete, disconnected, or not whole, come back to this place of shining luminosity and feel the warmth wash over you. Practice meditating on your heart.

Heart Beaming

When Chris brought Heart Beaming (Mason & Banks, 2014), which is similar to the heart meditation, to Conte Elementary School in Pittsfield, Massachusetts, students reported that connecting with their hearts in meditative exercises helped them feel calm and relaxed. One fourth grader said he likes the idea of doing more of this in school because "it makes me feel happy." Teachers report being thrilled that their students were able to share a moment of giving as they envisioned beaming love and caring to students across the globe. (See the Heart Physiology and Heart-Mind Connection Exercises: Letting Go of Anxiety, page 30, and Appreciation, page 31, in this chapter.)

Heart-Versus-Head Decisions:
Our Heart-Mind Connection and Coherence

Philosophers, researchers, therapists, and others have described the importance of adding heart to our decisions. Joseph Mikels is director of the Emotions and Cognition Lab at DePaul University. Mikels and his colleagues (2011) asked research participants to make a decision and, when doing so, to focus on their feelings versus details about presented options. They found that adding a feelings' component to certain sorts of complex decisions results in higher-quality decisions and that participants sometimes made *worse* decisions when they deliberated on the details, rather than trusting their instincts or considering their feelings. Perhaps you can recall at least a few times when your heart told you one thing and your head another. There are indeed times when it is hard to discern the next steps. Yoga teachers, *yogis*, might even say there are times when more balance is needed between the heart's power and strength versus the head's. When one of these is out of balance, you may find yourself driven solely by your heart *or* your head, without due consideration for the other.

While we strongly endorse heart centeredness, this is different than acting solely from an emotional space without considering consequences or the wisdom that comes from analysis and intellectual understanding. You can approach the balance—centeredness—by intentionally turning to thoughts or feelings, or by focusing a meditation on either the heart or the mind. Similarly, there may be times when you need more coherence. There are strategies—including mindfulness, yoga, and meditation—that may increase the quality of our decision making and our lives.

Sometimes when we are proceeding full speed ahead with our intellectual endeavors, we miss the beauty of the moment. In the classroom, teachers often feel the pressure to push ahead and push through the outlined state and national curricular standards notwithstanding the readiness of their students. When teachers are able to balance the strength of their head with heart, new pathways for learning evolve. Consider the possibility that the heart's intelligence can increase (Arguelles, McCraty, & Rees, 2003). According to Arguelles et al. (2003), the practice of yoga and meditation may enhance the wisdom that emanates from listening to our heart: "With every beat, the heart transmits to the brain and throughout the body complex patterns of neurological, hormonal, pressure, and electromagnetic information, which form a major component of the physiological backdrop that ultimately determines our emotional experience" (p. 15). Significant evidence indicates that we can impact our hearts with strategies such as breathing, mindfulness, and meditation (Childre & Martin, 1999; Vinay, Venkatesh, & Ambarish, 2016).

Imagine what a third grader's heart looks like as she struggles with multiplication, and what it looks like when her teacher finds a kind, effective way to reteach the concept to her, step by step. Heart Centered Learning isn't an either-or. Instead, teachers learn about their students and teach the necessary social-emotional and academic  skills components while realizing that there are no easy solutions or templates for motivating students and no standard procedure that ensures success. Instead, they are conscious and compassionate, purposefully reducing a student's anxiety and increasing positive sense of self, even as the student learns academics.

HEART PHYSIOLOGY AND HEART-MIND CONNECTION EXERCISE:
Letting Go of Anxiety

Source: Adapted from McCraty & Royall, 2015.

You can practice this as a meditative exercise for students in any grade to apply in a moment of anxiety. Help students through the exercise by reading the following steps to them.

1. Imagine a time when you have been anxious. It could be before a test or a performance, for example.
2. Notice and admit what you are feeling.
3. Try to name the feeling.
4. Tell yourself to *ease* and let go of that feeling as you gently focus on your heart.
5. Relax as you breathe and ease the anxiety out. Imagine the feeling floating away into the sky.

Consider students in your classroom, some of whom may be experiencing prolonged or generalized anxiety, stress, or fear. You can imagine their heart rates during moments of anxiety. If they were more relaxed, how might they experience both a stronger sense of well-being and a reduction in anxiety, stress, or fear? Explicitly teaching students about the coherence of their heart and emotional states can empower them to use mindfulness techniques to self-regulate thought patterns, emotions, and physiological responses.

Cambridge University researcher Barnaby Dunn and his colleagues (2012) describe related outcomes in a study they conducted on *interoception*—how well individuals can perceive changes in bodily function—with almost sixty adults. In this research, they measured heart rate and arousal in response to positive, negative, and neutral images. Dunn and his team conducted a second study, this time with just over ninety adults, on an intuitive reasoning task. For this study, they measured heart rate and dermal skin changes. They discuss the implications of both studies:

> Emotion experience and intuition are associated with individual differences in the ability both to generate and to perceive accurately subtle changes in the body, consistent with the thesis that how one thinks and feels sometimes genuinely involves following one's heart. Knowing when to trust and when to discount such gut feelings may relate to the extent to which individuals regulate their emotions and make optimal choices at crucial junctures in life. (Dunn et al., 2012, p. 1842)

HEART PHYSIOLOGY AND HEART-MIND CONNECTION EXERCISE:
Appreciation

This exercise works for grades 2–8, and you can easily adapt it for grades 9–12 by providing a more open-ended, higher-level-thinking response activity. You can adapt it for preK and grade 1 by completing the exercise together as a class, either aloud or with a recording done by the teacher.

1. Ask students to answer the prompts in the six squares in figure 2.1.

2. Ask students to refer to their squares and fill in answers to the three following sentence stems.

   - Today I am grateful for _____.
   - I appreciate _____ because _____.
   - I feel thankful for _____.

Someone in your life	Something in your life	Something you might take for granted (food, clothing, shelter, good weather)
Something at school	Something in your community	Something in the world

Figure 2.1: Appreciation form.

*Visit **go.SolutionTree.com/behavior** for a free reproducible version of this figure.*

3. Each student picks one of these thoughts, reads it silently several times, and then closes his or her eyes and meditates on the thought, considering details. For example, if a student appreciates his or her pet, perhaps he or she can picture the animal and consider the circumstance (a dog retrieving a ball or waiting by the door).

4. Say something like "Now that you have picked one sentence, close your eyes and repeat the sentence silently to yourself several times. Now take a few deep breaths and picture the thing or person that you care about and are grateful for. Imagine that person right with you. Feel a sense of peace or excitement and happiness. Take a few deep breaths and open your eyes." (See the Heart Physiology and Heart-Mind Connection Exercise: Heart Meditation, page 28, for how to guide students through a meditation.)

Elementary students can be seated in a circle, with one student holding a ball in his or her hands. He or she can toss the ball to another student who can say, "I am grateful for _____."

Middle and high school students can focus more on paying attention to how their hearts feel; on more details related to the event, the thing, or the person; and on considering more about why that person or thing is important to them. Students can also journal about the person, item, or thing they value (such as democracy or social justice).

Physiology: The Wandering Nerve

The functioning of the heart, like the brain, can be enhanced through specific practices and activities. Considering our heart, as our sense of fear or anxiety is eclipsed, we are more likely to feel a sense of well-being, peace, or even happiness. Thanks to a growing body of research, more evidence proves that reducing the negative effects of trauma and engaging in mindfulness, yoga, and meditative practices are associated with improved functioning of certain parts of the brain (Zelazo & Lyons, 2012). With this functioning comes a concurrent improvement in our sense of well-being and reduction in stress and anxiety.

The heart is also impacted at a physiological level by trauma and stress. Higher trauma rates result in increased risk of poor heart health in adulthood (Hendrickson et al., 2013; Kubzansky, Koenen, Spiro, Vokonas, & Sparrow, 2007). Strengthening heart coherence may have the added benefits of improving heart health as well as cognitive performance, a focus for many school leaders. For this reason, ideally more schools will see that trauma response and stress reduction are essential elements of improving academic performance.

To better understand how our hearts, thoughts, and feelings are impacted by trauma and stress, let's look at the vagus nerve. When we examine the physiology that impacts the heart and heart-brain connection, the vagus nerve plays a major role. As shown in figure 2.2, the vagus nerve extends from the brain stem into the carotid sheath in the heart, and then wanders down to the abdomen and farther down to the colon. The vagus nerve is part of the autonomic nervous system, which helps regulate heartbeat and breathing, control muscle movement, and transmit a variety of chemicals through the body.

You can determine your vagus nerve's tone several ways, including a measure of the variation in time between individual successive heartbeats. Although an average adult heart rate is seventy-two beats per minute, this is not a constant measure. It varies according to a multitude of factors, including physical fitness, stress, sleep and alert conditions, and age. The time between heartbeats, for example, might vary from .9

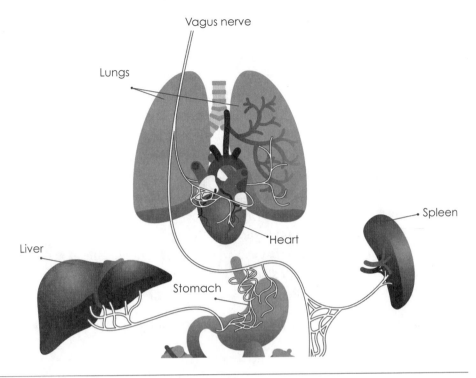

Figure 2.2: The wandering vagus nerve.

seconds to 1.1 seconds (Koester, 2017). Some tools, including a free app available at Elite HRV (https://elitehrv.com), allow you to measure this variability.

During emotional distress, the vagus nerve responds. Through the parasympathetic nervous system, the vagus nerve releases the neurotransmitter acetylcholine to help you relax. People with a stronger vagus response may recover more quickly from illness, stress, or injury. High vagal tone is related to social engagement and self-regulation, including monitoring and self-control (McCraty & Zayas, 2014; Reynard, Gevirtz, Berlow, Brown, & Boutelle, 2011; Segerstrom & Nes, 2007). The vagus nerve's tone can even impact traits such as self-directedness and coping styles (Geisler, Kubiak, Siewert, & Weber, 2013).

Could you learn to cope by toning your vagus nerve? If you are interested in knowing more about this, watch "The Healing Breath" video (www.sonima.com/yoga/yoga-articles/vagus-nerve), which includes author Deepak Chopra and yoga teacher Eddie Stern. In the video, Chopra (2017) explains that physical flexibility relates to adaptability and strengthens one's ability to cope, that stimulating the vagus nerve is how to encourage flexibility, and that "breathing is one of the fastest and easiest ways to activate the vagus nerve."

Heartbeat Awareness

Processing sensations is central to our physical sense of self, which encompasses heart rate awareness and internal bodily states and sensations interpretations. When researchers have examined these bodily states and sensations, yoga with movement has yielded slightly better results compared to yoga methods that relied more on static postures (Schmalzl, Powers, & Henje Blom, 2015; Streeter, Gerbarg, Saper, Ciraulo, & Brown, 2012). Yoga may also help individuals become more aware of stressors, and thus alter affective or physiological reactions (Kinser, Goehler, & Taylor, 2012). Over time, individuals who are aware of feelings and emotions may also develop a greater awareness of the relationship between their bodily sensations and reactions. Researchers report that "when individuals are aware of their internal experiences and more accepting of them as states that ebb and flow, they are also able to make choices about the most effective action to take in the moment, especially when relating to others" (Block-Lerner, Adair, Plumb, Rhatigan, & Orsillo, 2007, p. 511).

HEART PHYSIOLOGY AND HEART-MIND CONNECTION EXERCISE:
Heart-Focused Breathing

Heart-focused breathing, which works with all grades, can develop vagal tone (McCraty & Zayas, 2014). Following are the three steps to take.

1. Focus attention on the chest, the area of the heart.
2. Imagine that your breath is flowing in and out of your chest, and breathe a little slower and deeper than usual.
3. Continue for several minutes.

HEART PHYSIOLOGY AND HEART-MIND CONNECTION EXERCISE:
Loving Kindness Meditation

Several researchers reveal that loving kindness meditation produces many benefits, including relief from illness and improving emotional intelligence (Jazaieri et al., 2012; Seppala, 2013).

1. Focus on your heart, breathing long and deep.
2. Generate a feeling of loving kindness toward self.
3. Continue focusing on your *self*, removing any judgment, numbness, or self-hatred.
4. Consider your own health, well-being, and safety. You might silently repeat phrases such as, "May I be free from inner and outer harm," "May I be healthy," "May I be strong," or "May I be peaceful and happy."
5. Focus on someone you care about or someone you love. Feel unconditional love for that person.

Preparing to Teach Yoga and Meditation Exercises

When you instruct students in yoga, mindfulness meditations, or Heart Beaming, we recommend practicing the session and timing prior to instructing students.

Sometimes students will express some resistance or a sense of discomfort in closing their eyes and meditating or in practicing yoga or Heart Beaming. Tell them that they have a choice: they can choose to participate or not. However, if they choose not to participate at any given time, they must agree to sit quietly and be respectful of others.

- Begin by helping students to become comfortable. Consider where they are—at their seats, in a group circle, standing, or sitting.
- Let students know it is OK to do what they can. Often it is best to focus on those who are participating and either ignore those who aren't or gently suggest they try it. (Within a few sessions, most students are comfortable and participating.)
- Use a soft, calming voice.
- Speak somewhat slowly and meditatively, pausing between phrases so students can absorb and stay with a thought before adding the next component.

HEART PHYSIOLOGY AND HEART-MIND CONNECTION EXERCISE:
Heart Beaming Meditation

This exercise works for students in preK through grade 12, and it is also useful for adults. Read the instructions aloud to guide students at a slow to medium pace for about three minutes.

1. Make sure you are seated with eyes closed or focused on a fixed point.
2. Take a few deep breaths.
3. Put your left hand over your heart and your right hand over the left. Feel your heart beating.
4. Listen to your heart.
5. Imagine a friend you care about.
6. Send heart energy from *your* heart to your friend and back again.
7. End with a focus on breathing from your heart.

You can extend Heart Beaming so students beam heart energy to others. One way to do this is by suggesting they imagine beaming heart energy to someone who needs help—perhaps a child in a refugee camp.

You can modify the exercise for preschool students. Have students place their hands over their hearts and close their eyes; then ask them to think of someone they love—it could be a parent, a sibling, a relative, or even a pet.

Professional Development

The most critical aspect of professional development for this chapter is to practice the breathing and meditations. We recommend that an experienced meditator or professional yoga teacher spend at least two sessions with teachers, leading them through these exercises and helping answer their questions. If possible, at least one session should provide opportunities for teachers to team up and practice teaching each other.

♥

Reflection

To get the most out of this chapter, reflect on these questions after reading it.

- How do you see the heart influencing learning with your students in your classroom?
- How do you feel after you have practiced the heart exercises in this chapter?
- How can you help students understand how their hearts come into play when learning?
- Did you try any of the exercises with your students? If so, how did they react? How can you infuse these exercises into the natural flow of the classroom?
- What might you or your students do to make better heart-mind decisions?

PART II
HEART CENTERED COMPONENTS

In *Leading With Soul*, Lee G. Bolman and Terrence E. Deal (2011) end with this thought: "It comes down to the difference in asking, 'What works?' and 'What matters?'" (p. 239). We believe Heart Centered Learning leads us to *what matters*.

Chapters 3–7 guide us through an explanation of each of the five Cs of Heart Centered Learning as well as practical exercises for teachers to implement in their classes. Chapter 8 focuses on heart centered leadership for a broader, schoolwide perspective.

In each chapter, you will find exercises that you can adapt for students at all grade levels and ages. We recommend that you first complete the exercises, then reflect on their effects, and consider factors such as how this might relate to your grade- and subject-level curriculum. This will likely lead you to consider possible classroom adaptations. In many instances, we provide examples of how to modify the exercises for students of various ages.

In some instances (including the mindfulness, yoga, and breathing exercises), we encourage readers to practice these exercises several times, so they understand their true value before introducing them to classes.

To prepare you to implement the strategies in this part, we recommend that schools provide relevant professional development experiences to teachers.

— Notes —

CHAPTER 3

Consciousness

The world that we perceive is a reflection of our own states of
mind and reveals our own level of consciousness.

—Prem Prakash

key principle

Consciousness is a
prerequisite to entering
deeper levels of
understanding.

With limited consciousness, we are tethered to mis-
understanding and ignorance. We look around at our
planet and see conflicts, squandered natural resources,
hundreds of thousands of displaced people seeking
refuge from war and poverty, and some people barely
eking out a living, while others bask in luxury. While
some are living the good life, the plight of others is
ever-present. Exploring the concept of consciousness,
knowing why it matters and how to teach it in school,
discovering what it has looked like in the past, and
learning how to measure it can move us one step
toward mindful school communities.

What Is Consciousness?

Consciousness goes beyond cognitive or intellectual understanding. If there was
ever a time that was ripe for awakening to a better understanding of ourselves and
others, if there was ever a time for growing our comprehension of the multifaceted
realities of our existence, this may well be it. Artist Kelly Rae Roberts (n.d.) puts it
this way: "*Awaken* beckons me open my eyes as well as my heart to new possibilities,
new opportunities, or simply, a new day." With consciousness, we are invited to open
our eyes, our ears, and our heart to the lives of others—to their being, their voice,
their beauty, and their needs.

We have many opportunities for caring and compassion. However, caring, compassion, and, eventually, healing start with consciousness, or awareness, that fully

Practicing Consciousness: Connecting

In working with students in schools in Washington, D.C., therapist Atiba Vheir helps students understand more about themselves. Atiba provides individual and group counseling and support to students, often working in conjunction with teachers and staff.

Students—especially when they are identified as at risk, experiencing low self-esteem, or demonstrating disruptive behaviors—need connections. As Atiba works with students, she affirms connections in a nonjudgmental light, and interacts from a strengths-based perspective: "I matter, and I am important as a human being." She uses affirmative mottos on a daily basis with individual students and with classes to help support a seeding of positive consciousness and a positive alignment of purpose and well-being. From this perspective, Atiba indicates that students come to understand they have a purpose. She says, "When this discovery is acknowledged, and developmental supports are reinforced in both therapeutic and classroom settings, this unified learning affirms strengths within the individual, group, and classroom community." She goes on to explain that, depending on what is happening in one's livestream, as student strengths are honored, deep connections can be made as part of the "unfoldment process." For example, consider a student who is the so-called class clown. Atiba might acknowledge the powerful gift of humor while helping the student consider when and where to use that gift.

Over time, Atiba has seen how students' sense of well-being, self-esteem, ability to be comfortable with self, and joy unfolds, even in the midst of the challenges that are taking place (A. Vheir, personal communication, February 5, 2019).

opens our eyes, ears, and, most important, hearts to the world, environment, and people around us. Consciousness is the heightened awareness of self and that which is external to self. Brown and Ryan (2004) point out that awareness and attention are the primary features of consciousness. Consciousness is closely related to mindfulness; consciousness developed through mindfulness training contributes to positive mental health and the ability to adapt (Manuello, Vercelli, Nani, Costa, & Cauda, 2016; Paulson, Davidson, Jha, & Kabat-Zinn, 2013). Liu and Robertson (2012) are among those who focus on the value of an expanded consciousness. In practical terms, as we experience life events and pay attention to the world around us, we can do so with blinders on or we can be more fully present and aware.

Why Does Consciousness Matter in School?

Consciousness matters for teachers and students because it can be the difference between inaccurate and accurate understanding of self, others, and surroundings. It is particularly helpful to gain an understanding and awareness of how a teacher feels or what triggers certain unpleasant feelings in the classroom; one's own attitudes and interactions matter. Everything, positive and negative, in the classroom trickles down to affect the students and the classroom climate. For example, consider the teacher whose body language shows her irritation every time the class clown raises his hand or whenever she feels hurried to finish a lesson because students are clearly disinterested. Consider students who are listless, withdrawn, or irritable. The unaware teacher may chalk it up as misbehavior or disrespect—as something to be managed. With conscious awareness, the teacher may pause and reflect on possible contributing factors, realizing that something other than punishment may be needed. A conscious teacher will also be alert to students' academic struggles, the need to modify instruction, or ways to increase students' interest in learning. With this awareness, the groundwork is laid out for changes that are likely to improve not only the attitude students have toward learning but also their academic performance.

While teachers need to be conscious of themselves and their students, students can also benefit by becoming more conscious. Teachers can take steps to help increase their students' consciousness about their perceptions of self—their likes, dislikes, feelings, strengths, weaknesses, fears, and joys—and of others, much like the steps they take to increase their own consciousness. When students are more aware of their own emotions, they have a significant tool for deciphering circumstances and act in ways to enhance their own self-protection, resilience, and compassion for self. Consider, for example, sixth grader Carla, who wishes she had more friends. After her teacher discusses friendships and lets students practice friendship-making with role play, Carla realizes that sometimes she is anxious around other students, and that comes from the fear of being rejected. After a few sessions of deep breathing, positive affirmations, and practicing how to approach others, Carla feels more confident and approaches peers with a new sense of self-esteem.

Consciousness can help students understand more about their academic learning as well as their emotions. When students get opportunities to pursue their own interests and preferences, they gain more personal insights and are intrinsically motivated (Csikszentmihalyi, Rathunde, & Whalen, 1993; Deci, Ryan, Schulz, & Niemic, 2015; Hidi & Renninger, 2006). Allowing student choice can encourage motivation to learn because of students' innate sense of curiosity to explore a topic they value (Ryan & Deci, 2000). When students get the chance to reflect on their learning choices and outcomes, they can come to a deeper understanding of themselves as learners and people. For some students, especially those who are struggling to grasp topics, having some autonomy about how they pursue and demonstrate knowledge can lead to success (Ryan & Deci, 2000).

How Do We Teach Consciousness?

We can teach consciousness the following ways: four questions about self; service learning projects; free play in preschool and elementary classrooms; expanded understanding of fairness, discrimination, and equity; and mindfulness activities.

CONSCIOUSNESS EXERCISE: Four Questions About Self

There are a thousand and one ways to teach consciousness with strategies that begin with helping students become more introspective and observant on a day-to-day basis in the classroom. One place to begin is with asking students the following four questions.

1. "Who am I, really?"
2. "What do I value?"
3. "What do I know about the world around me?"
4. "What more do I need to learn?"

You can adapt these questions to various ages and grade levels. Elementary students can draw pictures and dictate sentences and stories. You can adapt them to be part of a specific unit, including social studies, language arts, or health, for example, and relate them to students' local community, country, or the world; a literary character; or human physiological development. Students in grades 4–12 can write essays on any or all of these topics. They can relate them to imagination exercises as well. One example is projecting their own values into a future state as they consider global health, sustainability, the daily experiences of people with various needs, and the moral dilemmas of characters in literature, history, or real life (including peer-pressure situations).

CONSCIOUSNESS EXERCISE: Who Am I?

You can adapt this exercise for elementary students by focusing on only one of the questions, or by having students draw responses to each question over a period of four days, responding to one question each day.

You can explore the concept of self a number of ways, with or without graphic organizers, leading questions, or a suggested experiential frame. Questions that reflect higher-level thinking can be introduced by asking students to compare and contrast who they *are* with who they would *like* to be. Figure 3.1 is one graphic organizer you could use.

How do others see me?	How do I see myself?
Which animal best represents me? Why?	Who would I like to become?

Figure 3.1: Who Am I? form.

*Visit **go.SolutionTree.com/behavior** for a free reproducible version of this figure.*

Take the following steps to complete the Who Am I? exercise.

1. Introduce the exercise, passing out copies of figure 3.1 or instructing students to fold a sheet of paper in half two times so there are four squares, and to label each square as you see in the figure. Tell students that the information is meant to be for each individual, and that no student should feel compelled to share everything or anything with other students.

2. Students add between three and five bullet points under each square, making sure to leave space for additional ideas. Students can illustrate each square with drawings if they wish. To help students understand how to complete this activity, begin by providing an example of what students could put in each square.

3. Students share the *How do others see me?* square with one or more peers, as far as they are comfortable. As students share, they can add bullets.

4. Students return to working individually, reviewing what they have added and checking to see if this prompts any additional bullet points for any of the squares.

5. Let students communicate as they wish with one or more peers in small groups.

6. At the end of the exercise, invite students to share as they wish with the whole group.

7. Give each student a small envelope on which to write their names and the date. Each student inserts his or her paper into the envelope and seals it.

8. Return the envelopes to students later in the year. Let them review what they have written about themselves and revise their statements. Students are free to add changes with one or more peers in a small group. The teacher could also lead a class discussion on how, over time, our concept of self sometimes shifts.

You could repeat a similar exercise with each of the original four questions.

CONSCIOUSNESS EXERCISE: Who Am I, Really?

After completing the Who Am I? exercise (page 42), students in grades 3–12 could take it to another level by writing a six-part essay about how others see them and who they really are.

When using this exercise in class, teachers may want to have a counselor close at hand. Some students may reveal that they have been bullied, that they are a bully, that they have experienced abuse, or that they have issues of gender uncertainty. In each of these cases, the teacher should consider whether follow-up may be needed. The follow-up could take the form of a private discussion with a student, a discussion with a parent, or a referral to a school or social service agency or counselor.

The steps are to instruct students to develop an outline with the following components.

1. Ask students to introduce themselves to readers in one paragraph, perhaps including age, gender, preferred pronouns, family, where they live, cultural background, pets, special skills, or interests.
2. Ask students to write about how they think they appear to others.
3. Add a component, asking students to write a paragraph that explains how they would appear to others if they really knew them. To help students with this part of the essay, provide possible sentence stems.
   - If you really knew me, you might be totally surprised to learn _____.
   - If you really knew me, would you like me?
   - If you really knew me, would you still be my friend?
   In this part, they can describe fears, doubts, or feelings of inadequacy.
4. Ask students to explain any dreams or intentions they have. Students can also include information about whether they have shared this with anyone before.
5. Ask students to finish with a conclusion. You can offer this sentence stem: If you really knew me, _____.

Students submit this initial draft to the teacher for feedback. They can then make revisions, illustrate their essay, or share it with family. Teachers could end with a discussion about icebergs and how we may think we know someone else, but sometimes what we see is the tip of the iceberg. Middle school and high school students may be able to write essays with less structure, perhaps focusing on fears and inadequacies or dreams and intentions.

CONSCIOUSNESS EXERCISE: Affirmations

To build a sense of positive self-regard, teachers work with students on identifying between one and three affirmations they can repeat daily. This exercise can serve as a good follow-up to the Who Am I, Really? exercise. The steps are as follows.

1. Ask students to write between one and three things about themselves that they may want to improve. These should be written as a positive statement, such as *I want to get better grades* or *I want to be kinder to my friends.*
2. Help students transform sentences to positive, present-tense affirmations, such as *I am getting good grades* or *I am kind.*
3. Give students three minutes each day to write down the positive affirmation they wrote in step 2. Students write the affirmation as many times as possible during the three minutes. Or, instead of writing the affirmation for three minutes, students could say their affirmation aloud for two minutes. Whatever format it takes, students can practice this affirmation at various times during the day over several weeks.

Include Service Learning Projects

Service learning is another way to help develop conscious awareness of self, others, and environment through exploration, expression, and reflection. The impactful significance of service pedagogy evolves from experiential, hands-on learning that connects meaningful life experiences with academic learning (Dewey, 1938, 2007). Service learning projects are one way to increase students' consciousness through real-life skills practice and purposeful community projects that can help facilitate wider community change and improvement (Rivers Murphy, 2013). Service learning fully embraces the contextual learning experience "from the premise that learning cannot take place in a vacuum, but should somehow be connected with real world attributes to make sense to learners" (Westera, 2011, p. 201). Hands-on experiences tend to have a lasting impact on students and the wider community as the interaction and development of shared awareness and ownership translates into what is needed to make sustainable change.

Practicing Consciousness: Service Learning

Partnerships and connections with teammates and community members are an essential element of many service learning experiences. For her 2013 doctoral dissertation, Michele M. Rivers Murphy studied service learning as implemented at Drury High School in North Adams, Massachusetts. Students embodied the values of teamwork, cooperation, and collaboration as they worked toward a common goal and overcame challenges such as public speaking, time management, and researching. During focus groups and self-reflective exercises, students expressed feelings of empowerment. They were surprised that they were given so much freedom and independence to make their own project decisions and have a strong voice in planning and implementation. There was an emerging sense of community awareness that evolved through students' involvement in their service learning project work within their own community.

Student B1 notes that "the most defining moments of this project are every time we collaborate, when we're all in the same place, at the same time creating new ideas. I like community interactions, finding our community partners, and talking with other people to get their input into our project" (Rivers Murphy, 2013, p. 106).

Student G26 summarizes the feeling of making a difference: "I feel like the most meaningful part of the experience was coming to the end and realizing that we can make a difference. We can help make the community better" (Rivers Murphy, 2013, p. 109).

Student G13 says, "This project has been very eventful and informative. I've learned much more about problems that our town struggles with. I have gained a much higher awareness of our town" (Rivers Murphy, 2013 p. 86).

Give Opportunities for Expression, Imagination, and Voice

Expression, imagination, and student voice are opportunities for developing a higher level of consciousness. This is valuable time for teachers to observe and just simply notice what students are doing, saying, conveying, or learning.

- In preschool and kindergarten, this may involve blocking out time for free and expressive play such as areas for dress-up, pretend cooking, nature-oriented items, and tactile elements such as water, sand, or clay.
- At the elementary school level, recess is essential to building a conscious awareness of others and of feelings, and for students finding their own voices as they navigate problems and make decisions on their own.

- At the middle school and high school levels, providing opportunities for expression, imagination, and voice may involve role play; student-generated free speech; content proficiency shown through song, dance, theater, or art; and dialogue circles (where students choose a topic of interest and create their own norms).

Practicing Consciousness: Awareness of Preschooler Skills

Orinthia Harris, a CEI trainer, shares the following:

> Teachers from several schools in Washington, D.C., have participated in a series of preschool STEM workshops I have offered over the past several years. These hands-on, experiential classes meet biweekly over a period of two or three months. Often, we will explore a topic during one session. Teachers return to their classrooms and implement the suggestions, and report back during the next class. Over time, I have seen teachers' "consciousness" or awareness of their students expand exponentially. For example, I recall teachers surprised at the idea that their preschoolers could develop their own engineering design challenges through play-based exposure to new materials they introduced in their classrooms.
>
> One teacher commented on how the simple incorporation of natural outdoor activity really engaged the curious minds of her preschoolers. She commented on how more exposure to free play in the natural elements—air, water, sunlight, and earth—brought more joy and order to her classroom, reducing the need to use as many behavior management strategies. (O. Harris, personal communication, January 1, 2019)

Expand the Understanding of Fairness, Discrimination, and Equity

Joshua Block (2016), a humanities teacher, describes a five-pronged approach to teaching consciousness. This approach can help expand students' understanding of fairness, discrimination, and equity.

Try Block's (2016) five prongs.

1. Gregory Michie's (2014) windows and mirrors strategy involves giving
   students windows into the lives of others and mirrors to reflect their own
   reality.
2. In Paulo Freire's (1970a) idea of *conscientization*, students take responsibility
   for their education, knowing that they can be honest and be heard.
3. Susan Lytle's (2008) *problematizing* approach to inquiry encourages students
   to question commonly accepted notions related to fairness and equity.
4. *Metacognition* helps students process their own learning.
5. Opportunities provide chances to authentically learn about and practice
   democracy in education.

CONSCIOUSNESS EXERCISE: Windows

Source: Adapted from Michie, 2014.

You can implement this over a period of one or two weeks with opportunities for
students to create, review, and reflect at least three times. This is most appropriate
for students in grades 4–8.

*We caution teachers that many issues, including gender identity, suicide, rape, sexual
molestation, or abuse, may trigger or re-traumatize students.* Issues such as racial discrimination, gang affiliation, or families seeking asylum in another country are very real
struggles that can equally evoke stressful responses in classroom discussion, because
this window mirrors students' own realities. If this is the case, it may be better to
modify this activity and present it to students as an opportunity to journal about
their circumstances.

The steps for this activity follow.

1. Prepare one or more robust examples. Possible themes or activities may
   include references to recent news, movies, or even cartoons. While you can
   use this exercise for various circumstances, it can be particularly relevant to
   learn more about people who have been marginalized, who have undergone
   some hardship, or who are facing dilemmas requiring difficult decisions.
2. Discuss the concept of windows and mirrors. You might open a discussion
   by asking students about the functions, similarities, and differences between
   the two. Teachers could ask students questions such as, "Which one lets in
   light? Which one lets in fresh air? Which one allows you to view an image
   of yourself?" Move on to discussing the topic for the day, asking students
   to consider how they might symbolically let in light or fresh air to further
   understanding of an event. Or another way is to consider looking into a
   window to see what is happening inside.
3. Begin with one of your examples and ask, "Looking in through the window
   as we get a glimpse of the person and the circumstance, what do we learn

about the individual's life and his or her family or friends? How does he or she feel? What might the person be thinking? Was anyone helpful?"

4. Let students choose how to do their work. It may be a piece of art to reflect the inner turmoil, or it may be a poem, essay, or story about someone facing a similar circumstance.

5. Over the next several days, give students time to research, review, revise, or continue working on their art or writing.

You can adapt this exercise to different times in history so students can write about refugees coming to Ellis Island, about slavery's Middle Passage, or about Native Americans who were forced onto reservations using an outsider's perspective looking inward.

CONSCIOUSNESS EXERCISE: Mirrors

Source: Adapted from Michie, 2014.

You can implement this over a period of one or two weeks with opportunities for students to create, review, and reflect at least three times. This is most appropriate for students in grades 4–8. The steps follow.

1. Discuss how mirrors can help deepen our understanding of self. Mirrors can come in any of a number of forms—someone who is our same age, who has the same or similar beliefs, who likes the same music, who has the same skin tone, or who serves as a role model (a teacher, a businessperson in the community, or even a character in a book).

2. Invite students to write down bullet points about who they are, the mirrors in their lives, and the role the mirrors play.

3. Students observe (or, if the mirrors are in a book, read and think about) their mirrors over several days.

4. Ask students to think and write about how the mirrors have influenced their thinking, including their views of themselves.

If a student seems not to have a mirror (consider a child who has just arrived from Somalia and finds no other Somalians at school), you can ask the student to write about the absence or to imagine and write about a person who could serve as a mirror.

CONSCIOUSNESS EXERCISE: A Realization of Oneness Meditation

After students have completed the Windows and Mirrors exercises, you can introduce the concept of oneness and unity. In essence, this is one world, and we are dependent on the kindness and goodwill of others, hoping that they are conscious of others and recognize the importance of sharing resources, supporting others in the time of need, and acting in ways that are altruistic and intended to extend help to others. This activity can be repeated several times. It is appropriate for students in grades 3–12, as well as for adults. The steps follow.

1. Introduce the concept of oneness as described in the preceding paragraph.
2. Indicate that students will experience a meditation that lasts between five and seven minutes.
3. Invite students to close their eyes and breathe long and deep.
4. In a soft, unhurried voice, say, "Imagine that you are holding a candle, its flame lit. Perhaps you can even see the flame waver back and forth as you breathe." Pause here.
5. In a few beats, say, "As you continue to breathe, imagine that this classroom is filled with lit candles—that each student is holding one." Pause again.
6. In a few beats, say, "Now imagine a world full of people holding a candle, each lit, and many candle flames wavering as you continue to breathe long and deep. You could even imagine each person who holds a candle breathing long and deep. It is almost as if there were one breath." Pause.
7. In a few beats, say, "Feel a unity with these people around the globe." Pause.
8. In a few beats, say, "Continue to breathe long and deep." Pause.
9. In a few beats, say, "Return your attention to yourself, to this room, to the candles lit in this room, and to the people in this room, breathing one breath. Now focus on your candle, yourself. Breathe long and deep and imagine the candle now centered inside your body, its flame glowing brightly." Pause.
10. In a few beats, say, "Feel peace. And when you are ready, inhale deeply, hold your breath, exhale, and open your eyes."

What Does Consciousness Look Like Historically?

Brazilian educator and philosopher Paulo Freire (1970b, 1996), in the *Pedagogy of the Oppressed*, presents an approach to individual and community self-determination (the ability to decide on a course of action) that asks educators to facilitate the elimination of suffering and oppression. Freire believed that educators could be transformative as they spread information about the power of democracy and that such an approach could reduce youth alienation, helping them find their voice and expose injustices.

CONSCIOUSNESS EXERCISE: Conscientization Project

Conscientization, in its strictest sense, may apply more to a way a classroom or school is set up and the underlying philosophy behind the educational approach. For this exercise, the teacher takes students through a series of activities that are based on Paulo Freire's (1970a) conscientization to help them understand intergenerational equity, where both the students and teachers learn, question, reflect, and participate in meaning-making. Students, with this approach, exercise personal responsibility, and the teacher acts as a facilitator.

The following exercise is most appropriate for students in grades 4–12. Students share responsibility for determining both what to study and how. Visit **go.Solution Tree.com/behavior** for links to projects on hunger and food insecurity. The steps for this exercise follow.

1. Introduce Paulo Freire, explaining his beliefs and asking students to consider ways people are oppressed and suffering. Students could review this in a historical context, studying the Brazilian society from which Freire's thinking germinated, or in a societal culture and context that students choose. For example, students could study the treatment of First Nations people in Canada, religious oppression in India, or the impact of anti-Semitism both during World War II and in 2020. You can modify this exercise to focus on the impact of waste management practices, recycling, or climate change.
2. Explain that students will decide on a class project that will be implemented over the next few months (or over the entire school year), and, for the project, students will study about a global concern and then learn about the impact on their local community. From that point, students will design and implement a solution.
3. Let students decide how they learn—individually or in teams, roles and responsibilities of various team members, whether they conduct local interviews or talk online with peers in other areas or locales, and the final product, including whether they prepare a presentation to deliver to a local community council, or invite community leaders to their school to hear about their work.
4. Ask students to develop a budget, figure out a timeline for implementation, and over a period of weeks, modify their solution based on what they learn.
5. At the end of the time period, students evaluate their results.

You can modify the exercise for preK–3 by tying the project more specifically to STEM or STEAM (science, technology, engineering, art, and mathematics) curricula and activities, reducing the scope of the work and the research. Critical components include the following.

- Student involvement in decision making about the project
- Active student engagement
- Reinforcing the link between what students learned and its impact on a group of people, whether it be people in their local community or elsewhere

CONSCIOUSNESS EXERCISE: Problematizing

French philosopher Michel Foucault (1991) describes *problematization* as an "endeavour to know how and to what extent it might be possible to think differently, instead of what is already known" (p. 76). In problematizing, Foucault relies on historical analysis to uproot common assumptions and to expand thinking. Susan Gasson and Jonan Donaldson (2018) explain how combining problematizing with *framing* (identifying or defining the context) can help students discover new ways of understanding a situation. For this exercise, we combine framing and problematization to increase awareness and understanding.

The following examples work best for middle and high school students, and you could easily conduct them in three class sessions. You can effectively use a shortened version with students in grades 3–6, where they discuss the challenge, create a frame, and reframe the situation, arriving at a new understanding or an alternative solution to the challenge.

Session one would include the following three steps.

1. Present students with a challenge, such as how to reduce gasoline consumption or how to reduce societal violence and help build a more compassionate culture.
2. Let students discuss the issue, including the societal context and the frame surrounding the challenge. During that time, students reframe the situation, examining it through a different lens. For example, with gasoline consumption, the students may consider the impact of shifting education and workforce resulting in most people working from their homes. You could also consider how much fuel is consumed in transporting food from one region of the country to another.
3. Ask students to elaborate on the framing they completed in step 2, helping understand the context, creating scenarios around the frame, and sharing online with each other.

Session two would include the following two steps.

1. Add problematizing, where students question the frame and common assumptions, and may even proceed to break the frame.
2. Reframe by re-situating the challenge with stories or analogies. Teachers briefly review the process they used, lead a discussion about the issue and context, ask students to recall how they reframed the issue (perhaps with *what if* statements), and provide or ask for some examples of elaboration, reframing, and problematizing. You can create a flowchart showing these steps, and then take students one step further by asking them to work in groups to create a scenario around one of the challenges and the solutions. Some of these stories may lead to analogies such as "It was almost like

waiting for the other shoe to drop"
or "They felt relief that was like finding your way home after being lost in the woods."

Session three would include the following step.

1. Share the scenarios and analogies.

CONSCIOUSNESS EXERCISE: Metacognition Exit Ticket
Source: Adapted from Owen and Vista, 2017.

A crucial part of understanding self and increasing awareness of self is knowing something about how you, as an individual, think and learn. Through metacognitive reflection, students can draw conclusions about such things as how they learn best, what they could do to improve their learning, or how to monitor their studying and learning to adapt to changing circumstances and needs. Metacognition can also help students plan and set goals for their learning.

1. During the last few minutes of class, give students a prompt to answer before they can exit the classroom. You can use the following prompts, the first three of which are suggested by David Owen and Alvin Vista (2017).
   - "Today my learning stopped because . . ."
   - "Today the question, new idea, or new perspective I considered was . . ."
   - "Today I understood and learned . . ."
   - "The learning activity I most appreciated today was . . . and I enjoyed that activity because . . ."
   - "I intend to complete today's assignment by . . ."
   - "The one study strategy I will use to prepare for an upcoming exam is . . ."

2. We recommend explaining to students that they have the option to respond to *one* of these prompts as they leave the class.

CONSCIOUSNESS EXERCISE: Democracy in Education

In an article on student ownership in education, Jonathan Scott (n.d.), director of policy for the Ontario Student Trustees' Association, describes the importance of students co-owning their education. Traditional student councils are one venue in which students can be empowered to contribute to and gain ownership of their schools. However, there are other ways to help students learn more about their options for experiences in practicing democracy.

- Ubegin (https://ubegin.com) is a website devoted to helping people connect to create communities and address worldwide issues such as poverty and hunger, affordable and clean energy, peace and social justice, and inequality.

- The Institute for Evolutionary Leadership (www.evoleadinstitute.com/connect) is designed to build a sustainable international community, and it offers workshops and retreats on topics such as global social evolution, addressing adaptive challenges, and evolutionary leadership.
- The Center for Collaborative Education (https://bit.ly/2YZW0lq) helps educators foster schools that are equitable, so that all students are enriched and engaged.

For this exercise, teams of high school students could review these websites and either elect to participate for a period of time in one of the websites' offerings or report to their peers what they discovered at the website.

To adapt this lesson for middle school students, review resources at one or more of the websites. For example, the Center for Collaborative Education has a report and slide presentation on fostering excellence and equity for black and Latino males (Tung et al., 2015).

CONSCIOUSNESS EXERCISE: The Five Ws of Conscious Living

This exercise can help students in grades 4–8 integrate consciousness into their lives. Introduce it after completing a number of the preceding exercises. The steps for this exercise are as follows.

1. Give each student a blank copy of the Five Ws of Conscious Living form (an abbreviated version of which is shown in figure 3.2).
2. In teams of three or four, have students identify between four and six issues related to their future and the planet's future. They list those issues down the side of the grid. If a single sheet is insufficient, students can work on large sheets of butcher paper, on poster boards, or electronically.
3. Students fill in who is involved; what the issue is; when this will be a critical concern; and where, why, and how the issue may be addressed.
4. After completing the form, teams go back, choose one issue as a priority, and make decisions about what they know and what they want to know. They could fill out a Know, Want to Know, Learned (KWL) chart, like the one in figure 3.3.
5. Give teams a few days to conduct research to fill in their knowledge gaps for their priority concern. Teams could consider potential solutions, how they are being researched, and what appears to be most promising and why. Teachers and teams may wish to use exercises such as framing and reframing, problematizing, or practicing democracy as students study an area and arrive at their recommendations or that priority concern.
6. Teams develop a presentation and give it to the class on their priority topic area.

Topic	Clean water	Clean water
Who	People living in areas impacted by a recent hurricane	Families in U.S. cities
What	How to obtain clean water and avoid diseases such as cholera and typhoid	In cities, the issue relates largely to lead in pipes
When	After a recent hurricane	A current issue
Where	Might be in the Caribbean, New Orleans, or Houston	Most prevalent in older cities and poorer neighborhoods
Why	To avoid illness and further health and well-being	For children's health, to avoid serious long-term problems
How	Short-term: what water sources to use and which ones to avoid; how to use iodine drops; how to get access to bottled water Long-term: how to purify water	Repair the infrastructure

Figure 3.2: Five Ws of Conscious Living form.

*Visit **go.SolutionTree.com/behavior** for a free reproducible version of this figure.*

Know	Want to Know	Learned
• After a hurricane, city water systems may not be working properly, so there may not be any safe tap water. • It might be difficult for people to get clean water after a hurricane. • People can get very sick if they drink water that's not clean.	• How do you know if you can safely drink the tap water or not after a hurricane? • Where should you get water if the tap water is not safe? • How do you purify water? • Can you purify water without electricity?	• There are cheap, easy-to-use tests to see if water is safe to drink. • You should stock up on bottled water when you know a hurricane is coming. • There are home kits and straws to purify water. Water filters that attach to sinks or are inside pitchers do not purify water, but merely remove just some toxins.

Figure 3.3: KWL for the five Ws of Conscious Living—example.

*Visit **go.SolutionTree.com/behavior** for a free reproducible version of this figure.*

How Do We Measure Consciousness?

The following tools measure consciousness: the Five Facet Mindfulness Questionnaire, the Mindful Attention Awareness Scale, and S-CCATE.

Five Facet Mindfulness Questionnaire

The Five Facet Mindfulness Questionnaire (Baer, Smith, Hopkins, Krietemeyer, & Toney, 2006; https://bit.ly/2mfXhYa) assesses mindfulness characteristics using a five-point Likert scale to assess nonreactivity, observing, acting with awareness, describing, and nonjudging. Examples of items that measure each of these factors follow (Baer et al., 2006).

- **Nonreactivity:** "I perceive my feelings and emotions without having to react to them."
- **Observing:** "When I take a shower or bath, I stay alert to the sensations of water on my body."
- **Acting with awareness:** "I find myself doing things without paying attention."
- **Describing:** "It's hard for me to find the words to describe what I am thinking."
- **Nonjudging:** "I make judgments about whether my thoughts are good or bad."

Mindful Attention Awareness Scale

The Mindful Attention Awareness Scale (MAAS), developed by Brown and Ryan (2003; https://bit.ly/2uKTYME), provides evidence that mindful thought leads to increased emotional awareness (Sivanathan, Arnold, Turner, & Barling, 2004). Numerous studies have confirmed the validity of MAAS for use with adults, and a few studies have been conducted with youth. Versions of MAAS are also available for students aged 9–12 (MAAS-C) and aged 14–18 (MAAS-A). A 2013 study conducted in Chengdu, China, confirmed that mindfulness decreases mental health concerns and also has the potential to reduce disruptive and inappropriate behaviors (Black, Sussman, Johnson, & Milam, 2009).

With MAAS, respondents use a six-point Likert scale to rate their own level of mindfulness for factors such as receptiveness and awareness to the present. The survey includes items such as the following (Brown & Ryan, 2003).

- "I find it difficult to stay focused on what's happening in the present."
- "I rush through activities without being really attentive to them."
- "I find myself preoccupied with the future or the past."

A short version with six items is also available.

S-CCATE

S-CCATE and the S-CCATE Supplement measure consciousness through items such as those in table 3.1.

Table 3.1: S-CCATE Consciousness Factors

Factor	In Action
Conscious communication	Teachers and school leaders help students understand the importance of practicing compassion (including empathy, humility, kindness, forgiveness, and caring). Per the Five Ws of Conscious Living exercise (page 54), this factor helps monitor teacher and administrator actions that improve consciousness.
Conscious awareness of emotions and stress	Students find out how to protect themselves when they are in vulnerable situations related to childhood trauma and stress.
Conscious awareness of emotions and stress	Teachers and school leaders teach students about neuroscience and neuroplasticity.

S-CCATE also includes items on a subscale about equity and justice.

- Students are aware of inequities (including discrimination, poverty, injustice, and gender) in their community.
- Students are aware of racial prejudice and racist actions in their community and elsewhere.

Reflection

To get the most out of this chapter, reflect on these questions after reading it.

- Which aspects of consciousness (awareness of self, awareness of others, or community consciousness and issues of understanding marginalized populations) are you most likely to focus on when implementing this in your classroom?
- Are there students in your class who you know have faced specific traumas? If so, what precautions might you take prior to implementation?
- What did you or your students learn about the importance of context, framing, and problematizing in terms of increasing consciousness?
- Are you using any metacognitive activities with students? If so, what is their impact?
- How did students respond to the other consciousness exercises? Are you likely to use them again or make modifications next time you use them?

— Notes —

CHAPTER 4

Compassion

Love and compassion are necessities, not luxuries. Without them, humanity cannot survive.

—The 14th Dalai Lama

key principle

Compassion is the underlying ingredient for developing an open heart and setting the right tone and environment for any classroom, school, district, or community.

❤

The 14th Dalai Lama embodies compassion, teaching all of humanity the essentiality of compassion in this world. Compassion is explained as a mutual exchange of exercising a genuine sympathy for others' suffering as well as the will to help minimize or reduce their pain, and, in turn, receiving a strength gained through this extension of love and caring (Dalai Lama, 2010). Compassion and love, as the Dalai Lama (2010) explains, bring us the "greatest happiness simply because our nature cherishes them above all else. The need for love lies at the very foundation of human existence. It results from the profound interdependence we all share with one another."

Compassion is essential for good health and well-being, learning, and loving. Consciousness is the premise on which compassion is cultivated, bringing an undivided attention and awareness to another's suffering or pain at a given moment. Building on heightened awareness or consciousness, compassion helps us focus away from our own issues and concerns long enough to pay attention to someone else's hurt and suffering.

Exploring the concept of compassion, knowing why it matters and how to teach it in school, discovering what it has looked like in the past, and learning how to measure it can move us one more step toward mindful school communities.

What Is Compassion?

To open our hearts and minds to others requires compassion. Compassion helps cultivate support and nurture mindful learning communities where students can thrive. Compassion is the ability to understand another person's suffering, pain, or emotional state. It is more than exercising empathy or identifying with another's pain; it is the inner desire to help alleviate or reduce the suffering of another person. Researchers Jennifer L. Goetz, Dacher Keltner, and Emiliana Simon-Thomas (2010) explain its neurological basis and how it is conveyed, and contrast it to related emotions and attributes such as love and empathy. They define compassion as "the feeling that arises when witnessing another's suffering and that motivates a desire to help" (Goetz et al., 2010, p. 351). Jazaieri et al. (2013), from a contemplative perspective, define four components, including (1) awareness of suffering, (2) sympathetic concern, (3) an intention to see relief, and (4) a responsiveness to relieve suffering.

The more love and compassion we demonstrate for others, the greater our own sense of health, well-being, and joy. When we understand that human suffering is universal and cultivate a heartfelt feeling for others and our world, we naturally are better able to put our minds and bodies at ease, reduce our own fears and insecurities, and gain newfound strength to cope with whatever comes our way. However, how we sense and express compassion is not only individual; it is also developmental, multitextured, and complex.

Child Development and Compassion

Several studies support the notion that compassion exists from the beginning of life. In one study of infants, their pupils widened, demonstrating their concern, when observing someone in need, but their pupils shrunk once someone else responded to the need, suggesting that they were no longer concerned (Dunfield, Kuhlmeier, O'Connell, & Kelley, 2011; Hepach, Vaish, & Tomasello, 2012). It was calming to see the person's suffering being alleviated, whether or not they were the ones who did it. In children as young as two, giving treats to others increases the givers' happiness more than receiving treats (Aknin, Hamlin, & Dunn, 2012). Similar research finds that the instinct of both adults and children is to help rather than to compete with others (Rand, Greene, & Nowak, 2012).

Compassion's Multitextured and Complex Elements

As British professor of clinical psychology Paul Gilbert (2017) explains, compassion is multitextured—reflecting an awareness of suffering, empathy, and desire for healing and to alleviate pain and suffering, as well as aspects of altruism, prosocial behavior, and neurobiological elements that may draw us toward or away from opportunities to be kind and caring. Compassion is complex in that it contains cognitive, emotional, attitudinal, and behavioral aspects. Compassion may be inspirational and also incorporate preventative components: "Compassion must involve evaluating and providing for needs that prevent suffering" (Gilbert, 2017, p. 10). Despite its many benefits, our experiences, cultures, and competing interests present barriers, making it easy to turn away from compassion. Gilbert (2017) reminds us that courage and devotion to preventing and alleviating suffering lead to compassion, which helps us make wise, rather than uninformed, decisions. This holds true for adults and children.

Patty Kohler-Evans and Candice Dowd Barnes (2015) summarize the essence of a discussion they had with colleagues, stating that the "one characteristic that stood out as both the most essential in humankind as well as that which is most missing in today's world was compassion" (p. 33). More policymakers, institutions, and organizations are recognizing the need for a more well-rounded, social-emotional, compassionate, balanced approach to educate our students, and rightfully so (Berkowitz, Moore, Astor, & Benbenishty, 2017; Brown, Corrigan, & Higgins-D'Alessandra, 2012; CASEL, 2018; Greenberg, Domitrovich, Weissberg, & Durlak, 2017). In school, compassionate learning environments become essential to help mitigate the myriad challenges associated with suffering and pain experienced by our students.

Why Does Compassion Matter in School?

Much of school experience is focused on making sure the individual student meets certain academic standards and excels. Emma Seppala (2013), science director at the Stanford Center for Compassion and Altruism Research and Education, points out that, somewhat paradoxically, self-centeredness does more damage than good. She reminds us of the scientific evidence confirming that having a compassionate mindset is associated with success and positive outcomes. Seppala (2013) then goes on to describe the physiological differences between being self-focused and compassionate:

> When our brains move from a modality of self-focus and stress to a new modality of caring, nurturing, and connecting, our heart rate accelerates, vagal tone—our ability to relax and return to normal after stressful events—is strengthened, and we release hormones that are key for connection and bonding, such as oxytocin. In this new state, we feel at ease. (p. 15)

Compassion is not experienced at simply a cognitive or emotional level. When we give or receive compassion, an invisible bond forms with other people that includes a physiological component that can calm anxieties and strengthen a sense of well-being. For children who have experienced trauma and may have difficulty forming attachments, these bonding experiences can be critical.

Compassion motivates us to be more accepting of others, to help in difficult situations, to be sympathetic listeners, and to create an environment of harmony and peace at school, work, and home. Considering the racism, discrimination, bullying, and suicide so prevalent in schools, these considerations are integral to ensuring student safety, self-esteem, happiness, and sense of purpose (CDC, 2019; Clark & Marinak, 2010; Coughlan, 2018; Federal Bureau of Investigation, 2018).

More schools are becoming interested in addressing compassionate responses to trauma. For example, in 2017, Watauga County, North Carolina, initiated a program that included collaboration with social service agencies and medical providers, and trauma-informed care training for staff. They also implemented what they call a *silent mentor* to ensure that each student had a positive connection with at least one caring adult at school and designated locations in classrooms where students could go to refocus and destress as they regulated their emotions (Presnell, 2018).

Compassion in school matters because it helps stress diminish, which enables learning, and because focusing on others helps us avoid mental illness.

Stress Diminishes, Compassion Enables

Research shows that compassion's benefits extend beyond the mind to the body in quantifiable ways. We can measure the relationship of compassion to happiness at the cellular level (Fredrickson et al., 2013). And there is a difference between *hedonistic happiness* (which occurs when your life is full of pleasure) and *eudaimonic happiness* (which occurs when your life has purpose or meaning). Eudaimonic happiness translates to living a life more focused on helping others than the self, a key aspect of compassion. Fredrickson and colleagues (2013), in researching happiness, expected to find that all so-called happy people would have low levels of inflammation (because inflammation is a common correlate of stress). However, their findings indicate that only those whose happiness derived from *living a life focused on helping others* had lower inflammation levels.

Abraham Maslow (1943) theorized a hierarchy of needs that has several levels. When a student's sense of belonging, security, safety, certainty, and self-confidence is strengthened in a classroom by scaffolding, a stronger basis for learning, motivation, self-discipline, responsibility, and the capacity to deal more effectively with mistakes is supported. In the absence of such compassionate support, a student's educational experience is diminished, and any joy or feelings of accomplishment that should occur are drastically reduced. Heart centered school environments that nurture and support social-emotional development in students "reinforce motivation and learning, and touch both hearts and minds of students" (Brooks, 2000, p. 1). While teachers are sometimes cautious about addressing significant social-emotional needs, Robert Brooks and Sam Goldstein (2011), coauthors of *Raising Resilient Children: Fostering Strength, Hope, and Optimism in Your Child*, point out that strengthening a student's self-worth through caring and compassion is not extra, but essential.

Researchers Shanetia P. Clark and Barbara A. Marinak (2010) believe that adolescent bullying and violence, which have risen to an alarming rate compared to previous generations, can be confronted with in-school programs that integrate "kindness—the antithesis of victimization" (as cited in Currie, 2014). While traditional antibullying programs tend to focus on the negative actions that result from bullying, teaching students how to transform their negative thoughts and actions better fosters a culture of kindness and compassion, leading to warmer, more inclusive school environments.

Focusing on Others Helps Prevent Mental Illness

Another benefit of compassion is that it gets us out of focus on self, something that can lead to narcissism and even depression and anxiety (Watkins & Moulds, 2005). Think about a time when you were feeling somewhat down and a friend called for advice. You may find that your mood lifted or you became energized as you shifted your focus to that person's needs. Also, when we are compassionate, we are less likely to be isolated, which contributes to depression, obesity, high blood pressure, and disease (Holt-Lunstad, Smith, & Layton, 2010). In a meta-analysis of one-hundred forty-eight studies, Julianne Holt-Lunstad, Timothy Smith, and J. Bradley Layton (2010) find that social connections, such as those that accompany compassionate responses, improve our immune systems and lead to faster recovery from illness. If you're unwell, it is often more difficult to learn. Caring for yourself becomes paramount.

How Do We Teach Compassion?

Compassion instruction begins with setting a positive and loving tone in school, modeling compassionate attitudes and behaviors. Teachers can also use any of a number of curricula or programs that highlight compassion, supplementing with books that have characters demonstrating compassion. School counseling, mindfulness practices, self-compassion, empathy, kindness, and positive discipline also further children's compassion.

Teach and Model Compassion

Compassion is taught and nurtured through example and role modeling. Teachers and school leaders need to exercise a true commitment to kindness as well as caring and heartfelt human interactions; set a positive and loving tone in the classroom, school, and district; and create a healthier and more loving educational learning environment. In a compassionate learning environment, students will feel inclined to help one another when needed, openly demonstrating a caring heart. Those who are suffering will feel more supported.

Teaching compassion is not like teaching mathematical formulas. It is something that must be woven into our daily school routine so that it permeates beyond the school boundaries, into the community and our homes, embedded in our hearts. How we answer students' questions, how we help solve conflicts on the playground, how we gently nudge or nurture their growing capacity to think about other people and their own actions—all help to develop compassion. Teaching about compassion also requires teachers and school leaders to help students develop a growth mindset—an understanding that abilities are malleable—leading to nonjudgment of self and others (Dweck, 2015).

Teachers can promote active compassion by maintaining positive expectations, exuding warmth (while remaining firm), being courteous to all students and faculty, allowing students to take ownership of their learning, and avoiding, at all costs, the temptation to make sarcastic and cutting remarks. Like any habit, compassion builds on itself; the more you practice active compassion, the more it exists in your life. In the midst of difficulties, teachers who can keep their cool, rather than lose their temper and reprimand, further a student's sense of self and ability to self-regulate. The compassionate teacher, rather than creating a tense and even hostile environment, can increase a student's sense of well-being and security.

Brooks (2009) observes that when teachers hover, micromanage, or control, there is increased chaos, unrest, and unease. Brooks (2009) urges teachers to shift their mindset to focus on the big-picture approach, examining why we are here and working in this teaching profession. The resulting heightened awareness moves teachers' concentration from taking student behavior personally toward gently guiding students through their distress and struggle to take the needed steps to improve and reach higher expectations within the classroom.

To teach compassion, adults need to model it and make it a part of classroom and school community expectations. Quickly setting a positive tone in the classroom may be one of the most indispensable factors in creating a healthy educational environment. Julia Thompson (2018), a public school teacher for more than thirty-five years, has the following suggestions.

- Smile at your students to show that you're happy to be with them.
- Be an active listener by paying attention when your students speak to you.
- Cheer students on at sporting events, choir concerts, and other events where students perform a talent.
- Show concern for and ask about students' families and other significant people in their lives.
- Ask students, "What can I do to help?"
- Verbally notice and encourage acts of kindness amongst students.
- Pay attention to signs that a student's basic needs are not being met and help the student meet those needs.
- Encourage students to succeed and assure them you want to help them achieve their dreams.

While many of Thompson's suggestions seem self-evident, her advice provides a reminder about how compassion can be furthered by little things such as a few kind words and your own enthusiasm.

Use Established Compassion Curricula

While infusing compassionate moments and policies into the school will increase some students' compassion, using a curriculum to directly teach the skill provides opportunities to practice in a structured lesson with guidance and feedback. Following are examples of five research-based programs available online that could be used as part of a compassionate school curriculum.

- The **Compassionate Schools Project** (www.compassionschools.org /program) includes ten principles of a compassionate school, such as empowerment, positive regard, and high expectations. It includes recommendations for becoming a trauma-sensitive school, helping students understand emotions and self-regulation, enhancing listening abilities and empathy, and building positive relationships (Kohler-Evans & Barnes, 2015).

- The **Compassionate Action Network** (www.compassionateactionnetwork .org) supports compassion initiatives on a global basis by partnering with schools and universities to share case studies, curricula, resources, and stories from institutions seeking to embed compassion into every aspect of the learning process. For example, the Children's Charter for Compassion provides a means for children and those around them to understand how to treat themselves and others with love and compassion.

- The **Compassion Games** (http://compassiongames.org) originated when a Louisville, Kentucky, mayor's challenge to citizens to perform acts of service in the community resulted in more than 90,000 acts of service recorded in one week. Now, it is an international initiative with several fun ways for kids to practice compassion. To be a secret agent of compassion, young participants receive a daily email during two weeks in September, urging them to commit compassionate acts and relay them by uploading a recording for others to view.

- The **Kindness Curriculum** (https://bit.ly/38iFbZb) teaches compassion by focusing on empathy, gratitude, and sharing through simple twenty-minute stories and practices that help students learn how to pay attention, regulate emotions, and cultivate kindness. A study of this curriculum's effects found that it enhances executive functioning and emotional regulation and increases social competence, cognitive flexibility, and delay of gratification (Flook, Goldberg, Pinger, & Davidson, 2015).

- **PeaceJam** (www.peacejam.org) provides a format for youth to engage in service projects. Five million students have participated in extracurricular

PeaceJam clubs since 1996. Since then, fourteen Nobel Peace Prize winners have collaborated with others to facilitate 65 million peace projects. The program combines service and diversity education. It has reduced bullying behaviors and gives us an in-depth understanding of empathy and volunteer work.

Practicing Compassion: PeaceJam

James S. Rickards High School in Tallahassee, Florida, uses PeaceJam (www .peacejam.org) to instill civic engagement, peacemaking skills, and the understanding of social justice issues in its students. Students work on a civic engagement project throughout the year, discussing different relevant lessons and concepts along the way. One group presented their project, a peace memorial built around their school's campus, to Nobel Peace Prize winner Rigoberta Menchú. Teachers say they are impressed with the wisdom, compassion, and connection they see between students in the club each year, where students are mentored by and dialogue with inspiring Nobel Peace Prize winners like the following.

- Óscar Arias Sánchez, a former president of Costa Rica who was pivotal in bringing peace to Central America
- José Ramos-Horta, a former president and prime minister of East Timor, who fought for freedom from oppression, developing a peace plan that resulted in the withdrawal of Indonesia from East Timor
- Mairead Corrigan Maguire, a peace activist in Northern Ireland
- Betty Williams, a peace activist in Northern Ireland and president of World Centers of Compassion for Children
- Adolfo Pérez Esquivel, an artist, writer, and activist who defended human rights in Argentina
- Sir Joseph Rotblat, a Polish-born British physicist who promoted nuclear disarmament
- Leymah Gbowee, a Liberian peace activist who led Women of Liberia Mass Action for Peace

At the PeaceJam website, you can uncover more about membership and curriculum options, such as the bullying prevention curriculum Compassion in Action, which prepares students at all grade levels to live with compassion in a multicultural world by exploring issues of diversity from personal, social, and institutional perspectives during lessons and discussions about Nobel Peace Prize laureates and by completing service projects inspired by their work.

Read Books About the Topic

In addition to being a model of compassion and introducing students to real-life examples of compassionate leaders, you can allow storybook characters to be peer models of compassion for students. Try integrating stories that provide examples of children showing compassion to others into your curriculum. Visit **go.SolutionTree .com/behavior** for more book ideas.

- *The Kindness Quilt* by Nancy Elizabeth Wallace (2006) describes one classroom's kindness project, giving many examples of acts of kindness students can practice in their daily lives. It might even inspire your class to make a kindness quilt of their own (for K–grade 2).
- *Crossing the Starlight Bridge* by Alice Mead (1994) is a story about a young Native American girl who doesn't want to leave her reservation and start over in a new place, until her grandmother shows some compassion by easing her into life on the mainland (for grades 3–5).
- In *Wonder* by R. J. Palacio (2012), a ten-year-old boy attends public school for the first time, as his jarring facial anomalies cause himself and other students to see him with their hearts (for grades 3–8).
- In *Children of the River* by Linda Crew (1991), a thirteen-year-old girl who fled Cambodia to escape the Khmer Rouge army arrives in Oregon, where she struggles to fit in at the high school (for grades 9–12).
- In *Speak* by Laurie Halse Anderson (2011), a high school student becomes increasingly isolated after an event at a high school party. She finds some solace in art class where she comes to understand more about the trauma she has experienced and is finally able to speak up for herself (for grades 9–12).

When students want a break from reading or being read to, visit the Compassion International channel on YouTube (www.youtube.com/user/CompassionIntl) and Mindful Teachers (https://bit.ly/2KEYb9e) for videos about this element.

Try School Counseling Programs

School counseling programs, one of the most direct pathways of addressing social-emotional needs, can infuse compassion into daily lives in innovative ways. One consideration is strengths-based school counseling, which focuses on the areas of a student's life where the student is experiencing some success, rather than approaching counseling from a problem-focused lens (Galassi, 2017). Such programs facilitate bonding, resilience, prosocial norms, and self-determination, which supports the development of compassion (Grant & Mason, 2017).

In elementary school, this approach could include a schoolwide program, presented by school counselors in classrooms and school assemblies, that encourages students to show self-compassion. In middle school, school counselors can lead one-on-one or small-group visualization exercises in which students imagine themselves using the skills they have or are developing to achieve a goal. School counselors at the high school level can develop a peer support group by training student leaders in compassionate conversation methods so that they can lend an empathic ear to students struggling with mental health issues.

Practicing Compassion: Comfort Dog Program

Middle School 88 in Brooklyn, New York—a school that serves a diverse population with a high incidence of trauma—uses the Comfort Dog program to reduce anxiety and reform behavior by learning life lessons in compassion and conflict resolution. Since the school started the Comfort Dog program, staff have noticed that the rescue dogs allow students who have difficulty with interpersonal relationships—with peers and school staff—to show compassion and vulnerability to another being. This is especially true for students with learning and physical disabilities (Border, 2017).

Practice Mindfulness

Neuroscientists have found that the brain experiences positive changes and people demonstrate more altruistic behavior after a short-term compassion training program using mindfulness techniques like meditation (Weng et al., 2013). As little as seven minutes increased participants' feelings of closeness and connection to the person about whom they thought while meditating. Researcher Barbara Fredrickson (2009) finds that a meditation program as short as seven weeks could increase positive emotions and life satisfaction and reduce the symptoms of depression. Try a loving kindness meditation with your students to boost the level of compassion in your classroom.

COMPASSION EXERCISE: Receiving Loving Kindness

Source: Adapted from Greater Good in Action, n.d.

Read the following steps to students from kindergarten to grade 12.

1. Say, "Keeping your eyes closed, think of a person close to you who loves you very much. It could be someone from the past or the present; someone still alive or who has passed; it could be a spiritual teacher or guide." Pause.

2. After a few beats, say, "Imagine that person standing on your right side, sending you his or her love. That person is sending you wishes for your safety, for your well-being and happiness. Feel the warm wishes and love coming from that person toward you." Pause.

3. After a few beats, say, "Now bring to mind the same person or another person who cherishes you deeply. Imagine that person standing on your left side, sending you wishes for your wellness, for your health and happiness. Feel the kindness and warmth coming to you from that person." Pause.

4. After a few beats, say, "Now imagine that you are surrounded on all sides by all the people who love you and have loved you. Picture all of your friends and loved ones surrounding you. They are sending you wishes for your happiness, well-being, and health. Bask in the warm wishes and love coming from all sides. You are filled and overflowing with warmth and love."

Show Self-Compassion

Teaching students how to be compassionate toward themselves helps them show compassion toward other people. Teachers and students can benefit from learning about and exercising self-compassion. When people are kinder and gentler with themselves, it becomes more natural to be kinder and gentler with others. As Kristen Neff and Christopher Germer (2013) state, "Self-compassion is associated with positive psychological strengths such as happiness, optimism, wisdom, curiosity and exploration, personal initiative, and emotional intelligence" (p. 28). They discuss how "judging oneself when things go wrong tends to exacerbate emotional pain, while self-compassion helps to alleviate that pain" (p. 32).

Several psychologists have researched and promoted a progression of steps for applying compassion in our daily lives. Koncha Pinós-Pey (2017), a contemplative psychologist, considered a model of compassion that expands beyond family to the larger community as she found a way to make compassion universally understood and applied. Pinós-Pey (2017) says she believes that a foundation for secular ethics of the 21st century begins with self-compassion. After mastering self-compassion, which we can cultivate during consistent meditation practice, we can learn to extend this compassion to those we most love, then those who we feel neutral about and, finally, those we feel negative about. Pinós-Pey (2017) indicates that this practice will take time as we work through the reactive emotions of fear, anger, envy, pride, and shame.

COMPASSION EXERCISE: Treat Yourself Like a Friend

Source: Adapted from Ackerman, 2017.

Sometimes, being compassionate with ourselves is one of the most difficult things to do. Often, we spend time reliving what we could have done or should have done differently. Without self-compassion, we can find our self-esteem shrinking. On the other hand, by practicing self-compassion with guidance, and in hypothetical situations, we can learn skills that will help us avoid the slippery slope of self-judgment.

The following exercise is appropriate for students in grades 2–8.

1. Explain the following to students: "Before showing compassion to people you have negative feelings about, you need to first practice self-compassion. Most of us are better at treating our close friends with love and kindness than treating *ourselves* the way we would like to be treated."

2. Lead a discussion, asking students the following questions: "Do you offer yourself the courtesy of love and kindness? Would you talk to a friend the way you talk to yourself?"

3. Pose questions. Students can answer on a sheet of paper or in an electronic document. For grades 2 and 3, ask one question at a time. You could ask the questions over several days, perhaps asking one a day, and follow with group discussion. For grades 4 and 5, you can provide a sheet with all the questions and ask students to answer them independently prior to a group discussion.

   - "Think about a time when a close friend felt really bad or sad about him- or herself, or perhaps was struggling in some way. How did you respond to your friend? Write down what you did and said."
   - "Now think of a time when you felt sad or bad about yourself and were struggling. How did you respond? Write down what you typically do and what you say to yourself."
   - "Did you notice a difference between these answers? If so, ask yourself why. What factors or fears come into play that lead you to treat yourself and others so differently?"
   - "How do you think you might change how you respond to *yourself* to match the way you usually respond to a friend?"

4. Teachers can end by asking this question: "Why not try treating yourself like a good friend and see what happens?"

You can use a modification with middle and high school students by introducing scenarios and role play that make the same points. While some students are role playing, others could make observations aloud about the differences in how students tend to express compassion for themselves versus for their friends.

Exhibit Empathy

Like many psychologists, we choose to carefully differentiate compassion and empathy. Empathy, being able to feel another's pain, is important but only part of the components that further compassionate action. Part of modeling compassion is modeling empathy with students, other teachers, and characters in the books you read. When you don't fully agree or sympathize with someone, you have a unique opportunity to teach your students about walking in another's shoes. Students feel valued and understood when teachers empathize with them. Empathy can also inspire social change. Author William Deresiewicz (2014) asserts that the goal of education should be "to leverage learning as an agent of social change" (p. 199) by cultivating leadership and citizenship beyond the use of buzzwords. Instilling empathy in students is one pathway to that goal.

While research has shown that our first instincts are to help one another, those instincts are not equal for all groups. Humans tend to exhibit higher levels of empathy for those who are most like themselves (Gilbert, 2010). Because of this, tribalist mentalities can lead to the bigotry and racism that, due to lack of empathy for those not quite like ourselves, sometimes result in violence. Cultivating empathy in your students, therefore, is an act of social justice.

When developmental psychologist Marilyn Price-Mitchell (2015) interviewed middle and high school students who engaged in social and environmental work, she found that empathizing with others and feeling compassion for oppressed and marginalized groups motivated students to serve the greater good. Her findings make clear how teachers can foster empathy in their students.

- Create meaningful relationships with students.
- Nurture students' self-efficacy through mentoring.
- Teach values associated with good citizenship such as caring, cooperation, kindness, service, and teamwork.
- Inspire students to be their best selves.
- Expose students to different opinions and worldviews.
- Link curriculum to real-world service activities.

Practicing Compassion: Mindfulness

Principal Doug Allen implemented mindfulness practices at Grandview Heights School and Bessie Nichols School in Edmonton, Ontario, Canada. The goal at Grandview Heights was to help reduce stress at an affluent school where students and staff were under extreme pressure to continue to raise achievement. Allen began with a period of exploration, research, and discussion, followed by implementation of the Mindfulness Fundamentals curriculum (https://bit.ly/33UrNaU) produced by Mindful Schools. Judy Aldous (2018) describes the protocol that Allen used at Grandview:

> It starts with the morning messages, which might involve a *Sesame Street* video about the importance of self-control. Throughout the day, teachers can lead "mindful minutes," often at the request of the children who are feeling overwhelmed by the pressure and noise of going to school. Children learn to do quick body scans, as a way to relax.

COMPASSION EXERCISE: Intentional Listening

Source: Adapted from Ackerman, 2017.

Showing empathy starts with intentionally listening and understanding how another person feels. Sometimes, it's obvious how someone is feeling by the set of the mouth, the tone of voice, or the tears streaming down. But sometimes, we misinterpret another's emotion. Asking how someone is feeling and being an intentional listener is the best way to truly understand another person's feelings. When two people are authentically listening to each other and feel listened to, it's like getting a psychological hug. The person talking gets more in touch with his or her feelings, can gain insight into a problem or conflict, and feels validated. The person listening gains a greater understanding of the talker and might have some confusion clarified. Intentional listening can be very useful during conflict resolution, which can become necessary with a student, a coworker, a supervisor, or a parent or guardian.

Try the following steps with a friend to practice intentional listening.

1. Set a timer for ninety seconds. The talker will talk about anything he or she wishes for the entire time, uninterrupted.
2. After ninety seconds, the listener summarizes what the talker said, making sure to include any feelings the talker explicitly mentioned, but not adding his or her own interpretation of how the talker feels.
3. Now, the two of you discuss what the experience was like and how it made you feel.
4. Switch roles and repeat the exercise.

There are many other ways to practice intentional listening.

Be Kind

It's essential that students learn how to be empathic to others; however, we want to take this mindfulness into action by *practicing* kindness. Teachers can encourage and help students put their empathy in action by teaching them how to be kind to others. We have several suggestions for how to teach kindness to your students.

Practicing Compassion:
Theater for Compassion

Nilo Nora at the Center for Educational Services believes that to cultivate caring communities in the future, we must proactively create global communities for learners, teachers, and other educators. Being considerate to others, even those who are miles away, is one of the best paths to changing hearts and minds.

The Center for Educational Services promotes the African concept of *ubuntu*, or no one to be left behind (Paulson, n.d.), through a drama program that offers exciting ways to build communication and collaboration skills. Drama can isolate a factor of human experience, allowing students to better explore emotions.

The Theater for Compassion program partners with schools and teachers to train teachers, convey lesson material for classroom storytelling, and provide a teacher handbook and in-person guidance. Often, a common story is divided into parts between grade levels so that the entire school can share a cohesive piece of Theater for Compassion (Golmohammadi & Kuusilehto-Awale, 2013, 2014).

COMPASSION EXERCISE: Temperature Check

Source: Adapted from Ackerman, 2017.

Don't underestimate the power of this quick, simple exercise to bring kindergarten to grade 12 students to a place of kindness. It takes one simple question as students walk in the door of your classroom: "How are you feeling today?" Try to ask as many of your students as possible and make sure you're practicing intentional listening so you can follow up with them later. If they mentioned they were nervous about a test, check in after they have taken the test and celebrate successes or coach them through struggles.

COMPASSION EXERCISE: Good Things

Have students turn and tell their neighbor something good in their life. This works with all grades. For elementary students, provide these positive sentence starters (Alber, 2017).

- One good thing in my life is _____.
- Something good that happened is _____.

If students struggle to come up with a good thing, ask them if they had any good food or if they had a chance to play on the playground. When all students have shared with their partner, ask volunteers to share their own or their partner's good thing.

Choose Positive Discipline

Being compassionate means thinking of the feelings not just of those we can easily care for, but also of those who challenge us. Instead of approaching classroom management difficulties with the attitude of Why won't they learn? or What's wrong with them?, we could instead ask ourselves, "What do they need to help them learn?" Or, we could simply ask, "What do you need?" We know that many students who exhibit disruptive behaviors are usually having trouble regulating their emotions, yet some students may simply be hungry, and this raging hunger can also impede a student's ability to learn.

Showing compassion to students struggling to pay attention means taking the time to have a conversation with them about what's going on with their hearts, minds, and bodies. Instead of punishing students for the ways their brains have been wired after experiencing trauma, work with them to brainstorm strategies for how to pay attention better. As Brooks (2000) notes, teachers should always start with the basic assumption that everything they do or say can have a major impact on a student's life—not only in the classroom but later in life.

Showing compassion for students who have experienced trauma can transform learning into positive experiences for the students and for those teaching them. Psychologist Ross Greene (2011) developed a discipline method that can help guide teachers. The Collaborative and Proactive Solutions model is a trauma-informed method, or compassionate action approach. It uses three components to place the burden on the adult, not the student, to facilitate learning:

1. **Empathy:** Adults ask questions to figure out what's going on with the student.
2. **Problem definition:** Adults take responsibility for solving the problem.
3. **Invitation:** Adults and students work together to think of solutions and make a realistic action plan.

Collaborative and Proactive Solutions (www.cpsconnection.com/CPS-model) has shown great results at schools, correctional facilities, and inpatient psychiatry units. At a juvenile detention facility in Charleston, Maine, incidents that resulted in an injury or restraint decreased by two-thirds after implementing the approach. Similarly, Central School in South Berwick, Maine, saw discipline referrals to the principal drop from 146 to 45 (Juvenile Justice Advisory Group, n.d.).

COMPASSION EXERCISE: Cultivation

Source: Adapted from Adams, n.d.

We know that people are born with an innate desire to help others, so how do we encourage them to practice what already comes naturally to them when their lack of impulse control can sometimes make them forget to put others first? There are several ways you can help remind students in kindergarten to grade 12 to practice compassion at all times. Try integrating a few of these into your classroom.

- Promote gentleness, a form of compassion, by showing students how to handle materials, toys, and animals. Show them that being rough with things can have consequences—like a broken crayon.
- Celebrate compassion when you see your students practicing it. You can say, "Way to go! Thanks for your kindness," for example.
- Give students many opportunities to explore their feelings. They could draw how they feel, describe how certain music makes them feel, write a song about how they feel, or exhibit any other creative expression of feelings.

Visit **go.SolutionTree.com/behavior** for links to resources for teaching your students how to be compassionate.

What Does Compassion Look Like Historically?

If we examine the history of the world, where does compassion stand out? Perhaps it is with Martin Luther King Jr. or Mother Teresa? How did these leaders make a difference? How did they build compassion? Why are the lives of people like Maya Angelou and Desmond Tutu so inspiring? Have you ever been moved to tears by seeing someone's loving and compassionate behavior?

Research by Jonathan Haidt (2005), a professor of psychology at New York University, suggests that seeing someone help another person creates a state of *elevation*, that warm, uplifting feeling we get in the presence of awe-inspiring goodness. In a research study, Haidt (2005) finds that participants who watch an elevating video of Mother Teresa rather than a control video report increased feelings of lovingness and inspiration. These participants also had a stronger desire to help and associate with others and were actually more likely to do voluntary humanitarian charity work after the study. Haidt (2005) goes on:

> When an elevation story is told well, it elevates those who hear it. Powerful moments of elevation, whether experienced first or second hand, sometimes seem to push a mental "reset" button, wiping out feelings of cynicism and replacing them with feelings of hope, love, optimism, and a sense of moral inspiration. (p. 5)

There also appears to be a multiplier effect: when we see or hear about acts of generosity, we tend to be uplifted and the happiness spreads to those around us (Fowler & Christakis, 2010).

COMPASSION EXERCISE: Define and Notice Compassion

Complete an abbreviated version of this exercise yourself before using it with students. You could use it as part of your grade-level teamwork or professional learning community, sharing findings for a few weeks prior to introducing the exercise to students. You can implement the exercise over several weeks or even months. Try this with grades 2–12. You can modify it for students under age seven by adding children's stories that include compassion and kindness. The steps are as follows.

1. Begin by talking with your students about kindness and compassion. Name a few recent incidents of kindness in your school or community.

2. Ask a few provocative questions, perhaps whether certain actions or statements were compassionate. Consider examples related to people living in poverty, perhaps workers who have lost their jobs, refugees, or people who have been released from prison.

3. Share definitions of compassion from this chapter and some of the research insights. Visit **go.SolutionTree.com/behavior** for a free reproducible version of this information.

4. Give students an assignment to notice incidences of compassion and kindness for several days. Passages can be shared from the internet, social media, television, news, or their own community.

5. Students keep their own list and each day select one story to share with others, placing their stories in a compassion treasure chest. A cardboard shoebox could be painted to resemble a treasure chest with a slit in the top. Discuss how we treasure good memories and that by sharing stories of compassion, we are furthering our own happiness.

6. At odd moments during the day, a student selects a story to share.

7. The class reflects on the story, on its value, and on how it helps nurture and keep compassion at the center of what we do.

How Do We Measure Compassion?

The following tools measure compassion: the Self-Compassion Scale, the Fears of Compassion Scales, and S-CCATE.

Self-Compassion Scale

The Self-Compassion Scale (Neff, 2003; Raes, Pommier, Neff, & Van Gucht, 2011; https://self-compassion.org/self-compassion-scales-for-researchers) focuses on assessing how people feel about showing themselves the kindness that leads to self-compassion. Survey participants rate their level of agreement with statements like "When something painful happens, I try to take a balanced view of the situation," or "When I fail at something that's important to me, I tend to feel alone in my failure," on a Likert scale ranging from 1 (*almost never*) to 5 (*almost always*). Before you can teach your students how to embody self-compassion, check your own level of self-compassion by completing the scale yourself. There is also a Compassion Scale at the site.

Fears of Compassion Scales

The Fears of Compassion Scales (Gilbert, McEwan, Matos, & Rivis, 2010; https://bit.ly/2kzpdWy) assesses the level of hesitancy some feel about expressing empathy to others and themselves. Using a Likert scale ranging from 0 (*don't agree at all*) to 4 (*completely agree*), users rate their opinions about how they express compassion toward others, respond to others' expression of compassion toward them, and express kindness and compassion toward themselves. Table 4.1 has sample statements from each subscale.

Table 4.1: Fears of Compassion Scales Examples

Subscale	Sample Item
Expressing compassion for others	"Being too compassionate makes people soft and easy to take advantage of" (p. 247).
Responding to compassion from others	"When people are kind and compassionate towards me, I feel anxious or embarrassed" (p. 247).
Expressing compassion toward ourselves	"I have never felt compassion for myself, so I would not know where to begin to develop these feelings" (p. 248).

Source: Adapted from Gilbert et al., 2010.

S-CCATE

To help administrators and teachers assess their progress, S-CCATE measures several aspects of compassion and related factors. You can see how central compassion is, with three of the five S-CCATE factors directly considering compassion in table 4.2.

Table 4.2: S-CCATE Compassion Factors

Factor	In Action
Leadership and a compassionate school community	Teachers and school leaders recognize students' courageous, compassionate acts on a regular basis.
Courage and resiliency	Students show empathy for others.
Confidence and positivity	Teachers and school leaders infuse the curriculum with positive compassionate values.

The two factors of S-CCATE in which compassion is not directly assessed measure teachers' and students' progress toward the mindset shifts necessary to self-compassion and compassion toward others through such items as "Students are aware of connections between their physical feelings and emotions," and "Students are aware of inequities (discrimination, poverty, injustice, gender) in society." Using S-CCATE in conjunction with CEI's professional development and action guides, schools can not only assess the level of compassion their school is showing, but better understand exactly how to improve it.

Reflection

To get the most out of this chapter, reflect on these questions after reading it.

- Have you gained a stronger sense of the importance of cultivating compassionate school cultures? If so, how?
- Which exercises did you use with your classes? Would you modify any of them for the future?
- Do you find any need to increase your own self-compassion?
- Do you think your school has a compassionate school culture? If not, how could you as an individual do something to change that?
- Are there any current events or popular world leaders you can use to talk to your students about compassion?

CHAPTER 5

Confidence

I learned this, at least, by my experiment: that if one advances
confidently in the direction of his dreams, and endeavors to
live the life which he has imagined, he will meet with a success
unexpected in common hours.

—Henry David Thoreau

key principle

Teachers, as part of their
pedagogy, are able to
weave a web
of experiences that
support student
confidence and success.

In chapter 4 (page 59), we described the importance of compassion and ways to further compassion in schools. However, by itself compassion only takes us so far. It is one thing to know about compassion, and it is another to live it day in and day out and apply it in a wide array of circumstances. What would it take to have the degree of confidence that Winston Churchill had? To be centered, with the confidence to persevere, to lead others? What if we decided to help students practice and gain more self-confidence, consciousness, and compassion? How can we be assured that our students are in the process of becoming more likely to make decisions in their own best interests or for the good of many? How can we be assured that they are less likely to bully or be bullied? Or that they have problem-solving skills to help them weigh alternatives, make good decisions, and be successful?

Why is confidence such a critical imperative in learning and teaching? Because ensuring the success of our students goes beyond a focus on curriculum that identifies skills for college and career readiness. Student success is cultivated in environments where they thrive and flourish—environments where teachers believe in the innate potential of students for transcendence: to develop personal strengths; high levels of cognitive, social, and emotional skills; and the habits to be self-determined. With self-transcendence, individuals are committed to applying their strengths to make personal contributions. Maslow (1971) explains:

> Transcendence refers to the very highest and most inclusive or holistic levels of human consciousness, behaving and relating, as ends rather than means, to oneself, to significant others, to human beings in general, to other species, to nature, and to the cosmos. (p. 269)

Yvette Jackson (2011) explains the importance of an environment furthering transcendence in her book *The Pedagogy of Confidence*:

> Teachers demonstrate their confidence in their students' capacity to learn through fearlessly articulating, supporting, and insisting upon these expectations that all their students will learn. Teachers are enabled to act upon these expectations by confident principals who demonstrate indisputable belief in the capacities of their students and teachers, who guide and support teachers to identify and build on students' strengths, who provide opportunities for teachers to develop their craft and their voice, and who inspire teachers to inspire students. (p. 5)

Exploring the concept of confidence, knowing why it matters and how to teach it in school, discovering what it has looked like in the past, and learning how to measure it can move us another step toward mindful school communities.

What Is Confidence?

We can be confident about many things, small and large. We can feel confident about the future of our planet, confident about the possibilities of a business success, confident that our students will do well, and confident that our cars get good gas mileage. When we are confident about something, we proceed without hesitation or worry. When we are confident in other people, we trust that they will succeed. Confidence is composed of many elements, including self-confidence and the inner core—the mind-body.

Self-Confidence

Self-confidence is a component of confidence that reflects the degree to which we feel secure about ourselves. The former means trusting our own abilities (Welford, 2012). Clinical psychologist Mary Welford (2012) says that with confidence, we are better prepared to try new things, to tackle *difficult circumstances*, and to be *assertive*. Along with trusting our own abilities comes a need to understand and accept our limitations. In other words, we must have a realistic self-appraisal and then acceptance of self—perhaps positive affirmations like "I am enough" and "I accept myself as I am" bridge that gap. According to the Search Inside Yourself Leadership Institute (n.d.), self-confidence is "an understanding and acceptance of those limitations, while having that understanding increase rather than lessen your self-worth. Your weaknesses become a strength." This relates to our professional lives as well as students in their academic lives. How much confidence do we have in the capabilities of students, in their capability to learn? How much confidence do we as teachers and educators have in our ability to be effective in creating the pedagogy to elicit and cultivate students' innate potential so their capacity to learn at high levels and be self-actualized can manifest? How much confidence do we have in our knowledge of learning and what affects it?

Aziz Gazipura (2009), a clinical psychologist and confidence coach, suggests that "Confidence is more important than money or good looks. It automatically causes others to feel safer and trust us" (p. 7). According to Gazipura, there is a system and science to creating confidence. Confidence is knowing what's expected and believing we have what it takes to meet those expectations (Jackson, 2011).

Mind-Body Connection in the Inner Core

Emotions are a part of our identity. Along with our awareness of our individual strengths and preferences, we each carry around a raft of images of ourselves that impact our feelings about ourselves. For too long, educators have tended to separate physical development from intellectual and cognitive development. We have expected students to sit for long periods of time with relatively little awareness of their comfort or discomfort, what their postures are telling us, or strategies to help improve their physical experience. In addition, students who have experienced abuse often hunker down in a protective posture, trying to fade into the background (Norton, Ferriegel, & Norton, 2011). To achieve the mental, emotional, and spiritual release that increases a sense of well-being, sometimes it works best to work on a physical level. Trauma and abuse are held at the bodily level (Cook et al., 2017; Levine, 2008) and can be released, freeing one's brain, heart, and body to be available to learn.

So, what is the relationship between emotions and the body? Many speak of inner strength and resilience as valuable traits worth developing. We often consider those who have inner strength as being better prepared and able to handle adversity. Linda Lantieri, cofounder of the Resolving Conflict Creatively Program, asks how we might "equip a child's inner strength to meet both the intense challenges and great opportunities that come their way" (p. 7) and says she "can't imagine how we will make it if we don't cultivate a child's inner life" (p. 141). Martin Seligman, with psychologist Mihaly Csikszentmihalyi (2000), holds similar thoughts about the importance of inner strength as he relates a firsthand narrative about a parent's role:

> First, I realized that raising Nikki was not about correcting
> whining. Nikki did that herself. Rather, I realized that raising
> Nikki is about taking this marvelous strength she has—I call it
> "seeing into the soul"—amplifying it, nurturing it, helping her
> to lead her life around it to buffer against her weaknesses and
> the storms of life. Raising children, I realized, is vastly more
> than fixing what is wrong with them. It is about identifying
> and nurturing their strongest qualities. (p. 6)

Seligman and Csikszentmihalyi (2000) elaborate on the importance of nurturing
inner strengths:

> Researchers have discovered that there are human strengths
> that act as buffers against mental illness: courage, future
> mindedness, optimism, interpersonal skill, faith, work ethic,
> hope, honesty, perseverance, and the capacity for flow and
> insight, to name several. Much of the task of prevention in this
> new century will be to *create a science of human strength*
> whose mission will be to understand and learn how to foster
> these virtues in young people. (pp. 6–7; emphasis added)

Why Does Confidence Matter in School?

How much thought do you give to your students' confidence, and senses of
self-confidence? Why does confidence matter in schools? How does confidence relate
to academic performance or social-emotional well-being?

Neuroscience confirms the mutual learning theory of eminent cognitive psychologists and learning theorists such as Reuven Feuerstein (Feuerstein et al., 1981), Asa
Hilliard (1992), John Dewey (1938, 2007), and Lev S. Vygotsky (1978) confirm: that
people learn when they are engaged. Engagement is the catalyst for motivation, and
motivation is deeply fueled by a sense of competence and self-confidence. When students are supported and guided to feel competent and self-confident, their attention
becomes focused, motivating them to search for and reflect on relationships between
their personal experiences and what they are learning so they can construct meaning,
which is requisite for the following.

- Intellectual processing, understanding, and learning
- Pursuing new interests and transforming them into personal strengths
- Overcoming the challenges in learning and problem solving they might
  encounter

Self-confidence is closely wound up with other related concepts such as self-esteem
(a sense of personal worth and value) and self-efficacy (a belief that we can have an
impact on situations and those around us). Educators can guide students through

developing self-confidence by incorporating activities that allow reflecting on worth and facilitating conversations about mindsets and how the way we think about our own abilities affects our performance.

- Students with higher levels of self-esteem exhibit higher academic achievement as compared to those with lower self-esteem (Mohammad, 2010).
- Lower levels of self-esteem during adolescence are associated with poorer health, financial insecurity, and higher levels of criminal activity as adults (Demirtaş, Yildiz, & Baytemir, 2017).
- Academic self-efficacy and perceptions of one's own competence in memory and reasoning abilities are predictive of confidence, mastery, goal orientation, and an overall believe in self and one's competence (Kleitman & Gibson, 2011).

In essence, the results from numerous research studies affirm that self-confidence prepares students for a better future.

Author and activist Gloria Steinem (1993) explains the critical roles teachers play in helping children develop confidence:

> If we think about our own classroom experiences—whether in schools that were far more privileged than Spanish Harlem or just as bad . . . we may also remember *that we became more or less smart depending upon our teachers' vision of us, that we learned better when teachers invested themselves in our subjects and expected us to do the same.* (pp. 42–44)

Steinem (1993) reminds us that some of us have more confidence when we are young than we have later in life, as our confidence is diminished by criticisms, life circumstances, failure, and, for some, misconceptions. As children, some of us were better received if we hid our intelligence, remained silent, and went along with the group decisions.

Self-confidence motivates self-determination, and self-determination steers self-direction so a person can stay on course for personal success. Teachers can cultivate the belief in students that they can accomplish their goals, and teachers can cultivate students' willingness to apply themselves by setting short-term goals (Dweck, 2016; Schunk, 1989), instilling a sense of self-determination, and dialoguing with them about their self-appraisals of their capabilities so that individuals develop realistic assessments of their skills (Maclellan, 2014). These supports in turn require us to provide mediated opportunities for engagement, challenge, reflection, affirming guidance, and nurturing feedback.

CONFIDENCE EXERCISE: Reflect on Your and
Your Students' Confidence

Reflect on the following questions and the implications for what may be most
needed for developing confidence during childhood.

1. Think about your own childhood. Were there times when you felt
   extraordinarily confident?
2. Were there times when you felt like a failure and your confidence waned?
3. How do you think your experiences as a child are impacting your feelings of
   confidence and success today?
4. Consider your students. Which students appear to have self-confidence?
   Which students seem to lack self-confidence? What do you think are the
   implications for their future?

Safety is another issue that relates to confidence and learning. Maslow (1943, 1971)
brought attention to the fact that before people can feel confident, they need to feel
safe. When safety is a concern, individuals contract, they are guarded, and their focus
is first and foremost on survival (Maslow, 1943, 1971).

To help students feel safe and secure, teachers can involve students in decision
making (empowering them and giving them a voice), set boundaries and routines,
and do what they can to ensure students' comfort. Students will feel a greater sense
of security when they help set expectations for both classroom behaviors and academic performance, when they realize that bullying is unacceptable and will have
consequences, and when the class includes specific routines such as check-ins, explicit
instruction, opportunities to begin homework, and a balance of teacher and student
talk (Deci et al., 2015; Goss & Sonnemann, 2017).

How Do We Teach Confidence?

We can teach confidence with positive communication, validation, and affirmations;
with support for positive emotions; by counteracting negative emotions; by developing
core and inner strength; and through metacognition.

Use Positive Communication, Validation, and Affirmation

While we like to think of ourselves as adults who help students prepare for their
futures, sometimes we construct barriers to their success. Sometimes, we might unin-
tentionally undermine a student's feelings of success.

- The questions we ask students can build or destroy confidence. When
  we repeatedly ask questions that are too difficult, we can increase their
  frustration and sense of failure. On the other hand, when we consider

students' background knowledge and skills and provide prompts and scaffolds as necessary, we can increase opportunities for student success.

- How we correct or reprimand students can either embarrass them or provide gentle guidance for a useful course correction.
- Encouraging comments elevate student confidence as opposed to red checkmarks that discourage engagement and squash creativity.
- Offering opportunities to improve, enrich, and self-correct work, rather than issuing letter or numerical grades, sends a strong *You are capable* message.
- Providing ongoing opportunities to retry with support helps students embrace the use of *yet* when they consider their success: *I haven't learned this* yet.

Board-certified high school teacher Jordan Catapano (www.teachhub.com/author/5939) offers several recommendations at TeachHUB for teachers to incorporate into their daily and weekly routines to help develop confidence. This includes several small but potentially powerful actions such as calling parents with positive reports, noticing things such as new haircuts or new shoes, finding aspects of a student's work to share, and making work public by posting it in hallways or the cafeteria or on school or class blogs.

In addition to increasing their own knowledge of how deeply students can be impacted by the traumas they experience, teachers can help students understand and name emotions. You can use literature (children's books and nursery rhymes for elementary students), fiction or nonfiction writing assignments, or apps like Breathe, Think, Do with *Sesame Street* (https://apple.co/2piuNPc and https://bit.ly/2OetoSs) or Stop, Breathe, and Think Kids (www.stopbreathethink.com/kids).

Students in grades 4–12 can write about their emotions in a daily or weekly journal. Periodically collecting journals and writing caring responses can help students feel that someone is listening and cares.

CONFIDENCE EXERCISE: Strategies

Jacquelyne Smith (2016), a psychologist, says parents should do eighteen things to raise a more confident child, and teachers can foster confidence in their students following these same guidelines—things like encouraging curiosity, helping kids learn from their errors, and celebrating success.

To consider the implications of Smith's (2016) recommendations for grade 5 classrooms, rank each of the strategies in figure 5.1 (page 86) according to whether you believe it is a strength in your classroom approach (+), satisfactory (0), or an area for strengthening (–).

Strategy	+	0	−
Encourage curiosity.			
Show appreciation for effort.			
Let students figure out solutions themselves.			
Increase student responsibilities.			
Avoid shortcuts.			
Praise often and be specific; correct with kindness (without criticism).			
Treat errors as building blocks to learning.			
Provide assistance when needed but allow students to find solutions or answers on their own.			
Celebrate the excitement of learning.			
Applaud courage.			
Provide new challenges.			

Source: Adapted from Smith, 2016.

Figure 5.1: Strategies to build confidence.

*Visit **go.SolutionTree.com/behavior** for a free reproducible version of this figure.*

Examine your results. What conclusions have you reached? Are there two or three strategies you want to focus on?

CONFIDENCE EXERCISE: Confidence Superhero Capes

Guide elementary students through a discussion about how superheroes are transformed into individuals with superpowers and feel their most confident when they put on their costume, mask, or cape and why those things help.

- Ask students to create their own cape or mask that they would wear to feel most confident. On their capes, students can write phrases that describe them, including mantras that make them feel good about themselves (such as *I am great, I am successful, I run,* or *I can do it*).
- Teachers can talk with students about how sometimes we put on imaginary confidence capes to help us feel confident.

For all grade levels, consider options such as the victory or power pose, shown in figure 5.2, by social psychologist Amy Cuddy (2014). In her video, (www .youtube.com/watch?v=C4ACeoqEjeA), Cuddy explains why our minds are so important to translating confidence messages to our bodies:

> We can change our own body chemistry for the better simply by changing body positions. Standing in a posture of confidence, even when we don't feel confidence, affects

testosterone and cortisol levels in the brain, and might even
have an impact on our chances for success. (as cited in
Mohseni, 2016)

Have pre K–grade 5 students practice the power pose even if they aren't feeling very
confident to develop the victor mindset. You can explain to reluctant students that
it's similar to the idea of faking it until you become it.

Figure 5.2: Victory or power poses.

Another worthwhile strategy is to acknowledge or validate a student's perspective.
This acknowledgment is critical for all students who need increased confidence—
especially students of color, whose perspective can be severely affected by how they are
made to feel in relation to how the world views them (Rychly & Graves, 2012). This
happens not only through explicit racial discrimination, but also through language
that is used to define or identify them that signifies *less than*. This language—such as
minority, *disadvantaged*, *low achieving*, and *language deficient*—marginalizes students.

Learning is not merely learning academic content; it also involves habits of mind
(Costa & Kallick, 2000) and metacognitive skills such as self-reflection and self-
appraisal, leading to improved decision making. As parents, this validation can occur
by acknowledging how a child is feeling rather than overriding the child's message
with dos and don'ts. Sometimes the most important part of validation is simply
saying, "I hear you."

Support Positive Emotions and Counteract Negative Emotions

Emotions can either further a student's sense of self and self-esteem or be a barrier to student growth and understanding of self. Each day teachers have opportunities to help students have positive experiences at school; experiences of success, joy, and delight all further positivity. The negative effects of emotions can be diminished by a teacher's support and also by helping students identify and label their feelings. Research shows that the more mindful or consciously aware you are, the more your amygdala (the flight, freeze, or fight center of the brain) is toned down, opening up opportunities for healing and creating a better balance in your brain (Wolpert, 2007).

CONFIDENCE EXERCISE: Acknowledging Negative Emotions and Supporting Positive Emotions

Teachers can build more positive emotions by being more positive themselves. We can consciously provide explicit opportunities to feel more positive. These might include the following.

- Greet students with a warm smile and kind word as they enter the class.
- Use de-escalating brain breaks if students are feeling angry or sad. This might include deep breathing; yoga stretches or postures; playing soft music; dancing; or playing fun action games.

Identifying our emotions isn't always easy, particularly if we have been suppressing the things we would sooner forget. This holds true for teachers as well as students. Sometimes in the middle of chaos, with students who have been disruptive, it is hard for teachers to be genuinely supportive or to turn their attention to something that is positive. However, there are two things to consider.

1. When we smile, we release endorphins and serotonin, which can elevate our mood—and moreover, when we smile, those around us are more likely to treat us well; smiling is contagious (Stevenson, 2012).
2. For both teachers and students, sometimes it is worth faking it until we make it (pretending we feel confident even in the midst of our fears). This might include specific yoga postures that can add to your feelings of confidence, including one of Cuddy's (2014) power stances, sitting or standing in such a way that our body takes up more space. Even such things as dancing or envisioning future success can lead to feeling more confident (Happily, n.d.).

In *Reclaiming Youth at Risk: Futures of Promise*, Larry Brendtro, Martin Brokenleg, and Steve Van Bockern (2019) tell the story of Richard Cardinal, a young Métis Indian in Canada who had been removed from his alcoholic parents' home at about the age of six, separated from his siblings, and shuttled among foster homes (usually with white families), youth shelters, and treatment facilities. A thoughtful youth, he withdrew, began describing himself as an outcast, and began avoiding relationships with adults. At age seventeen, he hanged himself. His story was told through the National Film Board of Canada (Obomsawin, 1986). The short award-winning film (www.nfb .ca/film/richard_cardinal) can be downloaded for classroom use. This excerpt from Richard Cardinal's diary reveals his awareness, his loneliness, and his despair:

> I didn't want no one to love any more. I had been hurt too many times. So, I began to learn the art of blocking out all emotions and shut out the rest of the world. The door would open to no one. I'm skipping the rest of the years because it continues to be the same. I want to say to people involved in my life, don't take this personally. I just can't take it anymore. (as cited in Brendtro et al., 2019, p. 35)

Educators can screen this movie with middle and high schoolers to frame a discussion about the power of unprocessed negative emotions and isolation *and* the power of a single peer or adult to make a meaningful connection that might buffer a youth. Analyze the journey Cardinal took before completing suicide; ask students to identify what friends, family, and school staff could have done to intervene in his life before it was too late.

Boost Inner Core Strength

Can we do anything on the physical plane to help nurture inner resources? There is some evidence that when we feel that we have physical strength, when we are confident in our bodies, we feel better about ourselves and better trust our own abilities to ride out life's storms. Yogis and fitness gurus speak of *core strength*, sometimes differentiating between the inner and outer core. The *outer core* is our skeletal and outermost layer of our musculature system, which supports large movements such as walking, running, and arm movements. The *inner core*, composed of abdominal, pelvic, hip, and back muscles, is essential to balancing, stabilizing, and supporting our spines.

From a yogic or fitness perspective, we have "five different components of core stability: strength, endurance, flexibility, motor control, and function" (Waldhelm, 2011). When we strengthen our core (both inner and outer), we reduce back pain and will find it easier to maintain good posture. This is important for everyone. The Mayo Clinic (n.d.) is one of several organizations that have online demonstrations of exercises for enhancing our core muscles. Yoga and Pilates instructors describe how "learning to be gently aware of our spine physically—and then inwardly, on an energy level—helps us to be more balanced and stable" (McCord, n.d.). Awareness of self and efforts to improve our physical self can lead to a greater sense of well-being. With specific exercises, we can also increase our sense of strength, which can add to feelings of self-confidence. As McCord (n.d.) states, "Trying to connect our mind and body, our thoughts and emotions and experience of a pose, gives us a chance to feel what our body, including our core, is doing . . . helping us find and live from that inner place of peaceful strength."

CONFIDENCE EXERCISE: Strengthen Your Core

Any exercise that strengthens the abdominal muscles is usually beneficial. We present exercises that will help students in kindergarten to grade 12 strengthen their cores so that they feel they have better muscle tone, their spine is supported by underlying muscles, posture is improved, and they become aware of a greater sense of balance in their lives.

- **Abdominal crunches** are a great place to start, perhaps followed by cross patterning, alternately pulling one knee to the abdomen. For all abdominal exercises, pull your navel point to your spine as you tighten your abs. For reverse crunches, lie on your back, bring your knees to your chest, pull your navel point to your spine, wrap your arms around your knees, and alternate pulling your knees closer to your chest and letting go, then continuing that cycle. For greater impact, combine a breath with the movement, exhaling up and inhaling as you release back down. Preschoolers and kindergarteners can simply bring their knees to their chests and rock back and forth. Proceed to alternating knees to chest. From the position for abdominal crunches, release your left leg, extending that leg out about six inches from the ground, pointing the toe and holding the right leg to your chest. Continue alternating, pulling one leg and then the other to your chest for two or three minutes. Suggest that students go at their own pace and take breaks as needed. Students as young as grade 1 can coordinate the breath with the movement, inhaling on one side and exhaling on the other.
- **Chair pose** involves squatting and reaching one's arms above one's head and holding (figure 5.3), perhaps for one minute. Students may be hard on themselves, thinking "This is so hard," "I can't do this," or "I'm not strong enough." Pause, releasing the posture, and then talk about the power of positive thinking. Ask students to do chair pose again, but this time telling themselves positive affirmations such as "I can do this," "I am capable," or "It's only one minute."

Figure 5.3: Chair pose.

- **Locust pose** replicates the insect. You may want to show students a picture of a locust as well as a student in the locust pose (figure 5.4). Begin on your belly with your feet hip-width apart. Arms are along your sides with your palms facing up. On an inhale, lift your head, chest, and legs up off the ground, bringing your shoulder blades toward each other. Elongate evenly through your spine, holding your head up for a count of three or four seconds—longer if you are able. Relax down, come back into position, and repeat three or four times.

Figure 5.4: Locust pose.

Foster Inner Strength

Just as it helps to develop a strong inner core, students will benefit from inner strength. Consider times when you felt a deep conviction and confidence in the actions you were about to take. Reflect on how you felt physically—did a sense permeating your whole being say that you were about to take the right steps? Ann Naimark (n.d.), a family counselor, suggests that "inner strength allows you to pursue dreams and goals and live life to your fullest." Naimark (n.d.) describes how inner strength evolves through knowing what you are feeling (good and bad); having boundaries (which takes willingness to set limits); finding the strength to go through challenges; asking for help when needed; and feeling love and acceptance for your body, your mind, and your emotions.

Meditation helps students become more confident by getting to know themselves better and by helping practice self-compassion to quiet that negative voice sending "I can't do it" messages. Mindfulness and self-compassion have been positively associated with confidence and with resilience (Olson & Kemper, 2014). In fact, the Search Inside Yourself Leadership Institute (n.d.), a team of leading neuroscientists and mindfulness experts, suggests that self-confidence can be better promoted through teaching mindfulness instead of trying to teach confidence directly. The self-awareness that is gained through meditation helps one identify strengths and weaknesses more easily. Meditation also helps us quiet our anxiety by letting go of unhelpful emotions.

Encourage Metacognition

One way to increase conscious awareness of individual student strengths, and hence ther confidence, is to help build student metacognition so they are aware of their own thinking. This can be done by providing time for students to reflect after their lessons (Cox, n.d.). They could reflect on what they did well and where they might do better and why, sharing their reflections in small groups. Teachers can help guide students to provide positive and helpful feedback to their peers.

To encourage metacognition, ask students to finish three sentence starters at the end of a lesson (Owen & Vista, 2017).

1. Red: *Today my learning stopped because _____.*
2. Yellow: *Today, I considered a question, new idea, or new perspective: _____.*
3. Green: *Today, I understood and learned _____.*

CONFIDENCE EXERCISE: Affirmation Meditation

Source: Adapted from Shapiro & Shapiro, 2012.

Affirmations are a way to reinforce confidence in one's capabilities. When we repeat positive phrases such as "I can" or "I am _____ (successful, healthy, smart, wise)," we are directly strengthening positive thoughts about self and counteracting negativity. The following exercise works well for students in grades 4–12.

1. Ask students to find a comfortable place to sit upright. Then say, "Take a few deep breaths and watch the flow of your breath."
2. Pause a moment and say, "Focus now on your heart. As you breathe in, feel as if your heart is opening and softening; as you breathe out, release any tension or resistance."
3. Tell students, "Now either bring into your heart an image of yourself or repeat your name and hold yourself in your heart, tenderly and gently." Pause.
4. Tell students to repeat after you: "May I be freed from self-doubt." Pause. "May I be happy." Pause. "May all things go well for me."

What Does Confidence Look Like Historically?

Before we take a deeper dive into ways to further confidence, pause for a moment and consider the confidence of leaders or those who have displayed remarkable talents, the innovative paths they pursued, and their ladders of success. In the biographies of almost any leader, superstar, inventor, scientist, or artist, we can find stories that might be instructive to our understanding of confidence.

As you read through these examples—Josephine Baker, Mary Wollstonecraft, Vera Wang, and Angela Merkel—we encourage you to further your conscious awareness of confidence. These diverse examples might be most helpful in considering the confidence that each leader developed as she beat the odds to reach a career pinnacle.

Josephine Baker

Consider Josephine Baker who, in the 1920s, used her confidence to promote women's emancipation and elevate society's perception of black people. Baker was so confident in her ability to outperform famous revue dancers, all of whom were white, that she began showing up at clubs that did not allow African American people in the audience, much less on the stage. Eventually, her impressive dance skills convinced club owners to give her a chance and she soon became so famous that she was able to refuse to perform in any segregated clubs, forcing club owners to allow black patrons if they wanted to see her dance.

Baker's confidence enabled her to bring both black and white women's voices to many spaces where none were previously heard. Two decades later, her courage animated her enough to employ her activism beyond entertainment and the U.S. boundaries to the battlegrounds of France during World War II. There she was awarded the Croix de Guerre by the French military and named a Chevalier of the *Légion d'honneur* (Legion of Honour) by General Charles de Gaulle for bravery as an intelligence liaison and ambulance driver for the French resistance. In 1963, after returning to the United States, she was the only woman to speak at the March on Washington for Jobs and Freedom, telling men and women of both races, "As I knew I had the power and the strength, I took that rocky path, and I tried to smooth it out a little. I wanted to make it easier for you" (as cited in Biondi, 2018).

Mary Wollstonecraft

Mary Wollstonecraft provides another example of confidence. During the Enlightenment, Wollstonecraft published *Thoughts on the Education of Daughters* (1787), *A Vindication of the Rights of Men* (1790), and *A Vindication of the Rights of Woman* (1793), in which she challenges the traditional method of educating girls and the individual rights of all people. Wollstonecraft believed that women were as capable as men and simply lacked the education. She spent her life advocating for the education of women to elevate their role in society through a context of human rights. While her life was short—she died at the early age of thirty-eight—Wollstonecraft was able to spark conversations about human rights and how women's rights were inherently equal through her fierce advocation of education. Wollstonecraft paved the way for future human rights activists to have the confidence to advocate for themselves and their space in society.

Vera Wang

Vera Wang began skating at age seven and competed at the 1968 U.S. Figure Skating Championships, but failed to make the U.S. Olympic figure skating team. However, she didn't let rejection define her, and she demonstrated an early ability to shift gears and succeed despite disappointment or perceived failure. Wang went on to graduate from Sarah Lawrence College with a degree in art history and was hired at *Vogue* magazine. She worked at *Vogue* for seventeen years but failed to become editor in chief. Once again, she showed confidence in her abilities. She shifted gears once more by going to work at Ralph Lauren, then opening her own bridal boutique and starting her own extremely successful fashion line.

Angela Merkel

Another master of confidence is Angela Merkel, the first woman chancellor of Germany, who was reelected three times (Connolly, 2015). Merkel showed confidence by attending and excelling at university during a time (the mid-1970s) and place (East Germany) where education wasn't prioritized, and by traveling to other countries when doing so was uncommon and, sometimes, unsafe because of political tension (Cupp, 2015). When West and East Germany reunited after the Berlin Wall's fall, Merkel was confident enough to begin working in government, even though her expertise was physics, because she wanted to be part of the political change that was happening (Cupp, 2015). Merkel says, "You could certainly say that I've never underestimated myself. There's nothing wrong with being ambitious" (as cited in Adams, 2011).

CONFIDENCE EXERCISE: Following Talent

This exercise will broaden grades 4–12 students' ability to enhance their own skills.

1. Share with students a few examples of how well-known figures (either current or historic) pursued their passions and perfected their crafts. Use the preceding examples or go to websites such as www.biography.com/people.
2. Give students an opportunity to research people in fields of interest to them. By using this technique, we are employing an evidence-based approach to build self-confidence by motivating students to apply their knowledge and skills that will give them tools that may directly impact their own futures.
3. Lastly, students demonstrate their comprehension through multimedia presentations, poetry, spoken word, and the like. This can be done individually or through cooperative learning, perhaps grouping students by topics. Suggested clusters include athletes, musicians, teachers, military strategists, politicians, scientists, and artists. However, these will vary with the interests of your students.

How Do We Measure Confidence?

The following tools measure confidence: the Rosenberg Self-Esteem Scale, the Piers-Harris Self-Concept Scale, and S-CCATE.

Rosenberg Self-Esteem Scale

The Rosenberg Self-Esteem Scale (Rosenberg, 1965; https://bit.ly/2KMV54d) is the most commonly used measure of self-esteem. It was originally developed for high school students, but additional studies have advanced its reliability and validity for adults as well. Both reliability and validity are high (with reliability scores of .85–.88 after two weeks). It includes ten items that measure negative and positive feelings about self with a four-point Likert scale. Items include statements related to feelings of uselessness, respect for self, and feelings of failure, for example.

Piers-Harris Self-Concept Scale, Third Edition

The Piers-Harris Self-Concept Scale, Third Edition (Piers, Shemmassian, & Herzberg, 2016), was designed for individuals between ages six and twenty-two. It was based on a nationally representative sample of 1,400 individuals and measures self-concept in children, adolescents, and young adults, and identifies individuals who need further testing or treatment. One of the premises is that individuals feel differently about themselves at various developmental stages. It includes almost sixty items, written at the first-grade level, measuring how people feel about themselves, with *yes* or *no* responses. It includes six scales: (1) behavioral adjustment, (2) freedom from anxiety, (3) happiness and satisfaction, (4) intellectual and school status, (5) physical appearance and attributes, and (6) social acceptance.

S-CCATE

The subtle difference between courage and confidence can be difficult to understand and measure. With S-CCATE, which differentiates between the two in distinctly rated factors, school leaders can see which aspect of positive sense of self is a more important focus for their building or district. When schools take the S-CCATE Supplement, they can better understand how confidence and courage act in concert for their school community.

There are two S-CCATE scales, both of which include measures of confidence. Three factors from these scales appear in table 5.1.

Table 5.1: S-CCATE Confidence Factors

Factor	In Action
Confidence and positivity	Students consider the teacher a good listener.
Confidence and courage	Students create affirmations and positive visualizations for themselves.
Confidence and courage	Students practice leadership skills.

Reflection

To get the most out of this chapter, reflect on these questions after reading it.

- Recall a time when you lacked confidence and how it felt. Did you have a strategy to help yourself through the situation? How successful were you?
- What strategies do you use in your classroom to help students feel successful?
- Of the exercises in this chapter for fostering confidence, are there specific exercises that you want to implement on an ongoing basis?
- Did you implement any of the exercises for building inner strength? If so, do you better understand the relationship between feeling strong and believing in oneself? How would you explain it to someone else?
- Which of your students could use the most guidance and support to help build their self-confidence? What specifically might you implement with them?

CHAPTER 6

Courage

Without courage, we cannot practice any other virtue with
consistency. We can't be kind, true, merciful, generous, or honest.

—Maya Angelou

key principle

Teachers and
administrators can
nurture courage
in classrooms, and
over time, it leads
to resilience, grit,
and higher levels of
achievement in school.

Confidence and courage are often viewed as preconditions for each other. In other words, some confidence is needed to be courageous, and we need some courage to be confident. What generates confidence is knowing what's expected and believing you've got what it takes to meet those expectations. A certain amount of confidence is essential to move beyond one's fears to be courageous and act courageously. In turn, courage instills or builds a certain amount of confidence in us as well, developing the sureness needed to help us confront our fears.

Exploring the concept of courage, knowing why it matters and how to teach it in school, discovering what it has looked like in the past, and learning how to measure it can move us even closer toward mindful school communities.

What Is Courage?

The ability to develop and gain the courage to live, learn, lead, and dream our best lives takes confidence—certainly confidence in ourselves and, to a certain degree, confidence in others and the environment that surrounds us. Singer-songwriter Bob Dylan (1985) says, "I think of a hero as someone who understands the degree of responsibility that comes with his freedom." As we gain a deeper understanding of how we can act with courage to better the world, our own lives, and the lives of those around us, we take on a responsibility to act consciously and compassionately. So, go quietly, be humble, be wise, and be courageous.

Courage requires a freedom to explore risk, a curiosity to discover, and also an innate belief and trust in one's own self and potential that can only be developed through confronting and conquering our fears. Courage is cultivated through confidence. Meditation sheds the cloak of fear or apprehension by providing the means, support, and deliberate and targeted intervention and structure that guide and nurture confidence (Jackson & McDermott, 2012).

Meditation fosters consciousness, which provides the constant and solid foundation that promotes our courage from within. Consciousness encourages the best within ourselves, helping us to steady and quiet our thoughts, overcome our fears, and develop the courage needed to excel.

Courage is multifaceted. It is associated with several traits and actions, is a natural response to fear, and can help us push through our fears. Courage also is not recklessness. One way teachers can help students learn about courage is by helping them consider superheroes and the inspirational figures that almost seem larger than life in terms of their accomplishments.

Traits and Actions Associated With Courage

Christopher Rate, a psychology professor at Yale University, has conducted a number of studies to attempt to define courage. According to Rate, Jennifer Clarke, Douglas Lindsay, and Robert Sternberg (2007), courage is:

> (1) a willful, intentional act, (2) executed after mindful deliberation, (3) involving objective substantial risk to the actor, (4) primarily motivated to bring about a noble good or morally worthy purpose, (5) despite the presence of the emotion of fear. (p. 95)

In one of their studies, Rate and his colleagues (2007) asked participants to list characteristics that they associate with courage. A few examples of the highest-ranked courageous characteristics follow. The percentage of respondents who identified a particular trait is presented in the parentheses.

- **Self-focused (internal characteristics):**
  - Endures tough situations (83 percent)
  - Can handle rough situations (82 percent)
- **Non-physical, socially oriented acts (internal motivation characteristics):**
  - Stands up to unjust social practices because of what one thinks is right (76 percent)
  - Stands up for the "right thing" against opposition (73 percent)

- **Sacrifices:**
  - Risks life to protect others (86 percent)
  - Sacrifices self to save another (85 percent)

Visit **go.SolutionTree.com/behavior** for a complete list.

In another component of their study, Rate and colleagues (2007) asked participants to sort items according to whether they exemplified an ideally courageous person. Averages (M) for the top-rated items follow, based on a ten-point scale.

- Risks one's own safety to save others in need (M = 8.15)
- Does the right thing, even if it is hard to do (M = 7.97)
- Fights for what one believes in (M = 7.89)

Has someone you know personally, or has any historical figure you have studied, exhibited these characteristics? Now consider your staff and students. Do any particular individuals come to mind? Who and why?

Cathy J. Lassiter (2016) defines four types of courage—(1) moral, (2) intellectual, (3) disciplined, and (4) empathetic—saying that everyday courage is about "facing the daily leadership challenges with a willful spirit to support the ideals of equity, excellence and inclusion of all students, even when it is not easy or convenient." Table 6.1 (page 100) provides examples of these four types of courage in schools.

Each of the traits that Lassiter (2016) portrays can be applied across an array of situations with adults and children. It is not only adults or leaders who need the four types of courage that Lassiter describes. There is the courage to go outside our comfort zones, to enter conflict when our values or beliefs are at stake, to resist conflict, to stretch ourselves, and to learn. It is interesting that some courage requires us to act in the moment, and other courage requires us to pursue a certain strategic path of action.

The Relationship of Courage to Fear

Being human, we have a natural tendency to fear—fear rejection, fear embarrassment, or fear being alone in our pursuits. These are all natural and human feelings. Fears can easily surface within us due to the uncertainty associated with any (new or old) situation or risk taken in life. Feelings of uncertainty can be mild, moderate, or severe—allowing us to tolerate them, sending us spiraling out of control, or inducing a constant state of fear if we let them.

Take, for instance, the anticipation from the moment students first step foot into a new school building. Varying degrees of anxiety and fear can quickly set in. This is especially true for students of color who live with the daily stress of the stereotypical perceptions or attributional inferences others have made about them because of how they are classified ethnically or racially (Jackson, 2011).

Table 6.1: Types of Courage in School

Courage Type	Summary	School Example
Moral courage	Standing up and acting when injustices occur, human rights are violated, or someone is treated unfairly	In a class discussion, a student takes an unpopular stance or brings up a subject that others find uncomfortable. It may be a transgender student who speaks up about bathroom preferences, a student who discusses reparations to Native Americans, or students who protest for changes in gun laws to improve school safety.
Intellectual courage	Challenging old assumptions and acting to make changes based on new learnings, understandings, and insights gleaned from experience and educational research	A student pursues a difficult project, spending hours researching and building a prototype to reduce pollution. With intellectual courage, a student elects to pursue a topic or project that presents challenges or may counter popularly held notions, rather than taking a more conventional approach.
Disciplined courage	Remaining strategic, deliberate, and reflective despite distractions or opposition	A teacher and administrator hear a student's version of a negative situation and arrive at a conclusion that is at odds with the school's zero-tolerance policy. It may take courage from both the student and educators to think outside the box when deciding on next steps.
Empathetic courage	Acknowledging personal biases and intentionally moving away from them in order to vicariously experience the trials and triumphs of others	A student undertakes a community service project to help people living in homeless shelters, organizes a school event in support of recent immigrants, or tutors students who need help with particular subjects.

Source: Adapted from Lassiter, 2016.

As educators with a trained eye, we sometimes readily discern the nervousness of students who exist in such an *otherizing* reality, or even the nervousness some of our students display as they begin the first day of school, start something new, or take a test. Some students may experience a heightened sense of fear when participating in a music, art, or physical education class. Other students may feel overwhelmed with the noise and anxiety of moving in busy corridors. However, other times students' feelings of inadequacy are far less obvious, perhaps hidden from plain sight and less noticeable to even an observant educator's eye. The degree of fear can vary from student to student and manifest itself in many different ways such as an inability to concentrate or focus, obsessive thinking, missing assignments or essential information, skipping class, or eventually dropping out of school. Being cognizant and empathic, making sure you're open to these less obvious cries for help, is important.

When fear collides with our ability to function at our best in life, we are forced to either retreat (flight), resist (fight), or confront our fear with courage. Life, in a sense, requires courage to move through it and get through it. In *Never Fear, Never Quit*, Joe Tye (2012) explains that if you care enough about something, you will find the courage to do what needs to be done. In life, sometimes, to understand courage, you must first face your fears to be reminded of why you care. Fear is an emotional state, implying you are afraid of something specific, while anxiety is a nonspecific state of dread. To bring the depiction of fear and anxiety to life, imagine a black cloud on the horizon as anxiety and the raging storm overhead as fear. It is fear we need to overcome through courage.

Courage is not the absence of fear. However, it takes courage to resist—and triumph over—fear. *Courageous* is often described as or used interchangeably with words such as *brave, heroic, daring,* or *fearless*.

- When learning or trying anything new, there is always a learning curve as well as an inherent amount of fear of the unknown or uncertainty attached.
- Feelings of anxiety and fear of uncertainty or the unknown can be even more pronounced in constantly changing and evolving environments like school.

Learning a new equation, worrying you will not have a friend to sit with at lunchtime, or anticipating being called on when you don't know the answer are minute occurrences in a school setting. More oppressive are the fear- and anxiety-producing, in-school realities of marginalizing terms such as *minority, low achiever,* or *special needs student* that students hear or see applied to them. However, the degree of fear or uncertainty is different with each person and in each situation, and in the absence of courage, we are often left with the fear alone.

Courage is an essential trait to acquire while growing up because our fears can hold us back from fully experiencing life's opportunities or reaching our full potential. In her 2010 TED Talk, vulnerability researcher Brené Brown discusses why we need to be courageous and overcome our fears. By being vulnerable and authentic, we open ourselves up to self-acceptance, love, belonging, stronger relationships, and a more fulfilling and meaningful life.

Many of our fears are based on our past experiences or past, current, or historical trauma (Courtois & Ford, 2012; Evans-Campbell, 2008; Nishith, Mechanic, & Resick, 2000). Courage is a valuable ally; it can help us conquer our fears, making it easier to find focus and explore the unknown or uncertain. Courage allows us to be the best version of ourselves, freeing us from frozen fear, as when our amygdala is in full bloom and freezes us with fright. But courage has to be nurtured in a safe environment in which students feel they belong and are valued. Sometimes, it is hard to even approach being courageous if one's fear is too great.

Consider a fear of heights. Sometimes it works to gradually acclimate oneself to heights, building one's ability and courage over time. However, if students are given a safe space to practice courage, how can they be courageous? The approach we recommend builds on what we know—how deliberate practice over time affects and overrides emotions to act more instantaneously in the moment. Karate and other forms of self-defense are examples of the impact of practice; they are practiced repeatedly so that they can be used when in danger. We are aiming for a similar automaticity.

Heroes and Superheroes

Courage and bravery are sometimes used simultaneously or in conjunction with one another. However, courage includes actions that may be preplanned whereas "bravery is fearlessness in the face of adversity without a thought to the danger to life" (Koshal, 2011). As Ralph Waldo Emerson (n.d.) wrote, "A hero is no braver than an ordinary man, but he is brave five minutes longer." Sometimes five minutes can make a world of difference. In five minutes, a fireman may rush into a burning building and save a child. In five minutes, we may answer a phone call and persuade a friend to keep on living. In five minutes, we may hit our own pause button and help a stranger.

We have all heard stories like this about people who have been courageous or brave. Many of us grow up revering courageous superheroes like Wonder Woman, Superman, and Black Panther—those who have extraordinary powers to triumph against evil and save the world. As we get older and are saturated by different socio-technological media, we begin to idolize the most courageous and inspiring sports heroes, both contemporary and past, such as Magic Johnson, Pelé, Billie Jean King, Steve Prefontaine, Pat Tillman, Roberto Clemente, Lou Gehrig, or Terry Fox, who made their indelible mark. Then there are sports figures who serve as role models of physical courage, like Peyton Manning, Amy Purdy, Tim Tebow, and Serena Williams, to name a few. Common to these athletes is their courage to persevere, to spend hours in practice, pushing their bodies to physical limits, always striving to excel and break barriers. There are many ways that we, on an everyday basis, can strengthen our own courage and bravery.

You will find that most students can easily relate to one or many of these courageous heroes through their own lives. The association with their story and the commonality of adversity, pain, or perseverance becomes something relatable and interesting to students. It also helps students to connect through mutual empathy, providing hope and encouragement.

COURAGE EXERCISE: Heroes

This exercise, for grades 3–5 asks, "Who are your heroes?" They could be historical or world leaders, modern-day athletes, movie or television stars, someone you know personally, or even fictional characters. Make a list of ten heroes. Discuss or write: Why are they at the top of your list? What was so important about their actions? What risks did they take? What difference did their actions make? Note that sometimes our heroes have flaws—they are imperfect, even as we continue to admire their courage.

You can ask younger students to think of a hero who comes to mind (superheroes or everyday heroes like firefighters) and list them on the board. You can modify this exercise for middle and high school students by asking them to focus on three things: (1) heroes who have recently been in the news, (2) students who have demonstrated remarkable courage, or (3) heroes whom they have recently learned about in their academic studies.

COURAGE EXERCISE: Conquering All Things

This exercise is for grades 4–8, but you can adapt it to other grade levels with different quotes and pictures. For lower elementary students, pick simple quotes—perhaps even some from action heroes. For students in grades 9–12, choose a lengthier or more complex quote, provide contextual information, and ask students to research and explain the quote's background and meaning. The steps follow.

1. Greet students and introduce the trait of courage and Ovid's quotes: "Courage conquers all things" (as cited in Lombardi, 2019) and "Happy the man who ventures boldly to defend what he holds dear" (as cited in Bradford, 2005, p. 14).
2. Hang pictures of courageous past and present figures students may recognize or with whom they may identify.
3. Have students bring in pictures of people whom they consider courageous.
4. Ask students the following questions and have them write their thoughts or share aloud with the class. As you listen to the answers, listen for limited perspectives of courage. Some students may focus solely on acts of physical courage, while others may not think of themselves as courageous. Additionally, some students may speak of their fears; you may find ways to help them consider courageous ways to address those fears. Other fears (such as of being left alone) may suggest a need for follow-up with families, a school counselor, or a social worker. As you lead a discussion, try to

broaden students' understanding by providing additional examples to more fully round out the picture of courage.

- "What does courage mean to you?"
- "What are some ways someone can show courage?"
- "Who are people you know or have heard about who show courage?"
- "Why are they considered courageous? What are the attributes that describe them? How do you think they developed these attributes?"

5. Ask students to create a table with three columns: Courageous Hero, Action, and Circumstance. The table should have five rows, and they should complete it.

6. From this table's contents, students can branch off into any number of tasks, such as discussing with classmates, choosing one of their heroes to write about, or even comparing and contrasting heroes to identify their similarities and differences. Students can also use this as a think-pair-share, where they share their findings with one other person and reflect together on similarities or differences.

You can extend the activity by asking students to research, develop reports on leaders, or even work in cooperative groups with students developing courage posters.

For elementary students, the discussion could occur at story time, after the teacher has read a story about courage. Numerous websites have lists of books on courage for all ages of children; visit **go.SolutionTree.com/behavior** for live links to resources. Teachers can also talk to students about the courage displayed by any of a number of cartoon heroes.

Discuss with students what it means to have courage, what courage may look like, why courage is important, and how having courage may feel in order for them to live their best lives and reach their greatest potential. Perhaps one of the most critical things we can teach our students regarding courage is that courage does not always feel the same on the inside as it does when we observe someone else exhibiting it on the outside.

On the outside, courage may appear to be thrilling, an adrenaline rush, or even reckless. You may even say to yourself in disbelief, "I can't believe he is doing that." From an insider's perspective, however, experiencing courage may or may not be accompanied by an adrenaline rush. Australian Psychologist Karen Young (2016) explains that while on the outside courage may appear impressive, powerful, and self-assured, it may not feel equally as thrilling when you are experiencing and feeling courage on the inside. It can feel more like a volcano erupting; an out-of-body experience; or a slow-motion movie frame, with anxiety, fear, or trepidation. Courage within us can come in waves, for seconds or for longer periods of time, but just long enough to be courageous enough to take on what truly frightens us.

Courage Versus Recklessness

We have all made foolish mistakes. Some of us have paid a dear price for impulsive decisions or actions. Sometimes we make decisions fully believing we are doing the right thing. Other times it is almost like walking right into the midst of a hurricane, knowing that was not our best option, and perhaps realizing we were not adequately prepared. Sometimes it is as if we are called by a circumstance and we simply go along with our peers—we proceed despite the nagging warning signs that are going off in our brain telling us to turn around and go back. Imagine a young child who takes risks on a playground, perhaps by climbing a tree or jumping off of a slide. Or consider a youth who is encouraged by peers who are planning to skip school, vandalize property, or join a gang.

- Are they reasonable risks or is the student ignoring safety and likely to be injured?
- Does the student need help assessing the risk and obeying an adult-imposed limit?
- Is the student responding to a dare by a peer and overriding his or her own sense of caution?

While educators must help young students learn the line between courage and recklessness, we caution against being overprotective. Experts suggest that we actually restrict children's growth and development by supervising them too closely and establishing too many rules (Tremblay et al., 2015).

Sometimes it takes a tremendous amount of courage to stand apart from your peers or to walk away from your friends. As we talk with students about courage, and review courageous options, teachers will want to help them learn to distinguish between the following differences.

- Minimal and significant risks
- True valor and false bravery
- Wise and foolish options

However, this is not always easy to do. For preschool and elementary students, it may be more a matter of helping them reason and supporting the eagerness to explore within the boundaries of safety. Consider the preschooler who very much wants to climb to the top of the slide and then get on her belly to go face down on the slide. The teacher might say, "Do you need some help?" or "Yes, you are really, really high up—look at you [celebrating the accomplishment]; I am here if you need me." And when the child reaches the top and is ready to go barreling down head first, the teacher could say, "Let's try it the other way first, OK? Sit down. Off you go." This type of language is supportive of the student while still considering safety needs.

For a student who is just a little older—perhaps up to age six—courage might be necessary for things like getting on an escalator, trying a ride at the amusement park, or climbing a tree. With each of these physical acts, teachers will use similar language to support safe risk taking, providing guidance or prompts as needed.

Many students might need the most courage for things like trying to make new friends or going to a new school or program. Teachers can be supportive by familiarizing new students with the new setting, introducing them to other people and the class as a whole, and encouraging elementary students to share toys or play together.

With elementary students, many of the unsafe things they try are related to impulsive actions, where they rush headlong into a situation without considering the options, possible consequences, or the help that might be available from adults or other children. Making yourself available, approachable, and supportive, reinforcing everyday examples of courage, and encouraging students to think through their actions are all great ways to foster courage in your students.

COURAGE EXERCISE: Guided Questions

Sometimes trial runs, role playing, or problem-solving options with students about how to handle or respond to tricky or challenging situations are some of the best practices a teacher or parent can provide. Try this with students in grades 6–8.

1. Students write the following four questions on one index card to think through situations before acting. Saying *no* is not always easy.
   • Will it break an important rule, or is it against the law?
   • Will it hurt someone?
   • Does it feel right for me?
   • What choices or options are the best for me?
2. Students work in teams and devise three or four scenarios where it may be difficult to decide on the best course of action. Consider things such as being offered an illegal substance, deciding to call out or challenge a bully (or a friend), or determining how to respond when they themselves have been threatened.
3. Students walk through the solution scenarios they developed in step 2 using their index cards (from step 1) to problem solve and decide the best options.
4. Students review the scenarios and solutions they developed in steps 2 and 3, deciding on one or two solutions they can strengthen through self-talk, reducing self-doubts, or taking positive actions.

COURAGE EXERCISE: Compare and Contrast

This exercise is for educators. First, examine the curriculum for the classes you are teaching. Then, consider the following questions, with reference to the different needs that appear in various situations that require courage.

- What examples of risks, fears, unbearable situations, and courage can you find?
- How could students delve deeper into the courage that was displayed, that could be displayed, or that is needed?
- What fears do you have?
- What fears have you faced?

Consider your students' fears and courage.

- What fears have they faced or are they facing?
- What students or people in your community have displayed heroic courage, and how?
- How is courage displayed whether one flees a dictatorship or stays and tries to help others?

Teachers can lead a class discussion of ways to further students' appreciation of the circumstances that a person might face in either of the scenarios from the final idea (such as the journey and plight of trying to escape or the hardships faced under a dictator with oppression and violence).

Raw Courage and Other Courageous Acts

Recall a time when you observed someone with raw courage, which seems to emanate organically, without practice, polish, or finesse. It is often fueled by emotions such as anger or desire, and may appear bold. It may have been a student standing up to a bully, speaking up in class to call out a peer, or just saying *no* to peers. Or it may have been a student placing him- or herself in harm's way when all the other bystanders walked away, cowered, or froze with fear.

What does courage look like? It might be bold, raw courage, or it may look like a student sitting on a bench, for example. Many elementary schools have adopted buddy benches in their outdoor spaces so that no student feels alone on any given day. The buddy bench is a simple way to help foster friendships for those students who are too shy to ask to join in. Sitting on the bench signals that a student would like to join a group, and other students respond by inviting him or her to play.

Courage can take many shapes and forms. As you explore courage with students, teachers may want to post a list of courageous acts that students will add to over the course of several weeks.

Why Does Courage Matter in School?

In the context of school, work, and life, courage is required to demonstrate our best, to reach our greatest potential, to be resilient, and to thrive. Exercising courage in school can take on many forms in the developmental cycle of maturation. It can mean riding a school bus for the first time, making friends with the new student in class, speaking up for something you are passionate about, trying out for the tennis team, or trying again after you have been rejected or have struggled through an academic lesson.

In a study of over 7,000 students in fourteen Australian high schools, researcher Andrew Martin (2011) found that teaching students how to bring courage into their day-to-day school lives improves learning, performance, and engagement. Martin (2011) reports that courage is more adaptive than avoidance, which means it leads to better outcomes and helps prepare individuals for what is to come. According to Martin (2011), strategies such as goal setting, prioritizing time, and managing their studies help students overcome their fears.

Courage matters in school because it helps us push through on tough days, and it propels us forward whether we are teachers or learners. Teaching and learning require courage.

Courage Helps Us Push Through on Any Given Day

Courage is something that benefits both teachers and students. Student success is directly related to the teacher's belief in students' innate potential for engaged learning and high performance as well as the belief and courage in their own ability to mediate students to demonstrate this potential (Jackson, 2011). Just as athletes push through to test their physical limits, students can also push through academic ceilings, testing their intellectual prowess and riding waves of challenges to reach ever-increasing goals and aims that enable them to focus and flourish.

Similarly, at the heart of every great teacher lies the ability to push through the challenges and fears that come with the teaching territory. Some days, it may be the choice between taking the time for a real teachable moment or sticking rigidly to the academic lesson and expectations set forth by the district or individual school. Teaching has become a constant balancing act, requiring consistent juggling of the school-, district-, state-, and national-level standards, mandates, and expectations. It takes confidence and courage to push through to what feels right on any given school day.

Teaching and Learning Require Courage

Parker Palmer (2007) talks about the risk that authentic teachers take in sharing about themselves and also in sharing leadership with students: What factors influence your courage? Look around you. Do you see any students, teachers, or principals who exhibit significant courage? How could we do more to build courage in schools? What would classrooms look like if a significant number of students demonstrated not only leadership but courageous leadership?

Whether it is a simple act of courage such as a student raising his or her hand in class, asking a question, or being called on to answer in class, or ordinary people demonstrating extraordinary acts of courage without a second thought, courage helps us to overcome our fear in that small moment of time. Courage is what propels people to higher ground and purpose, sometimes without giving it a second thought and sometimes after gathering all one's strength to resist the fear.

Teaching and learning have numerous risks. We often need courage to feel that it is OK not to be as highly competent as we are in the learning mode. This is true for students and teachers alike. For teachers, there is the risk of trying something new, being an innovator or early adopter, transforming entrenched practices to student-centered instruction, focusing on more than academics, or teaching new subjects, grade levels, or students. Each of these situations requires a certain degree of courage because the educator is leaving behind what is familiar. There are the complexities of maintaining a sense of order, introducing complex subjects in a way that matches students' capabilities and interests, and the ins and outs of relying on familiar instructional strategies while introducing new content, to name a few. Sometimes before we can teach in a new and different way, teachers may find themselves back in classrooms, getting another degree or taking advanced coursework. That requires the courage to balance things differently, and it can take a few trials to figure out how to best combine the old with the new.

What about you? Can you recall a time when you were afraid, needed courage to move forward, and took some risks?

COURAGE EXERCISE: Our Individual Courage

As an adult, reflect on one or two times in your life when you faced a fear and acted from a place of courage. What were the circumstances? How did you feel? What actions did you take? What were the outcomes? Looking back, is there anything you might do differently today?

Ask students in kindergarten to grade 12 to reflect on their own lives and answer these questions. This could lead to a writing assignment where students might even compare their own circumstances to someone else's—another student, someone they respect, a hero (known or unknown). Author Lauren Tarshis's *I Survived* book series (www.laurentarshis.com/i-survived) presents thrilling historical fiction from the perspective of a young adolescent who is there. These include books such as *I Survived the American Revolution, 1776* and *I Survived Hurricane Katrina, 2005*. Students could also develop a story, perhaps told in first person, about someone who displayed courage. Elementary students, instead of writing about courage, could draw pictures or select images of courage.

COURAGE EXERCISE: Safe, Nurturing Classrooms

When you consider a safe, nurturing, compassionate classroom environment, what do you envision? Pause for a moment and write down some of the key considerations. Consider the physical layout of the classrooms, the colors, the space, as well as activities and language that foster a sense of belonging and value. Imagine yourself in that peaceful, safe environment, teaching a room full of responsive students.

Now recall a specific incident in your own classroom. It may have been when you were faced with a difficult judgment call. Was punishment in order? What did you need to do to establish your authority or to send the message that the behavior was unacceptable? Looking back on that scene, was the environment safe and nurturing? Why or why not? Is there any way that you might rearrange the physical environment? Looking back from today, is there anything you might have handled differently? Did you have compassion? Did you have the courage to say or do what was needed? What of your students? How did they respond? What worked, and what did not?

COURAGE EXERCISE: Nurturing Courage in the Classroom

We suggest implementing the following six steps over a period of time—perhaps even as broad a time as three to six months—periodically reflecting on your progress and identifying what else is needed to enhance the courage quotient and your support of courage in your classroom.

1. Consider the physical arrangement of your classroom, language used, and the general tone and environment. Does your classroom support a feeling of safety, belonging, and compassion? If not, what could you do?
2. Engage students in exercises where they study others who have displayed courage. You might even discuss courage in the context of current events in your local community, nationally, or internationally.
3. Help students to understand more about themselves and courage. Take students through a mindful breathing exercise to bring clarity to how they feel when they are fearful and when they have courage. The next step then is what is called *thought replacement* (Krull, 2018), where students are given a suggestion to envision themselves being safe and courageous and the fear dissipating.
4. Be supportive of students. Organize and manage your classroom, instruction, and assessment in ways that help students develop a sense of confidence, value, and self-worth.
5. Find teachable moments where you can discuss courage with students. Could you relate discussions of courage, for example, to problems such as cyberbullying or current news and happenings in your school or community? The rise of youth activism after the Parkland, Florida, school shooting in February 2018 and the 1963 Birmingham Children's March

(www.tolerance.org) provide excellent examples for discussion of courage, civil protest, and how to impact change.

6. Over time, create and mediate with activities and assessments that develop an engineer's approach, so that students learn from their mistakes and start to think of errors as opportunities for growth and improvement. An engineering design cycle usually involves a process of some trial and error, learning from imperfect solutions and considering them *design failures* rather than *human failures*.

Practicing Courage: Alleviating Hunger

Kelly DeVarennes, a teacher at Lee Elementary School in Lee, Massachusetts, implemented a project-based learning initiative with her seventh-grade students to alleviate hunger. During the first year of the project, students learned about food insecurities in third world countries and then later focused on their own community.

Students educated themselves through a series of guest speakers (farm to table) and by planting herbs with younger students so that they could take home an herb to help them cook more healthily. Next, students designed and distributed a survey to learn the scope of their own school community's food insecurities, and they began to offer healthy snacks to those who needed more nutrition and food, even sending small snack bags home with students in need on weekends. One year later, their food bank grew into something even bigger—a separate room in the school, with community donations from a local supermarket and backpacks stuffed with meals for families in need to take home. Asked whether she ever expected her class lesson to grow into such a project, Kelly smiled and said, "I always hoped it would. I'm always looking for something bigger to connect [a lesson] to. If it's not relevant to the kids' lives, it doesn't feel the same" (as cited in Smith, 2018).

How Do We Teach Courage?

We can teach courage by making topics relevant to students; teaching assertiveness, grit, and resilience; helping them use their voices; providing space and opportunities to take risks; and teaching problem solving.

Make It Relevant

Author Paul Tough (2013, 2016) says that courage can be nurtured but not taught. We each have our own fears and varying comfort zones. Given this, one of the best ways teachers can mediate for student success is to lay the groundwork, have discussions that connect to students' cultural frames of reference (reflective of what is personally meaningful and relevant), share examples, and then provide opportunities where failure is acceptable and risk taking is encouraged. As Tough (2016) points out, the complex networks of our brains, immune systems, and endocrine systems are quite sensitive to cues from the environment. Creating a classroom environment that is safe and compassionate sends the right signal and conditions that help students better navigate and make sense of the world, decreasing stress and opening new opportunities for change, exploration, and enrichment. Similarly, teachers can further courage and confidence by intentionally building student resilience, where students gain practice handling difficult situations. Such practice fosters their ability to bounce back and move forward.

From time to time, ask students to identify a task that is difficult and then work toward a goal related to that task. It could be mastering a physical task, learning to play an instrument, learning a new complicated art process, mastering an online game, or getting closer to proficiency in an academic skill.

COURAGE EXERCISE: Visioning and Breath Work

This exercise is appropriate for students from preK to grade 12.

1. Have students close their eyes and take some deep breaths.
2. Lead them through a guided meditation, where they walk a distance, climb a mountain, turn a corner, find themselves in the midst of their dreamed-for environment, and see themselves engaged in their dream job.
3. After the meditation, students can share in think-pair-share groups, write a reflection in their journal, or develop a one- or two-page paper on their vision.

Teach Assertiveness, Grit, and Resilience

From time to time, we all experience conflicts and uncomfortable situations where we need to firmly say *no*—where we need to say that we are not interested, or that we will not tolerate certain behaviors or actions. Assertiveness is an essential tool. Some students seem naturally assertive and others are less so. Assertiveness presents the balanced middle between extremes of passivity and aggression and is an important tool to put into our mental health and well-being toolbox. As you plan for an environment that nurtures courage, resilience, and grit, consider how to embed activities and lessons on assertiveness into your curriculum. This might be through books, class discussions, or online investigations.

Courage helps fuel grit; the two are symbiotic, feeding into and off of each other. Indeed, when most people think of grit, they think of resilience—the ability to bounce back in the face of defeat, to respond proactively in the face of adversity, to show a spirit of not giving up.

How do we help students who have suffered from trauma show resilience? Consider discussing some stress openly. For example, teachers talking with each other about lockdowns with open awareness better prepares them to construct lessons to help students increase *their* awareness and resilience. When teachers discuss the impact of traumatic events, they give individuals permission to check in with themselves, rather than resorting to short-term defensive mechanisms like denial, which can exacerbate trauma (Rich & Cox, 2018).

From the positive end of things, researchers Angela L. Duckworth, Christopher Peterson, Michael D. Matthews, and Dennis R. Kelly (2007) say that grit is the "perseverance and passion for long-term goals." According to Duckworth (2016), author of *Grit: The Power of Passion and Perseverance*, high achievers who exhibit grit have long-lasting passion for their pursuits and demonstrate the following traits.

- Sustained effort
- Perseverance despite failure or obstacles
- Dedication to one's goals
- Deliberate practice of desired skills

High achievers and innovators often have an engineer's mindset, one that urges them to continue revising their solutions to arrive at a better and better product or outcome. In essence, grit and resilience provide us with survival skills and character traits to help us cope and adapt for our individual betterment. *Grit* and *resilience* are not terms reserved to describe high achievers. For students who are the most vulnerable and the most at risk for academic failure or social isolation, developing a growth mindset can lead to a stronger sense of self-worth and a greater likelihood that they will achieve some level of success (Dweck, 2016). This is because students will start understanding that they have the power to improve any skill or knowledge base through effective, focused practice.

Grit and resilience can be furthered through classroom and community projects. Master teachers structure classrooms, lessons, and supports so that all students have the opportunity to develop resilience through real-world problem solving. Through inquiry and long-term projects, students are able to address challenging situations, while eventually discovering and implementing viable solutions. Many of the exercises are most appropriate for students in middle and high schools. Take the following steps.

1. Begin by ensuring that students have had practice with the exercises earlier in this chapter for building courage.
2. Pose challenges that will require that students stay with a project for a longer period of time, perhaps even intentionally imposing obstacles. This

can be done hypothetically by inserting steps: "Now imagine that you have lost financing. Or perhaps after collaborating to raise $200,000 from crowdsourcing, you find out that you have been scammed and that only $10,000 is available to you." Or for a community service project, establish steps where students need to appear before a town council, secure support from their local PTA, or get buy-in from local businesses. These additional steps will increase their need for extra preparation and perhaps even extra effort to address recommendations made by parents or local organizations.

Remember that no one develops these characteristics in isolation. Supportive, guiding individuals, opportunities, or organizations help to keep the hope and confidence needed to strive to keep a goal alive. How do you provide these supports to your students? What supports have been most meaningful to you in times of adversity or challenge?

Practicing Courage: Grit

Principal Jessica Jenkins at the West End Secondary School in Manhattan uses expeditionary learning, which engages students and teachers in work that is challenging, adventurous, and meaningful so that learning and achievement flourish. Teachers focus on developing three dimensions of student achievement—(1) knowledge and skills mastery, (2) character, and (3) high-quality student work (Beesley, Clark, Barker, Germeroth, & Apthorp, 2010). Jessica has created a learning environment where her students can solve real-world problems using the information they learn in the classroom.

Teachers at the school challenge students by having them think critically about their lessons. Students are asked to figure out how to apply grit to an issue that they once thought was impossible to solve. Students embark on projects that last up to twelve weeks. Their projects combine a wide variety of subjects such as mathematics, filmmaking, and environmental justice. For example, students were given a project that focused on the health of the Hudson River. They made graphs on the water quality of the river, created a documentary about it and even started a Change.org campaign to update the river's sewer system. At first, they expressed their doubts due to the length and difficulty of the assignment, but they persevered over time, using the supports and guidance provided or found and now they look forward to grappling with new problems every day. Activities such as these can increase grit by teaching students that with a little perseverance, they can solve any problem that they encounter (Marzano, 2017).

Sometimes students will understand more about grit if they learn about how others have displayed it. You might assign longer-term projects, which require some degree of persistence and tenacity. While students may sometimes be discouraged by these more difficult assignments, timing is critical. These projects are geared toward older students, who have demonstrated success with shorter-term projects. The following ideas for longer-term projects will help as well.

- Establish checkpoints to provide formative feedback to students and help them examine options for next steps.
- Identify or provide the materials and guidance needed.
- Practice with hypothetical projects prior to beginning actual community service initiatives.

Help Them Use Their Voices

One of the best ways to help students find their voices in the midst of adversity or fearful experiences is to practice using their own courageous words during role play and scenarios. The following exercise helps students practice what to say, how to say it, and when to say it.

COURAGE EXERCISE: Finding Your Courageous Voice

This exercise works for elementary, middle, and high school students.

1. For elementary students, make up age-appropriate scenarios for them to act out and rehearse their responses. Middle and high school students can submit real-life scenarios that they would like to work through. As an example, here is a scenario for middle and high schoolers.

    A friend is smoking pot at a party and pressures you to take a hit. How do you find the words or the verbal courage to confront your friend?

2. Ask students what the right thing to do is in this situation.
3. Make a list of choices they suggest on the board.
4. Have students pair up, practice each response, and provide feedback to each other. The teacher helps students find their words during the role playing. For example, a student may respond in several ways.
    - Escape clause: "My parents would never let me out of the house again if I did," and walk away.
    - Caring friend: "Drugs can kill you—even one hit. You don't know what is in that pot. I am leaving. This is crazy stuff."
    - Strong voice: "I don't do drugs—they can kill you—and you shouldn't either. You are being stupid. I'm out of here."

The more students (young and old) practice the words they will use, the easier their courageous voice comes in times of adversity, fear, and challenge.

Give Space to Take Risks

While everyone prefers feeling safe, we also have a responsibility to balance safety and comfort zones with new opportunities to grow, learn, experience, and explore. Opportunities that involve uncertainty, fear, and discomfort are needed to develop true courage.

Psychologist Peter Gray (2014) describes why it's important to give space to take risks:

> Children are highly motivated to play in risky ways, but they are also very good at knowing their own capacities and avoiding risks they are not ready to take, either physically or emotionally. Our children know far better than we do what they are ready for. When adults pressure or even encourage children to take risks they aren't ready for, the result may be trauma, not thrill. There are big differences among kids, even among those who are similar in age, size, and strength. What is thrilling for one is traumatic for another. When physical education instructors require all of the children in a gym class to climb a rope or pole to the ceiling, some children, for whom the challenge is too great, experience trauma and shame. Instead of helping them learn to climb and experience heights, the experience turns them forever away from such adventures. Children know how to dose themselves with just the right amount of fear; for that knowledge to operate they must be in charge of their own play.

So, one good way to help students develop courage is to give them space to learn about their own courage. Are your playground rules or other school policies giving students adequate freedom to take risks and learn about their own capabilities and limits?

Brené Brown (2015) provides an additional perspective: "Our willingness to own and engage with our own vulnerability determines the depth of our courage and the clarity of our purpose; the level to which we protect ourselves from being vulnerable is a measure of our fear and disconnection" (p. 2). How willing are we to risk our own vulnerability? Cultivating bravery and courage will help students prepare for success, adulthood, and life with all its twists and turns and ups and downs.

Amanda Blaine (2014) describes how practicing nonviolent communication inspired her:

> to share something I find scary to inspire courage in my stu-
> dents. By trusting myself in front of the class, by going forward
> even though I was vulnerable and afraid, I was showing that
> they were worthy of trust. This was how I was choosing to
> exercise my role as the leader in my classroom: setting the
> tone of productive risk-taking.

COURAGE EXERCISE: We Are Vulnerable

This exercise works for students in grades 4–12. We are taught to be tough and to act with confidence. Sometimes this works well and can help us get through a difficult situation. However, as Brown (2015) explains, we must use care so we don't end up in denial or overlook important clues that our bodily reactions are giving us. Here is an exercise to identify, own, and work through vulnerability.

1. Students write down the following headings on a sheet of paper, leaving about two inches between each heading: Situation, Feeling, What I Did, How It Turned Out, What I Could Do Next Time. Or, you can give each student a blank copy of figure 6.1 (page 118).
2. Introduce Brown's (2015) concept of vulnerability, having the courage to be authentic and imperfect, and how it is good to admit when we feel fear or anxiety. You can read a quote from her website (https://brenebrown.com), books, or videos.
3. Ask students to consider a time when they felt overwhelmed, afraid, or a sense of foreboding proceeding into a dangerous space. Ask them to describe the feelings they had.
4. Ask students to identify what happened next.
   - "Did you make plans to handle your fear? Did you stop, reflect, and rethink them, or did you need to act in the moment?"
   - "If you made plans, did you follow through with them?"
   - "What was the result of your action, and how did you feel about the outcome? Brave? Successful? Discouraged?"
   - "If you faced a similar situation in the future, what might you do?"
5. End with a discussion of why it's a good idea to be able to recognize when we are feeling vulnerable (that by recognizing that feeling we may make different, healthier decisions).

You could relate vulnerability to a story in literature, a scientist, an athlete, or a leader in history for a follow-up discussion or students could write a story or a biographical essay on vulnerability.

Situation	Feeling	What I Did	How It Turned Out	What I Could Do Next Time
Having to do several homework assignments in one week	Overwhelmed, afraid I would fail	Made a plan for what to do every night and did it	Bs on everything I did; felt pretty good about it since I had so much to do at once	Nothing different, I am OK with this
Passing a large dog with a loud bark on my way home	Scared	Took a different route	Takes a little longer but I don't get scared every time I walk to and from school; safer	Maybe try to be brave and just go on the other side of the street
Having to read a poem in class	Anxious, afraid other people might laugh at me	Picked the shortest possible poem to read	Relieved; glad I lived through it	Pick a longer poem

Figure 6.1: We Are Vulnerable exercise form—example.

Visit go.SolutionTree.com/behavior for a free reproducible version of this figure.

You can modify this exercise for students in grades K–3. Rather than exercises and activities, perhaps one way to address vulnerability is by accepting fear and anxiety, rather than rushing to assure the student that everything is fine or suggesting that the feelings are invalid (Lindberg, 2018).

Encourage Problem Solving

Teachers can discuss issues using a problem-solving format so that students think through the longer-term implications and the multiple layers of complexity that are often introduced over time. This problem-solving format could be as simple as the following steps (Beecroft, Duffy, & Moran, 2003).

1. Define the problem.
2. Generate possible solutions.
3. Evaluate and select a solution.
4. Implement and follow up on the solution.

One method is to have students look at a local problem—drought; forest fires; homelessness; teen suicide; substance abuse; or inequities related to wealth, gender, or sexual identity. In groups, students could look at one problem from different perspectives or each person could choose a unique problem to define before producing potential solutions for the group to evaluate and attempt to implement.

Here is a specific example from science and history. When studying the impact of climate change on icebergs in Antarctica and the ripple effects, teachers can introduce some of the original explorers, such as Sir Edmund Hillary or Ernest Shackleton, and discuss their grit and determination. As reported in *Time* magazine (2003), Shackleton placed this ad to find his crew for the *Endurance* expedition: "Men wanted for hazardous journey. Low wages, bitter cold, long hours of complete darkness. Safe return doubtful. Honour and recognition in event of success." Despite the realities described in the ad, men who had honed the grit and resilience needed were prepared to participate in the arduous trials they were warned they would encounter!

COURAGE EXERCISE: Assessing Grit and Resilience

One way to begin nurturing grit and resilience is to assess your grade 4–12 students' knowledge of these concepts. Several scales are available for students (some of which work with students as young as nine) to assess how these characteristics show up in themselves (https://positivepsychologyprogram.com/3-resilience-scales). Review the scales, take them yourself, and consider using one or more with your students after talking with a school psychologist about their administration and use.

What Does Courage Look Like Historically?

For teachers in the classroom and in life, momentous actions, both current and historical, provide a great platform for helping students understand courage. There are times when individuals—activists, everyday heroes, and world leaders—rose to meet the demands of the time.

Activists

Consider Rosa Parks's sit-down for civil rights in Montgomery, Alabama and Nelson Mandela's dedication to justice, anti-apartheid activism, and leadership of the African National Congress. Whether we consider these or other heroes (Harriet Tubman, Dietrich Bonhoeffer, Pushpa Basnet, or Malala Yousafzai, for example), we find leaders who demonstrated courage, acted boldly, often defied common logic, and made hard decisions.

Rosa Parks and Nelson Mandela both broke the law when they had experienced enough injustice, knowing that the consequence could be jail or imprisonment, threats to their lives and their families' lives, and even death. Malala Yousafzai defied authorities by simply going to school. These examples demonstrate the power of doing the right thing and the importance of sometimes challenging rules and laws because of the bigger stakes. In each case, the person's actions both called attention to injustice and led to change.

Courageous leaders overcome fear, show a mental toughness or grit, and often display the perseverance to stay with their vision even when confronted with seemingly insurmountable obstacles.

At Marjory Stoneman Douglas High School in Parkland, Florida, students launched a historic March For Our Lives movement after surviving a mass shooting and losing seventeen classmates and teachers. Within five short weeks of this tragedy, students organized a two hundred-plus city march for reducing gun violence, seeking accountability from elected officials, and new gun legislation. All heroes, including ordinary people like you, me, and the students at Marjory Stoneman Douglas High School, exhibit a certain amount of everyday courage and bravery.

COURAGE EXERCISE: Quote Sort

You can use quotes from famous people in any grade's class many ways: introduce topics, summarize a topic, or stimulate student investigations. Read through the following quotes.

- "Bran thought about it. 'Can a man still be brave if he's afraid?' 'That is the only time a man can be brave,' his father told him" (Martin, 2016, p. 178).
- "Fear and courage are brothers" (Guillemets, n.d.).

- "I learned that courage was not the absence of fear, but the triumph over it. The brave man is not he who does not feel afraid, but he who conquers that fear" (Mandela, as cited in CNN, 2008).
- "There is no living thing that is not afraid when it faces danger. The true courage is in facing danger when you are afraid" (Baum, 1900, p. 153).

Now, consider the following questions.

- Are any of their quotes relevant to topics you are studying in your academic curricula? Consider things such as time period, historical significance, leadership, and cultural influence.
- Which quote speaks to issues you are trying to convey as you nurture courage in your classroom?
- What quote might you post on your classroom walls?
- Are there any quotes you might want to share and explain to your students?
- How could you build a lesson around one of these quotes?
- Could students select quotes to journal about in a daily free write?
- Would it be worthwhile for students to select a quote and study the quoted person and the relevant time period to learn more about the context and the idea?
- Can students match these quotes with Lassiter's (2016) types of courage?
- What else could students do with these quotes?

Visit **go.SolutionTree.com/behavior** for more quotes about courage.

Everyday Heroes

Along with courageous current and historic figures, there are also everyday heroes such as firefighters, rescue personnel, and servicewomen and -men who support order and safety. Ordinary people among us have also displayed extraordinary courage. Consider the bystander who jumps on the train tracks to save a person from an oncoming train, a person who risks his or her life to save a person from a burning car just before it explodes, or a brave soul who fights the floodwaters to rescue a person trapped on the roof of a house.

How Do We Measure Courage?

The following tools measure courage: the Connor-Davidson Resilience Scale, the Predictive 6-Factor Resilience Scale, Academic Resilience Scale, Resiliency Scales for Children and Adolescents, and S-CCATE.

Connor-Davidson Resilience Scale

The Connor-Davidson Resilience Scale (CD-RISC; Connor & Davidson, 2003; www.connordavidson-resiliencescale.com) is a self-report measure of resilience used by clinicians dealing with individuals who are struggling with post-traumatic stress disorders. It assesses resilience as a function of five interrelated components.

1. Personal competence
2. Acceptance of change and secure relationships
3. Trust/tolerance/strengthening effects of stress
4. Control
5. Spiritual influences

The CD-RISC was originally developed for adults, but numerous studies have reported use with students ages ten to eighteen. It includes twenty-five items and takes between five and ten minutes to complete. Shorter versions of the scale are also available. The scale measures such things as ability to adapt to change, ability to use humor in the face of stress, whether you are easily discouraged, and whether you consider yourself to be a strong person.

Predictive 6-Factor Resilience Scale

The Predictive 6-Factor Resilience Scale (Rossouw & Rossouw, 2016; https://bit .ly/2KuqgRi) is based on the neurobiology of resilience and the relationship with health and hygiene factors such as exercise, nutrition, and sleep and measures factors that lead to well-being and personal success. The online scale includes sixteen items and can be completed in three minutes. Originally developed for adults, the authors are planning a scale for children.

It measures resilience as a function of six domains.

1. **Vision:** Self-efficacy and goal-setting
2. **Composure:** Emotional regulation and ability to identify, understand, and act on internal prompts and physical signals
3. **Tenacity:** Perseverance and hardiness
4. **Reasoning:** Higher cognitive traits like problem solving, resourcefulness, and thriving
5. **Collaboration:** Psychosocial interaction, such as secure attachment, support networks, context, humor and health (physiological health)
6. **Health:** Eating well, getting enough sleep, and regularly exercising

Academic Resilience Scale

Academic Resilience Scale (ARS-30; Cassidy, 2016; https://bit.ly/2XuGRwZ) assesses resilience in the context of academic success. The scale uses a vignette describing a significant academic challenge and a Likert scale from 1 (*likely*) to 5 (*unlikely*). Three factors are assessed with ARS-30.

1. Perseverance
2. Reflecting and adaptive help-seeking
3. Negative affect (feelings) and emotional response

With this scale, respondents rate the likelihood that they would do such things as work harder, keep trying, and use feedback to improve their work (show perseverance); think about their strengths and weaknesses to help them work better (use metacognition); seek encouragement from family and friends; seek help from tutors (reflect and use adaptive help-seeking); and get annoyed, depressed, and think everything is ruined and going wrong (negative affect and emotional response).

Resiliency Scales for Children and Adolescents

The Resiliency Scales for Children and Adolescents (RSCA; Prince-Embury, 2007; https://bit.ly/2kc1ICu) is designed for ages nine to eighteen and is written at a third-grade reading level. It contains three stand-alone scales of between nineteen and twenty-four questions, and each takes about five minutes to complete.

1. The Sense of Mastery Scale, which measures optimism, self-efficacy, and adaptability
2. The Sense of Relatedness Scale, which measures trust, support, comfort, and tolerance
3. The Emotional Reactivity Scale, which assesses sensitivity, recovery, and impairment

S-CCATE

As you move forward mindfully into the realm of courage and take steps to embed courage into your classrooms and instruction, we encourage you to consider how courage applies in the numerous studies you share with your students. Table 6.2 has three of the factors from S-CCATE for the area of courage.

Table 6.2: S-CCATE Courage Factors

Factor	In Action
Understanding of equity	Students learn about the role of peaceful protests, media, and litigation for obtaining justice or reducing inequities.
Confidence and courage	Students create affirmations and positive visualizations for themselves and others.
Courage and resiliency	Students seem eager to approach challenging situations.

Reflection

To get the most out of this chapter, reflect on these questions after reading it.

- What does courage mean? Do you see any one type more than another during your workday?
- What is the importance of courage?
- How can you develop courage in yourself? What type would help you most at school?
- How gritty and resilient are you? Do you have the tenacity and perseverance for the long haul?
- How can you act and lead courageously?

CHAPTER 7

Heart Centered Community

Community building must become the heart of any school improvement effort.

—Thomas J. Sergiovanni

key principle

It takes time to build a heart centered school community, through infusing and weaving consciousness, compassion, confidence, and courage into the classroom, school, and beyond so that every community member feels its sustaining effect.

While schools are places for learning, they are also places for students to connect and socialize. In an ideal world, deeply engaged students would experience a sense of joy, delight, and happiness at school. A growing body of research increasingly supports the link between learning and students' mental health and well-being (Bergin & Bergin, 2009; Centers for Disease Control & Prevention, 2014) and the importance of building mindful school communities (Schaps, 2003; Wang & Holcombe, 2010). However, while this seems self-evident, many schools still have work to do. It takes effort to create positive school environments.

When schools purposely choose to build respectful relationships and meaningful connections with students, staff, and families, a sense of safety, belonging, and trust takes hold. When students feel valued, connected, and supported by their school community members, mental health and well-being are just two of many improvements. Student attendance, educational outcomes, and participation in the school community also increase (Bergin & Bergin, 2009). Cultivating a heart centered community is an effective way of fostering those connections and building bridges into the hearts and minds of students as they grow to appreciate, value, and love learning with their peers and teachers within the structure provided by academic curricula.

Exploring the concept of community, knowing why it matters and how to teach it in school, discovering what it has looked like in the past, and learning how to measure it can take us that much closer toward mindful school communities.

What Is a Heart Centered Community?

Beyond the school is a wider community—families, neighbors, and local businesses. The larger community also includes social services agencies and other organizations and individuals networking with your school. Whether you work in an urban, suburban, or rural setting, you will benefit by approaching community building as a process that extends beyond the walls of your school. In these cases, all that we have described previously—being aware, building trust, expressing compassion and empathy, having courage to stand up and speak out, developing confidence and courage in yourself and others, and just being a source of communication and support for each other—applies. Building the kind of community that cares for everyone, students especially, requires cultivating a heart centered community.

A heart centered community is the wraparound hug or the invitation into the "circle" that makes everyone feel as if they are being listened to because of the embedded sense of safety, belonging, and importance. Building compassionate, heart centered, mindful school communities requires all stakeholders to move in the same direction to cultivate a place where each and every person feels valued and heard. *Gemütlichkeit*, the German-language word used to convey a state or feeling of warmth, friendliness, and good cheer, speaks to what a *sense of community* should feel like. It means a sense of purpose. Other qualities associated with this term include "peace of mind," a sense of belonging and well-being springing from social acceptances, and a "heart, mind, temper, feeling" (Gemütlichkeit, n.d.). *Gemeinschaft* refers to this heart of a caring community—when members are committed to thinking, growing, and inquiring— where learning becomes an attitude as well as an activity, a way of life as well as a process (Sergiovanni, 1999).

In heart centered communities, we make a conscious effort to refocus our schools and school cultures so that students become immersed in environments that consider social-emotional well-being and the needs of self and others. We envision this awareness and goodness being extended to a wider school community, "embracing our ability to educate with both our hearts and minds" (Mason et al., 2019, p. 2). With conscious consideration of the needs of students and staff, school leaders are better positioned to develop a sense of trust and goodwill. Similarly, when teachers are consciously aware of student needs, they are better positioned to develop healthier expectations, facilitate student self-esteem and resilience, and further community building. When this happens, students feel that they belong to a caring, compassionate learning community, that they are worthy, and that their voices will be heard.

At the core of a heart centered community lies supportive, nurturing, and compassionate relationships. There can't be one set of norms for teachers and another for students. Rather, a mutual exchange that includes respectful, supportive interactions is crucial. Teachers who are building heart centered communities do the following.

- Actively cultivate respectful, supportive relationships among students, teachers, and families; see Build Strong, Healthy Relationships and a Sense of Belonging (page 135) for more.
- Emphasize common purpose and ideals, such as "We are all in this together" and "All for one and one for all."
- Provide regular opportunities for service and cooperation. Incorporating high-quality service learning and problem- or project-based learning regularly into curricula helps students develop and experience the heartfelt satisfaction of contributing to improving the well-being of others and community. Through meaningful interactions and cooperative work, students are fulfilled by working to improve their own communities.
- Provide developmentally appropriate opportunities for autonomy and influence. Having a voice in creating an agenda, classroom norms or expectations, and a positive classroom climate is intrinsically satisfying and helps prepare students for the complexities of citizenship in a democracy (Schaps, 2003).

Why Does Community Matter in School?

People want to belong. Inherent in a sense of belonging is the fulfillment of the need for relatedness. Feeling securely connected to others in the community allows us to feel worthy of love and respect (Osterman, 2000). When we feel securely connected with support from peers, a sense of safety increases (Cowie & Oztug, 2008). In a study of the relationship between middle school students' perceptions of teachers and students' feelings of alienation or belonging, Tamera Murdock, Lynley Anderman, and Sheryl Hodge (2000) find that "reports of teachers' disrespect and criticism as well as of teachers' long-term expectations were related not only to students' beliefs about themselves (including academic self-concept) but also to the values that students developed about school" and that "students who do not feel valued by the schooling process are not apt to value schools" (p. 344). Murdock and her colleagues also reported that patterns of negative behavior and experiences in early adolescence between grades 7 and 9 contributed to risks of dropping out of school.

Community matters in school because belonging alleviates alienation; caring social connections are crucial. Communities nurture learning, as teachers and students benefit from collective efficacy. Further, attuned teachers increase student bonding and motivation, and within a mindful school community, physical health increases, disruptive behaviors diminish, and stress-handling skills improve.

Alienation Is Alleviated

Caring social connections are crucial. While many youth enjoy academic learning and pursuit of knowledge, many also want a sense of intimacy, time for collaboration with peers, and social clubs. One of the primary reasons that youth join gangs, for example, is for the sense of belonging (Estrada, Gilreath, Sanchez, & Astor, 2017). In gangs, youth find others who play the roles of adults, dishing out expectations, rules, and even punishments. Youth who are feeling alienated or isolated may find in gangs a community filled with activities and structure—meetings at specific times, celebrations, and clearly defined roles. They also find others who reward them for taking risks and defying norms, as well as the thrill or adrenaline rush that may come with outsmarting authorities, planning and plotting with others, getting away with crimes, and engaging in exciting activities. These components—thrill, structure, planning with peers, and celebrations—are specific conditions that could be introduced into classroom and school communities.

A 2017 study, *What Teens Want From Their Schools*, finds that teens have a "greater need for connection at the school level and therefore tend to prefer smaller schools with fewer students who all know each other, not large institutions that might sacrifice intimacy for more courses and extracurricular options" (Geraci, Palmerini, Cirillo, & McDougald, 2017, p. 6). One group of students, making up about 20 percent of the respondents, "was particularly inclined toward social engagement" (Geraci et al., 2017, p. 62). They preferred "collaborative assignments (pairs or small groups) and other group projects" (Geraci et al., 2017, p. 212) and were interested in extracurricular activities, sports, and social clubs that provide opportunities to develop close relationships with peers and teachers outside of class.

Belonging to a school community also has an impact on teen suicidal ideation and behavior. According to a Texas survey of 2,530 students, youth suicidal behaviors are reduced by a sense of belonging to a school community (Olcoń, Kim, & Gulbas, 2017). Katarzyna Olcoń and colleagues (2017) found that in comparison, school bullying, feeling unsafe at school, and being threatened or injured at a school increased the risk of suicidal behaviors.

Other researchers report that young students who have close relationships with teachers and peers are more likely to experience a positive transition into secondary school (Waters, Lester, & Cross, 2014). These students also reported fewer emotional problems, feelings of depression and anxiety, and antisocial behaviors.

Interest in Learning Increases

What can teachers do to help students form bonds with peers and connections with schools? When Chris Mason worked as a resource teacher at Glasgow Middle School in a suburb of Washington, D.C., she conducted an array of high-interest, exploratory activities with her seventh-grade students. Several of her students were gang members or at risk of joining gangs. She relied on her knowledge of their interests to help shape their sense of belonging and commitment to school and learning.

Stimulating Interest in Learning: Simulated Court Trial

One of the concepts in the seventh-grade curriculum at Glasgow Middle School in Alexandria, Virginia, was the role of the judicial branch and classroom justice. While the school did not have a student council, Chris met with student leaders to consider juvenile crimes to be tried by a simulation of a trial by their peers. Students studied the roles of judges, lawyers, and juries, as well as court reporters and courtroom artists. In an inclusive environment, students with varying needs and capabilities, from students who were academically advanced to students with individualized education programs (IEPs) and students who were English learners worked in cooperative learning teams as they prepared for the trial. Students in each class presented the cases they had prepared as other students played the audience. When all teams had completed their presentation, everyone, including the judge, jury, and audience, used a rubric to discuss what went well and, in their view, whether it was the defense attorney or prosecutor who excelled in pleading the case. This simulation allowed students to engage in higher-order thinking while also challenging their notions of justice. Students were able to get to know each other in a different context and a deeper way.

With clearly defined roles, a common goal, and a framework to provide structure, students feel safe to be vulnerable around one another. Students at Glasgow were highly engaged in this project and it served not only as a doorway to academic learning, but as a way to establish a greater sense of cooperative learning and community.

COMMUNITY EXERCISE: Adding Excitement to the Classroom

Building on what we know about student engagement, this exercise is designed to heighten a student's sense of excitement, connection, and celebration within classrooms. You can adapt this activity for preK–12 students. Many teachers use a version of this when they specifically introduce celebrations to reward completion of units.

- In planning, teachers consider students' developmental levels and age-appropriate interests to reflect on how to engage students in activities related to the curriculum goals in ways that will increase students' sense of thrill, excitement, structure, peer collaboration, and celebrations. Teachers may even want to meet in grade-level or subject-level teams or professional learning communities to plan.
- When teachers have three or four options, they meet with a small group of student leaders who help make decisions about their choices and plan the activity. Planning will include identifying the objectives, activities, number of sessions, reading, homework, resources, and ways to celebrate completion and evaluate success (perhaps through a student rubric).
- Teachers find an exciting way to introduce the activity. It could be a video, a field trip, or inviting a speaker to talk on a particular subject.
- Students complete the activity, conduct the celebration, and evaluate success.

For elementary students, the complexity, number of roles, celebration, and evaluation of success can all be adjusted to be developmentally appropriate. For example, first- and second-grade students could visit a farm or zoo, study animals, and write or act out group or individual stories about an animal of their choice. Upper elementary and middle school students might watch an entertaining, educational video about animals. High school students could do a brief open-ended mini-research project to create a product like a slideshow, poem, or song. A creative writing or art project could introduce students to a new learning topic.

Teachers and Students Benefit From Collective Efficacy

Teachers also benefit from creating heart centered school learning communities. Peter DeWitt (2017), a former K–5 teacher and elementary principal, suggests that a sense of collective teacher efficacy can be supported by collaborative inquiry, authentic collegial learning communities, staff meetings where teachers investigate a problem of practice, and teacher coaching and mentoring that provides additional support and caring to peers. Heart centered learning communities are, in fact, both small and large teacher teams and professional learning communities in schools.

Heart centered communities value the importance of teachers' collective efficacy. In these communities, teachers and other school staff work toward mutually established intentions, purpose, and outcomes that are achieved through use of the S-CCATE (Mason et al., 2018). When teachers cultivate a Heart Centered Learning community where all teachers feel they belong and are cared for by their peers, they are better able to support each other in creating a sense of belonging among their students as well. Teachers who have worked through the ebbs and flow of committing to a Heart Centered Learning community at their school will be better positioned to establish positive, healthful, and heartfelt communities in their classrooms and in the larger school community.

Attuned Teachers Increase Student Bonding and Motivation

Teachers can use their position as classroom leaders to buffer against mental health issues by transforming classroom and school culture to be less supportive of bullies while supporting individual students who may be victims of bullying (Farmer, Lines, & Hamm, 2011; Rodkin & Gest, 2011). Understanding student social dynamics, especially bullying, allows teachers to be more attuned to their students. Teachers who have increased their level of attunement have been able to better identify students identified as bullies (Farmer, Hall, Petrin, Hamm, & Dadisman, 2010). When aggressive students are identified as bullies by both teachers and students, bullies' social status decreases (Ahn & Rodkin, 2014).

Interventions to enhance teacher attunement are crucial, because levels of attunement to bully-victim dyads is low, especially in large class sizes (Ahn, Rodkin, & Gest, 2013). When teachers are not aware of their students' bully culture and have low levels of responsive teaching (teacher sensitivity, quality of feedback, positive climate, and quality instructional formats), school bonding and motivation diminish over time (Gest, Madill, Zadzora, Miller, & Rodkin, 2014). Researchers Amy E. Luckner and Robert C. Pianta (2011) conclude from studying fifth graders that when teachers provide both a well-organized structure *and* emotional support, students show less aggression. This may be because these traits make it easier for students to self-regulate their behaviors. Also, results from a study of student self-reported perceptions showed that positive peer relationships as well as positive student perceptions of the school environment both appear to be strengthened by teacher attunement (Farmer et al., 2011).

Students who have a connection with their school community are more likely to have better academic achievement, higher grades and test scores, and better attendance, and they tend to stay in school longer (Allen, Kern, Vella-Brodrick, Hattie, & Waters, 2018).

Physical Health Increases

There are also physical health benefits to creating a heart centered community. A strong community often—though not always—can help create a physically healthy school environment. Often that physical health starts with funds from the surrounding communities (in the form of taxes) resulting in safe, updated buildings and available health resources at school. When students attend schools in buildings in desperate need of renovation and few health resources, their health suffers (Crosnoe, 2005; Huang, Calzada, Cheng, & Brotman, 2008; Pianta, La Paro, Payne, Cox, & Bradley, 2002). That said, not all strong communities need to be fiscally wealthy. Financial wealth isn't a requirement for making a community heart centered. Internationally, students who are part of non-dominant cultures are more likely to attend poor-quality schools (World Health Organization, 2012), so several factors must be considered when attempting to eliminate disparities along racial and ethnic lines. These include the physical maintenance and upkeep of school buildings, hazardous environmental concerns, and available health programs, resources, and policies.

Disruptive Behaviors Decrease

As a specific approach to improve the well-being of students, heart centeredness also shows promise as a way to reduce disruptive behaviors and increase a sense of calm. Students learn emotional and behavioral regulation through breath work, yoga, and meditation. Mindful moments rooms are created to allow students to re-center in times of emotional distress, and restorative justice is used in response to infractions in lieu of suspensions and detentions. Administrators, educators, and students work together to find solutions to the root causes of disruptive behavior instead of punishing the behavior repeatedly. Students who perceive school authority as legitimate and teacher-student relations as positive are less disruptive (Way, 2011).

Stress-Handling Skills Improve

Clinical psychologist Rick Hanson (2018) recommends an approach to teaching methods for staying calm and happy in the face of stress that is highly compatible with mindfulness. Hanson provides a rationale and exercises for developing strengths such as grit, gratitude, and compassion. Practicing these skills on a regular basis can be a buffer against the negative impacts of stress and help cultivate a heart centered, compassionate school community.

COMMUNITY EXERCISE: Sensing Beneath the Surface

Source: Adapted from Hanson, 2018.

To cultivate a compassionate school culture, have K–grade 4 students learn to sense what's beneath the surface by truly imagining what it feels like to be someone else. Teachers can help them do this by leading them through a visualization exercise. For example, help students understand how aggressive behavior can be a defense mechanism for fear by imagining the bodily sensations of someone acting out because of fear by reading the following script to them.

The steps for this exercise follow.

1. Read this script to students: "Close your eyes and imagine you are all alone, coming into a brand-new school where you don't know anyone. You really want to make new friends, but you're nervous and shy. Is your heart beating fast? Are you sweating?"

2. After a pause, say, "Imagine that you've gathered your courage and walked up to one of the other kids in your new school to ask if you can sit down next to him. The other kid says his friend is going to sit there, so you walk away feeling sad, lonely, and rejected. How does your body feel now? Do you have a stomachache? Is your face warm and red?"

3. After a pause, say, "Now, imagine a different kid starts walking toward you. You think he is going to make fun of you and you're scared all of the other kids are going to laugh at you. Are all of your muscles feeling tight? You turn your back to this kid to try and hide your fear. He taps you on the shoulder, startling you, so you turn around and push him. Why did you push him? Are you mad or scared?"

4. After the final pause, ask students to "open your eyes slowly and notice how your body feels."

5. Lead a class discussion and have students identify how their bodies, minds, and hearts felt at different points of the story. Ask students to indicate how many of them think the person who pushed the other student did so because he was mad or sad. If you have introduced other mindfulness techniques, ask students what advice they would give the new student: Do some breath work to calm your body? Get an adult and ask for help finding communities based on your interests? Discuss why it is important to have systems and routines for welcoming people into our community.

How Do We Teach Community?

We can teach community the following ways: giving students voice; building strong, healthy relationships and a sense of belonging; encouraging positive, respectful relationships; using restorative justice; considering parents' and families' needs; and fostering effective communication.

Give Students Voice

Parker Palmer (2014), founder of the Center for Courage and Renewal, reminds us that "community is not a goal to be achieved but a gift to be received." The best way to obtain the gift of community is to open our hearts. He urges us to tap into our integral capacity for connectedness to create a space for everyone to grow. Palmer (2014) suggests that teachers penetrate "the illusion of separateness and [touch] the reality of interdependence." In fact, he urges us to embrace our relation to all members of our community from our closest family members to the neighbors with whom we must get along to the strangers we'll never meet.

In a classroom setting, this requires the teacher to take a step back from lecturing and allow the students to do more of the talking. At the district level, this may involve inviting students to participate in decision making as well. This can be done by visiting their schools or by asking for student representatives to meet with key central office administrators or come to a board or committee meeting or hearing. Students then have the opportunity to tap into their own resources, perhaps even some that they did not know they had. This method of teaching inspires critical thinking and a sense of the community at the classroom or district level. When students work together to solve problems rather than simply hearing the solution from the teacher, they get the sense that they are being taken seriously.

Building Community: Messaging and Actions

To appreciate the importance of listening to students and valuing what they have to say, Carole Siegel, psychotherapist and former school psychology director for Pittsfield Public Schools in Pittsfield, Massachusetts, relates this story:

> One morning, two boys came to my door and asked to see me. One, John, said that he was "really messing up." He said he was using drugs and had moved out of his house. I was amazed at his clear explanation of his situation, particularly because he had never been one of the boys in the group who spoke easily or regularly in group. He went on to explain that he had nobody who listened to him or whom he could talk to. There was no family mealtime, so he just waited for group time each week. Since I had less of a sense of John than probably any of the other of the seven boys, I asked him what made the group so important to him. "It's the only place that I have people who I trust and who listen to me." His simple explanation was a powerful reminder to me of so many truths about schools, students, and the culture. Many young people have no adults who they see regularly (family mealtimes almost never occur in many homes). I think the most amazing thing about his revelation was that something which seems at first so minimal is, in reality, so significant. (Siegel, 1995, p. 54)

Schools can strengthen a student's sense of community by infusing commonsense, practical approaches that feel natural and welcoming. Staying in the moment and being aware of the many burdens and loads students carry allows teachers to focus on community building that will help students achieve their academic and social-emotional potential. Mindful teachers meet students where they are academically, not where they think they *should* be. They also provide feedback in a timely manner and celebrate with heartfelt recognition to demonstrate that the students' voice, opinions, and work matter. Being conscious about not only verbal responses but also body language ensures that we don't show students irritability or aggravation.

Build Strong, Healthy Relationships and a Sense of Belonging

Source: Adapted from Learners Edge, 2016.

Humanistic psychologist Carl Rogers believed that in order for individuals to grow, they need an environment that provides positive relationships and interactions with healthy personalities, along with genuineness (openness and self-disclosure), acceptance (being viewed with unconditional positive regard or love), and empathy (being listened to and understood; McLeod, 2014). As Saul McLeod (2014) explains in a discussion of Carl Rogers and self-actualization, much like a flower that needs sunlight and water to grow, people need nurturing. How do we nurture both ourselves and others as community members?

Teachers, administrators, or a committee of parents, teachers, and community representatives can review the following list and assess whether the participating school follows the guidelines. If not, they can determine whether the school can adopt them.

- Make an inviting environment for anyone entering the school building.
- Model calm, respectful behaviors and consistently, fairly enforce rules with appropriate non-punitive consequences.
- Consider replacing in-school referrals or in-school suspensions with mindful moments rooms and suspensions with in-school engagement sessions that allow students to make connections, complete homework, or perform other productive and reflective exercises.
- Encourage teachers and school leaders to authentically get to know their students and families.
- Identify ways of improving communication with families and a variety of venues to meet individual family needs. For example, teachers can send a form asking how parents would like to communicate: by phone, email, or hard copies sent home.
- Focus on student and family strengths. Recognitions, awards, and celebrations are a great way to do this, on a semi-grand scale. On an

Encouraging Consciousness: Mindful Moments Rooms

Mindful moments rooms (Holistic Life Foundation, 2016) are the opposite of what a detention room looks like. A mindful moments room is an inviting, safe environment that encourages deep thinking, reflection, and calm so that students can work through emotions like fear, anxiety, or anger that are precipitated by stress and pressure. The room is filled with soft lighting, decorations, and comfortable seating such as beanbag chairs or large fluffy pillows, rocking chairs, and rugs or mats. Students use this room to practice breathing, guided meditation, or imagery to help calm and quiet their minds and bodies before they discuss what happened to them and return to class.

individual scale, however, we can do this by consistently pointing out strengths—including those of an individual student, family, or culture.

- Clearly communicate school policies regarding safety, well-being, and discipline so students and families feel supported rather than blindsided.

Positive, respectful relationships are at the heart of it all. Transitioning from often disruptive home environments or violent previous evenings that result in little sleep and much worry places students in a very vulnerable state when they arrive at school each morning. Greetings, *I wish my teacher knew* _____ writing prompts, and morning circles invite all students to the circle of conversation and community.

Community and classroom circles help foster responsibility, cooperation, mutual respect, and ethical student, classroom, and community behavior (Rimm-Kaufman & Sandilos, 2011). These circles promote a sense of civility and openness for community members when communication is at eye level with peers, teachers, and other stakeholders.

Here are some guidelines.

- When held daily, they especially help students transition from often hectic home lives and into a calm, supportive, consistent learning environment.
- Dedicating the first ten to thirty minutes of each day to circle time provides great returns, as it helps build social-emotional management and positive relationships from the start.

- Establishing group norms and expectations together as a class community at the beginning of the year, as well as discussing how and why these group norms help students be respectful, stay safe, and care about others, helps set the stage for a healthy classroom environment.
- The stronger the sense of community, the fewer conflicts students experience.
- When problems do arise, this strong foundation allows students, teachers, and school communities to find real solutions.

Stimulating Interest in Learning: Knowing Student Needs and Desires

Knowing your students means understanding their needs, interests, and desires, and using this knowledge to better understand how to engage them in the natural flow of the classroom. At Taconic High School in Pittsfield, Massachusetts, veteran mathematics teacher Donna Quallen looks for ways to regularly and skillfully infuse student names and interests into problems, scenarios, and problem-based learning projects. If Donna's students are in the health care program, for example, she relates real-life health care scenarios such as taking a person's vital signs and how to calculate and analyze that information.

This is the real-life, relatable, and practical application that connects what students are learning to what they need to know to be college and career ready. Her classroom also differs from a traditional classroom with desks and chairs. Instead, she purposely arranges her tables and chairs into a boardroom-like setting, conducive to conversation, cooperative learning, and mutual exchange for project- and problem-based learning. Donna sets up a learning environment based on successful student-student and student-teacher relationship building while cultivating an interactive and engaging learning community that helps them prepare for college, career, and life (D. Quallen, personal communication, October 5, 2019).

Use Restorative Justice

A valuable part of a heart centered community is the discipline within the school and classroom. In "Restorative Justice," Thomas Ryan and Sean Ruddy (2017) describe a value-based approach to responding to wrongdoing and conflict. Restorative justice considers the offender, victim, and community with the intent of answering wrongdoing "by healing the harm, particularly to relationships, that is created by the harmful behavior" (Ryan & Ruddy, 2017, p. 254).

Ryan and Ruddy (2017) present the following guiding questions to use with a restorative approach.

- Who has been hurt?
- What are their needs?
- Whose obligations are they?
- What are the causes?
- Who has a stake in this?
- What is the appropriate process to involve stakeholders in an effort to put things right? (p. 254)

As they explain, when there is inevitable friction or conflict within a community, restorative justice uses that conflict as a learning and healing experience consistent with our heart centered work. While there are many ways in which teachers can systematize their use of restorative justice practices, Cathy and Peyton Erb (2018) present a Making Amends binder, which includes a subject and picture of the offensive action on the left page, with five sentence frames on each of the right pages. Students use the binder to help decide how to make appropriate amends. Include a verbal apology template with the question "Is there anything I can do now?" This self-reflection helps begin a dialogue with the individual who has been harmed.

> **Verbal apology:** I am sorry that I _____. It is wrong because _____. Next time I will _____. Is there anything that I can do now?
>
> **Apology letter:** Dear _____. I am sorry that I _____. It is wrong because _____. Next time, I will _____. Sincerely, _____
>
> **Help the classroom:** I would like to make amends to our class for _____ by _____ in the classroom. I think this is an appropriate way to make amends because it will _____.
>
> **Show appreciation:** I would like to make amends for _____. I will show my appreciation to _____ (person) by _____ (action).
>
> **I create:** I would like to make amends for _____ by _____. I think this is an appropriate way to make amends because it will _____.

COMMUNITY EXERCISE: Heart Centered Community Building

Source: Adapted from Connell, 2016.

This exercise is for grades 3–5. During it, the teacher guides students in a process of sharing information on vulnerabilities to give another person a deeper insight into him- or herself.

1. The teacher begins by showing a letter she has written to introduce herself to students, sharing information about her talents, fears, weaknesses, and dreams.

2. Students write their own letters, addressed to the teacher, each other, or someone else such as a neighbor or relative. The teacher could help with letter starters such as this:

    Hi Grandma. I have been thinking about you and realized that you may not know that I am now on the basketball team. While I have scored a few points, I also have a lot to learn! I am enjoying this. While I have a dream to one day play on a pro team, I know I need a back-up plan . . .

3. Students share letters and the teacher provides feedback. The letters can be used for a general discussion about who we are and what we are feeling— the joys and sorrows and ups and downs of our lives.

This exercise could be adapted for younger students by drawing three pictures: (1) who I am, (2) my dream, and (3) one more thing about me. The third picture could be something positive or negative. Perhaps you just had a birthday party, or perhaps you have just moved and are missing friends.

For students in middle and high school, the exercise could be adapted to be a longer essay, perhaps asking students to focus on one thing they want to improve, one fear, or one thing they are working on. In these cases, students could start by writing the essay in week 1, and then returning to the essay one month later and adding an update.

Consider Parents' and Families' Needs

To feel a sense of security, students need healthy relationships with their caregivers—in and out of the classroom. However, many parents don't have a lot of time to engage in the school community because they must juggle work, household chores, children's extracurricular activities, and more. Even though they may be stressed out and short on time, parents are still interested in learning more about child development and how to be a good parent. In fact, 79 percent of parents want more information about raising children, yet 65 percent of them never attend a single parenting class (Zepeda, Varela, & Morales, 2004).

To help parents and families get the information that could help them strengthen their relationships with their children and model heart centered behavior, schools must get creative in their methods of delivery. For parent education to be effective, it must target specific skills, give parents materials they need to implement the strategies, be digestible, and not take up too much of a parent's time (Magnuson & Schindler, 2016). While many parents' hectic work schedules won't allow them to attend school events frequently, most parents can spare half an hour, especially when the parenting information can be accessed from the comfort of their homes simply by logging onto the internet.

Two parenting supports are consistent with and complementary to our heart centered approach.

- **Parent in the Moment** (www.pitmnyc.com) is a Brooklyn-based parent education company that helps families learn how to use mindfulness to reduce stress, better regulate emotions, and strengthen the bond of love by teaching parents quick, easy, actionable ways of infusing mindfulness into family routines. Most of their parent education happens on the internet. Parents can fill out a quick questionnaire online that includes which parenting struggles they're experiencing.
- **Peace at Home Parenting Solutions** (www.peaceathomeparenting.com) will deliver a web-based workshop or consultation that shows parents how to use mindfulness to reduce their stress, helping them become more responsive parents who can better meet their child's needs.

In a collaboration with Peace at Home Parenting Solutions, Parent in the Moment also offers thirty-minute live webinars, sometimes free, during the evenings, when most young children are in bed. During a webinar, parents are taught how to cultivate mindful habits for their families by weaving mindfulness into normal family routines; parents learn things such as how to help kids regulate their own emotions using fun breath-work exercises and kid-friendly yoga poses.

Foster Communication

Several daily routines can further positive communications, support for peers, and engagement with parents. The Child Development Project provides guidance on the regular use of several key activities (Schaps, 2003) that are appropriate for students in K–12 classrooms.

- **Class meetings:** To enhance a sense of belonging in a community, use class meetings to collectively set goals and expectations, identify problems, and come up with solutions. When students are involved in these processes, they feel heard and are more likely to follow rules and pursue goals they had some agency in creating. Regular class meetings help students and teachers grow together.
- **Buddy programs:** Partnering younger and older students for mentoring gives older students an opportunity to teach social skills they have recently mastered to the younger students while contributing to the sense that all grade levels in a school are part of a larger community. Buddies can read to

each other, complete art or service projects, or spend time playing together. Some schools decide to record buddies' relationships in a portfolio that demonstrates how the students got to know each other throughout the year.

- **Homeside activities:** Providing parents and caregivers with quick conversation starters and interview prompts to use with their children at home can reinforce the community-building work being done in the school. For example, children can interview a parent or grandparent about acts of service he or she did when younger, or parents can begin a conversation about bullying with their children. Connecting students' learning with their home lives will deepen their knowledge.
- **Schoolwide community-building activities:** Inviting families to spend time with their children in the school building can enhance the feeling of belonging in that school community. This can promote inclusiveness and foster new school traditions. Community-building events can be as simple as family film nights or as challenging and rewarding as creating a family heritage museum that celebrates the diverse backgrounds of students' families.

These activities give all members of the school community the tools they need to foster compassion and belonging. The result can be a significant change in invisible norms, practices, routines, and policies that may have been a barrier to creating a heart centered community.

COMMUNITY EXERCISE: In Our Community

Source: Adapted from Feltis, personal communication, December 19, 2018.

Lindsey Feltis, a youth counselor at Safe Haven Youth Shelter, designed this exercise, which works for grades 1–8. Middle school and high school students can handle additional constraints. For example, seventh and eighth graders could solve the problem with only $25 to get started.

The activity increases student awareness of community problems, promotes collaboration, and helps students think critically about how they engage with the world around them (L. Feltis, personal communication, December 19, 2018).

1. Teachers begin by introducing the activity, letting students know that today you will be talking about communities; you will be talking about the great things about your communities and also the ways you believe your communities could be improved.
2. Begin a class discussion about community. Ask the following questions.
   - "How would you describe our community? Big or small? Loud or quiet?"

- "What types of things are in our community? Do we have one school or ten schools? Do we have one shopping mall or five shopping malls? What types of things do you like to do in our community?"
- "What is your *favorite* thing about our community?"

3. Thank your class for participating and continue with a discussion about problems in your community by asking the following questions.
    - "This question is a little bit trickier. What are your least favorite things about our community? Maybe you don't like seeing litter on your walk to school, or maybe you feel sad when you see someone experiencing homelessness downtown."
    - "What are other problems we have in our community?"

   If students are struggling to think of problems in their own small community, encourage them to think bigger than their neighborhood. Example problems could include homelessness, mental illness, pollution, and littering.

4. Ask students to choose between three and five problems they think are the most relevant to their community.

5. Write one problem each on large poster board paper.

6. Split your classroom into smaller groups and assign each group to one problem in your community.

7. Give your class twenty or thirty minutes to work together to talk about how they would solve the problem after saying the following to them: "In your small groups, I want you to work together to solve this problem. I'd like you to think big. Let's say I just handed you one million dollars to solve this problem. Use your poster paper to make a plan. Think about how you are going to spread awareness. How are you going to help people, if there are people involved? How are you going to create sustainable change?"

8. After the allotted time, have students present their ideas to the classroom.

Visit **go.SolutionTree.com/behavior** for more community-focused exercises.

What Does Community Look Like Historically?

Community can grow from different kinds of circumstances and take many forms. Communities can come together around a common goal in order to make something in their town or city better or more just. Sometimes schools are buffeted by the goodwill, enthusiasm, and support from local business owners. At other times, local communities come together in times of crisis, uniting to rebuild after a natural disaster, for instance. For example, tragedy combined with resilience resulted in activists in Newtown, Connecticut, forming organizations to help students feel safer. In times of crisis and in everyday situations, wraparound service providers coordinate from area agencies to service students in various economic, social-emotional, and academic ways. Different agencies and organizations are motivated to collaborate in temporary or long-lasting communities to accomplish something or make meaningful connections.

Today, many of those connections occur online. Teenagers and preteens spend hours each day on their phones, computers, and tablets. While some worry that teens may be missing out on genuine human connection by spending so much time online, young people often find a sense of community online. It's important that teachers talk to students about internet safety, physical health needs, and social media literacy to help them engage with online communities in a healthy way. Many activists have expanded their campaigns and influenced politicians and the general public by organizing and spreading their message online. We can learn a lot about 21st century communities from some of these organizations' success.

Sandy Hook Organizations

In the years following the mass shooting at Sandy Hook Elementary School in Newtown, Connecticut, families and community members have banded together to overcome their grief. My Sandy Hook Family (https://mysandyhookfamily.org) is a platform for individuals to share the unique ways that they chose to memorialize their lost ones. Children's books, animal sanctuaries, and funds to support art programs are a few of the efforts made by parents to keep their children's spirits alive. Organizations such as Safe and Sound Schools (www.safeandsoundschools.org) and Sandy Hook Promise (www.sandyhookpromise.org) promote increased school security, mental health reform, and violence prevention programs by providing a space for students, teachers, and other community members to process their grief and rebuild a sense of safety together.

Despite the wide range of responses to such a tragedy, it is clear that love and togetherness are themes that run through each one. Every victim was honored for the kindness that he or she shared with others, and the tragic loss of their lives inspired those they left behind to ensure that their kindness lives on in their community. It has been made clear by the Sandy Hook community that even in the midst of a disaster, love can serve as a strong foundation that makes each member of the community feel heard, loved, and a sense of belonging.

Wraparound Service Providers

Wraparound services are much like a wraparound community hug for students and families. They are provided by an array of community agencies and are meant to ensure that students have access to physical, mental, and emotional supports. However, as therapist Carole Siegel (1995) points out:

> Obviously, schools are not mental health centers, nor should they be. Children come to school to learn, to develop, to grow. They do not come primarily to be "fixed" as they do at a mental health center. The schools' task is primarily to develop, not to remediate. But these children who come to learn bring with them everything which is part of them. They do not leave their problems at the front door as if it were baggage that is checked at an airline counter.

Such services help students spend more time in their regular classroom, daycare, and home settings rather than being put in more restrictive environments. Trained staff work with parents and teachers to design an individualized program that addresses the specific needs of each child by giving him or her the tools to solve behavior problems that are a barrier to academic and social-emotional success. Wraparound services can help students suffering from problems related to substance abuse, anger management, or mental illness feel empowered to change their behavior so they can be active members of their home and school communities.

Wraparound services are also more effective than standard mental health services for children who have experienced adversity that results in welfare custody. In one study, after just eighteen months, 82 percent of youth receiving wraparound services returned to environments that were less restrictive and less costly, while only 38 percent of those receiving traditional mental health services did (Bruns, Rast, Peterson, Walker, & Bosworth, 2006; Rast, Bruns, Brown, Peterson, & Mears, 2007).

While co-treatments from outside resources and agencies are critical to improving many students' overall health and well-being, wraparound services are often underutilized because families experience transportation issues and other challenges, complicating their ability to get their children to services. Schools can help with this challenge of continuity and consistency of students' services by arranging for services to come to schools instead of students going to service locations. When wraparound services or co-treatments are offered and delivered at school, the fidelity of implementation and continuity of care increase exponentially. In addition, parents and families already have to deal with compounded stressors. Setting up services within the school day helps alleviate parents' additional stress and anxiety associated with having to ensure their children get to and from a variety of services.

Wraparound services are a team effort, and effective teamwork requires that all team members work together to use their individual skills and knowledge to create a holistic therapy experience that mirrors a healthy family (Bloom, 2015). Defining each member's roles and tasks eliminates redundancy and competition (Walter & Petr, 2011). In Pennsylvania, for example, when a student receives wraparound services, a dedicated team of three staff members is assigned to the individual case. A therapeutic staff support person uses the treatment plan to teach the student how to change problematic behaviors using redirection and behavior modification. A mobile therapist meets the student where the student is comfortable—in the home or another community location—rather than in an office setting to provide individual therapy addressing the student's emotional concerns. Working with the other two team members, a behavioral specialist consultant writes, plans, implements, and revises the treatment plan throughout the course of treatment (Pennsylvania Health Law Project, n.d.).

How Do We Measure Community?

The following tools measure community: the Student-Teacher Relationship Scale, the Teacher-Student Relationship Inventory, and S-CCATE.

Student-Teacher Relationship Scale

The Student-Teacher Relationship Scale (STRS) is a self-reported tool designed to capture a teacher's perceived conflict and closeness with an individual student (ages three to twelve) in his or her classroom (Pianta, 2001; https://at.virginia.edu/2k IU96w). Items are rated on a Likert-type scale ranging from 1 (*definitely does not apply*) to 5 (*definitely applies*). The conflict subscale is comprised of seven items and survey participants respond to statements like "This child is sneaky or manipulative with me" and "This child easily becomes angry with me." The closeness subscale is comprised of eight items, including statements like "This child spontaneously shares information about herself" and "It is easy to be in tune with what this child is feeling" (Pianta, 2001).

Teacher-Student Relationship Inventory

Similar to the STRS, the Teacher-Student Relationship Inventory (TSRI) is a self-report measure that assesses teachers' perception of the quality of their relationship with students from fourth grade through junior high (Ang, 2005). The TSRI is a fourteen-item tool with three dimensions: instrumental help, satisfaction, and conflict. Teachers indicate agreement with each of item using a Likert scale, ranging from 1 (*almost never true*) to 5 (*almost always true*).

Instrumental help refers to how willing a teacher perceives a student is to seek advice, sympathy, or help from the teacher. Five items on the TSRI focus on instrumental help and include statements like "The student turns to me for a listening ear" (Ang, 2005). Satisfaction involves feelings of contentment and positive regard. Satisfaction is covered with five statements on the inventory, including "If this student is absent, I will miss him/her." Conflict, with four items on the TSRI, refers to negative feelings about the relationship that may decrease the desire for interaction with a student.

Teachers will rate their agreement on statements like "I cannot wait for this year to be over so that I will not need to teach this student."

S-CCATE

Community is measured in S-CCATE and the S-CCATE Supplement through multiple items that were validated as some of the most critical indicators of a compassionate school community. Three samples from these scales appear in table 7.1.

Table 7.1: S-CCATE Community Factors

Factor	In Action
Leadership and a compassionate school community	Teachers and administrators further participation and a sense of belonging (connectedness to the larger school community) for all students.
Leadership and a compassionate school community	School culture reflects a spirit of happiness and joy.
Culture and school community	Students from diverse cultures are welcomed at the school by everyone, including teachers, administrators, and peers.

Reflection

To get the most out of this chapter, reflect on these questions after reading it.

- What elements of heart centered community building are strengths in your classroom, school, or district?
- What elements of heart centered community are challenging and need further work?
- Is your school community inclusive, welcoming, and supportive? If so, how? If not, what could turn it around?
- Have you implemented restorative justice, mindfulness, or other specific strategies such as wraparound services? If so, what value, if any, did these programs bring to your school? If not, do you have plans to implement any?
- What are the two most important elements of building a compassionate school community that supports learners, teachers, and the wider school community?

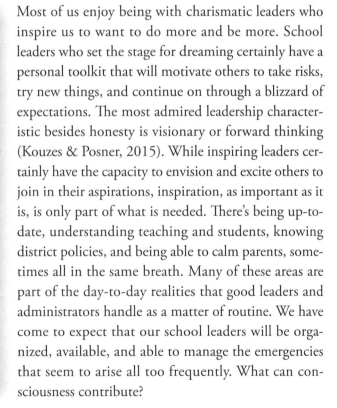

CHAPTER 8

Heart Centered Leadership

If your actions create a legacy that inspires others to dream more, learn more, do more and become more, you are an excellent leader.

—Dolly Parton

key principle

By opening their hearts and minds, stimulating their own intellect, fostering health and well-being in the school community, and bringing best practices to schools, expressing gratitude, recognition, and encouragement, heart centered leaders have the capacity to bring out the best in those who follow.

Most of us enjoy being with charismatic leaders who inspire us to want to do more and be more. School leaders who set the stage for dreaming certainly have a personal toolkit that will motivate others to take risks, try new things, and continue on through a blizzard of expectations. The most admired leadership characteristic besides honesty is visionary or forward thinking (Kouzes & Posner, 2015). While inspiring leaders certainly have the capacity to envision and excite others to join in their aspirations, inspiration, as important as it is, is only part of what is needed. There's being up-to-date, understanding teaching and students, knowing district policies, and being able to calm parents, sometimes all in the same breath. Many of these areas are part of the day-to-day realities that good leaders and administrators handle as a matter of routine. We have come to expect that our school leaders will be organized, available, and able to manage the emergencies that seem to arise all too frequently. What can consciousness contribute?

Exploring the concept of heart centered leadership, knowing why it matters and how to teach and practice it in school, discovering what it has looked like in the past, and learning how to measure it can move us one more step toward mindful school communities.

147

What Is Heart Centered Leadership?

Heart centered leadership is a conscious journey without an ego and with a purposeful intention to place others before one's own self-interests: "Schools are communities, and what fuels them is a matter of choice" (Jackson & McDermott, 2012, p. 131). By integrating the heart centered principles of intention, self-reflection, and compassion, school leaders can transform school communities, increase creativity, and inspire their faculty and staff to improve positivity and build a more heart centered, compassionate school culture that better supports all school community members' needs. Incorporating consciousness into their leadership styles helps principals interact and attune to others more easily. It also helps leaders maintain perspective, bolsters confidence, and makes them appear more trustworthy (Wylson & Chesley, 2016). Conscious leadership embraces self-reflection; pairs action with awareness; involves listening, reflecting, and problem solving; takes a policy perspective; incorporates social-emotional learning; and merges conscious and traditional leadership.

Self-Reflection

Heart centered leadership requires self-reflection, examining our inner motivations for being a leader. Being a conscious leader requires being able to take an honest, hard look at oneself on a daily basis while asking self-reflecting questions (Dasa, 2017).

- What is my motivation for leading?
- Why am I in leadership? Do I enjoy people, community, and making a difference, or do I enjoy the power, control, and attention?
- Am I leading to serve or am I leading to be served?
- Am I willing to put the interests of our school district and community ahead of my own?

Heart centered leadership for school leaders includes traits of compassion, empathy, and trust within the school and school district. It is these qualities that professor Caryn Wells (2015) at Oakland University in Michigan describes as advancing leadership "by responding *with presence,* with fully attending and responding to the concerns that surface" (p. 12). As Wells (2015) notes, the "differences of mindful leadership may appear subtle at first, but they provide a powerful mosaic that may influence a school organization, all enhanced by elements of emotional and social intelligence" (p. 12).

Heart centered school leaders can keep a realistic check on all that is happening within the school, district, and greater community. Conscious leaders are keen observers involved in continual reflection. This includes seeing the good, the bad, and the ugly and not shying away from what we would really like to avoid. With conscious awareness, we may even, as Wells (2015) suggests, head into the eye of the storm, "facing into the conflict for understanding, insight, and . . . power . . . . The power is in influence as opposed to directing or delegating" (p. 12).

Heart centered leadership also includes the following behaviors and traits.

- **Leading by example:** Heart centered leaders have an awareness of the profound influence their attitudes and actions have on those they lead and the school culture as a whole. A leader's words and actions matter. Heart centered leaders only expects from others what they would be willing to do themselves. Otherwise, a disconnect or deterioration of trust will occur.

- **Showing gratitude and recognition:** Heart centered leaders purposely look for meaningful and intentional opportunities to notice and appreciate educators and staff's hard work and contributions. Heart centered leaders consider the "flowering within" of school staff. Michael Bunting (2016) describes this as "watering the ground of their being with sincere, heartfelt praise and encouragement" and watching staff flower within (p. 153). Keep in mind that gratitude and recognition of accomplishments and hard work are viewed as equally important as a paycheck—and perhaps even somewhat more important since a leader's behavior increases staff engagement and job satisfaction while also helping to balance any corrective feedback along the way (Kouzes & Posner, 2015).

- **Leading with humility and kindness:** Heart centered leaders lead with a certain graciousness and humbleness. Humble leaders recognize their strengths as well as weaknesses. Author, speaker, and business consultant Ken Blanchard explains it this way: "Don't think less of yourself, just think of yourself less" (as cited in Schakohl, 2019). To do this, leaders need to ask for help when it's needed and be aware of personal shortcomings in relation to school or district successes or failures.

- **Communicating with compassion:** Heart centered leaders communicate with intentional, compassionate-minded thoughts after careful consideration and pause, not with quick reactive words fueled by negatively charged, raw emotion. Words can make a powerful and lasting impact on others and your school culture. Heart centered leaders pause, pay attention, and notice how they are feeling or thinking at any particular moment before thoughtfully constructing and delivering an honest and beneficial response that ensures a positive and intended outcome for all.

- **Showing equanimity of emotions:** Heart centered leaders lead with clarity of thought and calmness in words, body, and behavior. Practicing mindfulness regularly and intentionally each day helps leaders to be aware and notice how they feel and how their emotions may impact their thinking and ability to lead (adapted from Bunting, 2016; Dasa, 2017; Williams, 2015).

Awareness helps school leaders to be in control of their responses. Schools have a barrage of incoming distractions, disruptions, and disturbances that school leaders must manage on any given day. All of us regret reactive responses that we wish we could take back the moment they are released. Mindfulness practice is paramount for school leaders as it helps improve emotional intelligence, allowing leaders to be more aware of and compassionate toward teacher, staff, student, and family needs and concerns and less focused on their own. When school leaders are mindful and responsive to school community members' needs and concerns, more positive and trusting relationships are cultivated. However, as internationally known researcher and educator Andy Hargreaves and his colleagues have pointed out, changes that occur with the introduction of mindfulness will not happen overnight (Hargreaves, Moore, Fink, Brayman, & White, 2003). Trust is also built over time—and significant time may be needed to achieve targeted gains in student achievement.

Action Paired With Awareness

Awareness, relationships, and trust—all traits we see in positive, mindful school communities—take time. From our perspective, we might also add that it makes sense to define heart centered school leaders as leaders who not only listen and are aware of needs, but also act on their awareness. We might expect them to demonstrate confidence in their staff and in the roads they choose. We might expect these leaders to have the courage to take on the battles that may be needed to promote justice and equity. We might expect that heart centered leaders would take extra steps to build positive school communities. In short, we might expect that heart centered leaders would display the traits and talents that we advocate with Heart Centered Learning: they would have consciousness, compassion, confidence, and courage, and they would cultivate heart centered school communities.

Practicing Heart Centered Leadership: Sustainable Change

Melissa Patschke, principal at Upper Providence Elementary School, in Royersford, Pennsylvania, shares this about heart centeredness being an opportunity for sustainable change:

> When mindfulness is framed as a classroom strategy to improve student achievement and allow children to feel more controlled, both teachers and parents buy in. It didn't happen overnight, but our school has worked for several years to build a high level of resilience in students and staff.
>
> During a two-hour information session, staff learned about the practice and science behind mindfulness, including the positive impact on student behaviors and focus. The next step was to continue to bring these messages into every faculty meeting.
>
> To reduce costs, two teachers, a guidance counselor, and I got training to become resident experts in (1) yoga, (2) resilience, (3) mindful practices, and (4) verbal de-escalation. To this day, I open faculty meetings with a mindfulness or yoga activity that teachers can use in classrooms. The four of us take lessons we learned into classrooms such as mindfulness jars, deep breathing, chill skills, and controlled attention work. (M. Patschke, personal communication, April 1, 2017):

Listening, Reflecting, and Problem Solving

Consider the research of W. Sean Kearney, Cheryl Kelsey, and David Herrington (2013). In a study of the mindfulness of principals, conducted in one-hundred-forty-nine schools in Texas, they identified relationship building, principal reflection, and perpetual renewal (staying current and a willingness to try new things) as factors positively influencing student achievement. From interviews with a sample of these principals, they reported that:

> Mindful principals spoke of taking the time to reflect, collaborating with teachers to analyze data on the effectiveness of teaching and learning in specific areas of interest, taking the

> time to listen, considering multiple voices, integrating them into
> any definition of a problem or solution, taking time to think and
> reflect on possible solutions, and avoiding the tendency to rush
> to judgment to implement quick fixes that might not address
> the real problem, or worse. (Kearney et al., 2013, p. 325)

Kearney and his colleagues (2013) also discuss the importance of learning from mistakes and how principals build resilience through openness and a willingness to examine, reflect, and provide support for teachers, students, and staff. By being aware of and open about their mistakes, heart centered leaders are constantly learning, refining their actions, and building trust within their community.

Equity-Conscious Policy Perspective

What are some of the policy issues that conscious school leaders are addressing? Irma Zardoya (2018) says it is important for leaders to understand equity issues and concerns:

> A school or district leader cannot help others address bias
> until she is able to recognize and talk about her own. So, the
> first critical step—consciousness—involves becoming aware
> of one's own biases, understanding how life experiences have
> shaped those biases, and how they have affected interactions
> with students, families, and teachers, as well as their leadership
> decisions. We have seen effective training push leaders to own
> up to and challenge their own racial biases. (p. 18)

Addressing biases is critical for equity. It teaches staff what fuels the social and emotional barriers that stifle achievement by otherized students: factors such as stereotype threats associated with race or ethnicity (Steele & Aronson, 2004), feelings of failure, absence of enrichment, and stigma associated with marginalizing labels relegated to the students of color, English learners, or students with special needs. But heart centered leaders realize that policies designed to dismantle barriers perpetuated by biases do not animate the spirit of staff to create environments that mitigate the negative impact of biased barriers and enable each and every student to thrive and flourish.

Heart centered leaders understand that the antidote to bias is inspiring equity consciousness—educating in a way that is rooted in the belief that all students are innately wired for high intellectual performance and engagement, to demonstrate strengths, and to be self-determined enough to develop these strengths for self-actualization and personal contribution.

Equity-conscious leaders are compassionately mindful of two transformative principles of Jean Piaget (1950): (1) students shape themselves to fit their world and (2) high intellectual performances are mediated by high-level engaging tasks. With these two principles as beacons for their mindfulness, these leaders will ask themselves the following questions, following up with actions as necessary.

- "Have I explicitly affirmed and made apparent my belief in the innate potential of all my students for high intellectual performance and personal contribution?"
- "Have I explicitly inspired, guided, and supported my staff to act on and incorporate into their thinking my expectation that all pedagogy, practices, and opportunities should reflect this belief?"

Heart centered superintendents respond to these self-reflective questions with acts that affirm and create equity consciousness among their staff and community. Some examples follow.

- Fearlessly stating that they perceive their schools as not having an overabundance of low achievers, but rather underachievers with numerous strengths and vast intelligence who are dependent on school to tap into those strengths (Jackson, 2011)
- Dismantling practices of disbelief (including tracking, instructional focus on so-called weaknesses, ignoring strengths and interests, and lack of access to enrichment or personalized learning) that perpetuate marginalizing, low-level instruction that deflates engagement and stymies intellectual development, achievement, and self-determination
- Aiming their intention on writing a district vision of student success like superintendent John Baker of Redwood City School District in Redwood City, California, does to generate a vision that describes the intended characteristics of Redwood City graduates, implying that these characteristics will be cultivated in each and every student (J. Baker, personal communication, December, 2019)

Heart centered principals enact the vision of such equity-conscious superintendents by inspiring a culture of belonging. They do this by guiding their staff and students to first surface their commonalities, recognizing humanity and fostering powerful group affiliations, strong relationships, empathy, and compassion for other cultures. By bonding through relationships, students and teachers begin to confidently recognize, appreciate, and build on the value and power of their diverse perspectives and experiences for enhancing the community's creativity, problem solving, and decision making. Teachers build on these skills, along with the desire all students have for group engagement and high levels of independent and interdependent learning to design pedagogy that achieves its original purpose: self-actualization and self-transcendence (Maslow, 1943, 1971). That includes self-actualization that enables students to thrive in society and self-transcendence that motivates them to contribute to that society (Chen, 2014; Freire, 1996; Gladwell, 2008; Jackson, 2011).

Another major concern of school leaders is how to address tragedies happening on school campuses. Whether it is violence, school shootings, or mental health conditions, trauma is prevalent. In 2018, there were twenty-three school shootings resulting in 113 deaths and injuries (Coughlan, 2018). Suicide is the second leading cause of death among teenagers (CDC, 2018). The Mental Health Technology Transfer Center Network (2019) offers educators help preparing for and handling the emergencies that they face in schools.

- Put students at the center by not only seeking their needs and ideas for solutions, but engaging them in planning and making decisions.
- Provide grief-specific and trauma-specific professional development training for the whole school community.
- Develop a crisis-response team and protocol that includes ways that schools will address youth suicide and other school emergencies that may traumatize youth and adults. Identify the roles and responsibilities of crisis team members.
- Have policies and protocols for maintaining confidentiality, tracking and monitoring high-risk situations, antibullying and cyberbullying, parent notification, and referrals.
- Have suicide prevention plans, including screening, networking with community-based behavioral health agencies, and implementing a substance use program, as well as a protocol for assisting students who are most at risk. Support protective factors by offering opportunities for students to connect with caring adults.
- Include a self-care program for school personnel with education about toxic stress and strategies for alleviation.
- Develop peer-support programs that give students the tools to listen to one another and provide lifesaving assistance to one another when they are processing a tragedy.
- Network with families to involve them in prevention efforts and co-create a protocol for handling school crises.
- Have plans for intervention and *postvention*. Make sure your school knows what to do if a tragedy occurs and is able to navigate its aftermath. Know who will be involved, how they will be involved, and how the school will announce programs such as counseling options (DiCara, O'Halloran, Williams, & Brooks, 2009; SAMHSA, 2012b).
- Engage the media. They are critical partners when it comes to suicide, violence, and contagion. Assign a media spokesperson, develop safe messages, and build relationships with media prior to a tragedy

(American Association of Suicidology, 2018; American Foundation for Suicide Prevention, & Suicide Prevention Resource Center, Education Development Center, 2018).

Social-Emotional Learning

Social-emotional learning (SEL) is a related area of interest and concern. The Collaborative for Academic, Social, and Emotional Learning (CASEL, 2019) scorecard shows that all fifty of the United States have policies incorporating SEL into preschool standards; however, only eighteen states have SEL standards, and only twenty-one states have SEL-related pages on their websites (https://casel.org/collaborative-state-initiative). In describing progress toward meeting SEL policy standards, CASEL showcases results from some of the districts, as well as national and state initiatives. These standards recommend that policies do the following.

- Incorporate clear, free-standing learning goals with age-appropriate benchmarks for students in preschool through high school.
- Integrate and align SEL standards with academic content standards.
- Incorporate guidelines for teacher practices.
- Include guidelines for creating positive learning environments.
- Be culturally and linguistically appropriate.
- Link to policies and tools to enhance implementation.

A few examples of SEL policies and procedures initiatives follow.

- Ask small-group breakout questions: "How might I incorporate SEL and cultural competence approaches into the planning of academic and social-emotional interventions that I develop? What seeds can I plant to encourage students to recognize both their emotions and strengths" (Restorative Schools Vision Project, 2015).
- Include familial and cultural stories to help students build strong, positive identities, especially if theirs is different than the region's predominant culture (Alaska Department of Education and Early Development, 2009).
- Teach social-emotional standards, such as respect for self and others, including those found in established frameworks such as the West Virginia Student Success Standards (West Virginia Department of Education, 2014).
- Establish a team, create a vision and logic model, routinize procedures, differentiate supports, build a shared understanding, and develop family-community partnerships (National Center on Safe and Supportive Learning Environments, n.d.).

HEART CENTERED LEADERSHIP EXERCISE: Policy Recommendations

Take the opportunity to reflect on how to implement policy recommendations at your school or district by following these three steps.

1. Review the information presented in the section of this chapter on "Equity-Conscious Policy Perspectives" (pages 152–155).
2. Compare your school or district policies and procedures with the suggestions on racial equity guidelines (Zardoya, 2018), how schools handle tragedies (SAMHSA, 2012b), or SEL policies (Dusenbury & Yoder, 2017).
3. Note the differences that you see. Do you have a school tragedy-response plan? Have you considered how to ensure cultural competence at your school or district? Are there areas of your school or district policies you might explore and perhaps update or revise?

Heart Centered and Traditional Leadership

To understand more about the benefits of heart centered leadership, table 8.1 compares how traditional practices impact some of the key goals and responsibilities of principals and teachers. As we have shown throughout this book, heart centered leadership adds another avenue for facilitating growth, health, and well-being.

Table 8.1: Comparing Traditional and Heart Centered School Leadership

	Traditional School Leadership	Heart Centered School Leadership
Raising academic achievement	More mathematics and reading; eliminating arts, music, and special projects	Neuroscience and executive function education
Helping struggling students	Response to intervention (RTI), multi-tiered system of support (MTSS), individualized education programs (IEP), reading coaches	Stress and trauma impact alleviation through mindfulness practices
Keeping students engaged	Extrinsic rewards, incentives	Student interest, self-determination, goal setting
Incorporating visionary leadership with stressed-out teachers	Focus on what schools can become	Shared decision making, teacher empowerment, collaborative role in developing a vision
Responding to parents and community	Open houses, school conferences, parent-teacher associations	Consciousness of and responding to family and community needs, stresses, trauma

In some cases, the traditional approaches that were a part of education since the No Child Left Behind Act of 2001 have ended up harming students and teachers by adding layers of stress and reducing opportunities to ignite students' interest in learning (Ravitch, 2016). In other cases, traditional leadership has included many components that have furthered education such as RTI, MTSS, and positive behavioral intervention and supports (PBIS). However, even in these cases, heart centered leadership provides additional and complementary support that can benefit students, teachers, and the wider school community.

Principal leadership and mindfulness are associated with several interrelated constructs (Wells, 2015). Figure 8.1 synthesizes information from various sources to compare leadership actions to heart centered practices. In this case, emotional intelligence includes self-awareness, self-regulation, social awareness, and inspiring and developing others.

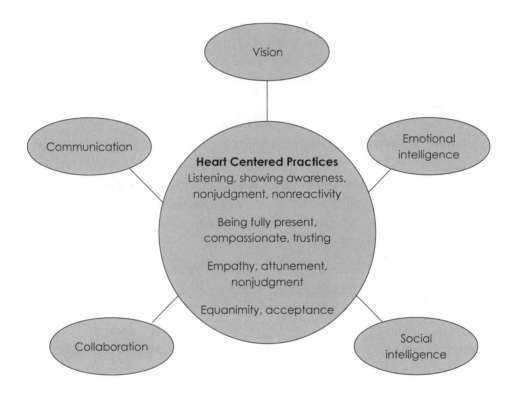

Source: Adapted from Goleman & Boyatzis, 2008; Goleman, Boyatzis, & McKee, 2002; Wells, 2015.

Figure 8.1: Comparing leadership actions to heart centered practices.

Why Does Heart Centered Leadership Matter in School?

In schools, principals are responsible not only for themselves but also for others. Principals are impacted by a multitude of stress points: raising academic achievement, handling complaints and concerns, maintaining order, dealing with the everyday logistics, having courageous conversations, finding time for students, and addressing dictates that come from the district and state, to name a few. School leaders can expect that some of these stressors will be exacerbated by teachers who may be resistant to new ideas or suggestions for change, or who lack adequate resources, and have competing demands. Principals' jobs are high stress by their very nature. Principals can benefit from heart centered practices (such as mindfulness) simply to lower their own stress. Likewise, superintendents of school districts have similar high-stress workloads and a variety of venues and people maneuvering for their attention and response. Benefits from heart centered practices can go a long way toward self-care.

Heart centered leadership matters in school because consciousness develops awareness of being. It lets leaders press the pause button as healing increases, responsibilities become shared, and awareness of student needs is enhanced.

Consciousness Develops Awareness of Being

Sometimes, to get to point B, we need to start at a specific point A. Try as we like, in some cases it will be hard to reach a certain destination if we haven't already covered some ground beforehand. William George (as cited in Silverthorne, 2010) points out that leaders who lack self-awareness and self-compassion often lack self-regulation, making them less able to acknowledge their own mistakes, feel compassion for others, or establish "sustainable authentic relationships." Under such conditions, these leaders will have difficulty furthering a sense of trust or being supportive of teachers at the points when they are most in need, leading to reduced teacher morale.

On the other hand, "developing a more aware and considered approach helps leaders to respond to situations (whether internal thoughts or external events), rather than react to them" (Rezek, 2013). Conscious or mindful leadership has been shown to boost employee engagement by 25 to 50 percent through building stronger relationships, improved communication, and decreased emotional reactivity (Bunting, 2018). The reason? A mindful leader makes for a better, more present, compassionate, and healthy work environment. With over three decades of scientific research around the globe, mindfulness-based stress reduction has been found to positively and profoundly reduce physiological and psychological stress (Chiesa & Serretti, 2010).

Not surprisingly, heart centeredness and character strengths can positively impact one another while relieving trauma and increasing achievement. The more time spent using strengths significantly correlates with mindfulness (Jarden et al., 2012). Mindfulness can help an individual express character strength in a balanced way that is sensitive to the context and circumstance. For example, "character strengths such as curiosity can help bolster a person's mindfulness practice, helping them overcome obstacles and barriers in maintaining a regular practice" (Niemiec, 2012, p. 24).

You Can Press the Pause Button

School leaders grapple with finding the time for their own professional development and self-care. Leadership stressors can wreak havoc on our minds and bodies, compromising our full potential to lead or make sound decisions and respond with clarity. Pressing the pause button and learning how to relax, re-center, and re-focus to be most present and productive can mean winning the fight for survival on any given day. Short, guided meditations—between four and fifteen minutes long—provide opportunities for school leaders to find balance and equanimity by infusing mindfulness into their often turbulent and hectic school day. The Institute for Mindful Leadership has meditations on two sites: www.instituteformindfulleadership.org/category/guided-meditation and http://soundcloud.com/inst-for-mindful-leadership. Ten to twenty minutes of mindfulness practices throughout the day can yield big returns for those who lead.

In addition to reducing stress, mindfulness can also strengthen leaders' self-awareness, empathy for self, energy management, and listening (Inam, 2012). Mindful school leaders are better prepared to engage with others and have improved intuition, clarity, focus, and ability to adapt (Inam, 2012). With intention, self-reflection, and compassion, school leaders might find that transforming schools can become less urgent and demanding and more rewarding. By increasing creativity, inspiring their staff to improve positivity, and fostering a school culture that better supports students', staff's, and families' needs, leaders may find greater enthusiasm among key stakeholders.

Responsibilities Become Shared

Additionally, heart centered leadership is collective. Michael Chirichello (2018) explains how collective leadership transcends shared or participatory leadership. *Shared leadership* broadly distributes responsibility, so people on a team or in an organization lead each other, while *participatory leadership* requires at least some input from people who are affected by the decisions. With collective leadership and a higher consciousness, as relationships are built, staff learn from the collective experiences of each other and "a collective culture emerges as followers become leaders and leaders step out of the way to become followers" (Chirichello, 2018). Chirichello goes on to say that:

> collective leadership *may be likened to a stream that comes to the beginning of a desert terrain.* The stream allows itself to be absorbed by the wind as its essence is carried over the desert. When the desert ends, it becomes a stream again on the other side. Like a stream crossing the desert, collective leaders recognize that they gain power only by giving it up,

by sharing it with others to create a culture that promotes the collective efficacy of followers.

With a social justice framework, we shift the deficit discourse of school failure and troubled communities to one of collective, shared responsibility. By shifting accountability, the focus on behavior management of so-called problem students is replaced by a critical examination of the social conditions that create suffering for our children and youth. With an integration of antiracism and critical pedagogy, heart centered educators can ensure that education builds a practice of freedom (inspired by Brazilian educator Paulo Freire) rather than a technology of compliance (Cannon, 2016).

To address academic deficits, it is difficult not to revert to old habits and head down the remediation path. Likewise, there are many reasons that, without sufficient investment, schools will continue teaching to remedy weaknesses rather than trying to achieve more fundamental changes. We must also ask that students put forth their best effort and remain open to trying different strategies to learn new skills and information. When everyone feels an equal responsibility for learning, teamwork enhances the sense of community between students and educators.

The question we ask is, "What is the relationship among trauma, student achievement, and classroom practices that acknowledges student strengths and supports Heart Centered Learning?" Yvette has centered her professional development around student strengths, Chris has investigated student self-determination, and Michele has implemented positive disciplinary approaches to eliminate traditional in-school suspension and to dramatically decrease out-of-school suspension. Our approaches honor student strengths, views, culture, values, and health and well-being, acknowledging that social responsibility is a shared responsibility.

Sensitivity to Student Needs Is a Must

Educators have finally arrived at a time when we recognize we have no choice but to identify the critical effects of the barriers or deterrents to learning that arise outside of school so we can determine how to mitigate the impact of those effects inside school. These adverse childhood experiences (ACEs), which span the spectrum from physical, sexual, emotional, and drug abuse to race-related violence, domestic issues, and other family dramas, have produced levels of stress and trauma that have caused severe breakdowns in the cognitive, emotional, and neural circuitry of the brain, wreaking havoc on learning, causing major achievement dysfunctions and underperformance (Felitti et al., 1998; Harvard University Center on the Developing Child, n.d.b). Consider the layers of the onion (the complicated needs) and the extraordinary stress students have.

Layers of the Onion—Complicated Needs

Schools are filled with students who have serious needs that are not easily remedied. Think of these serious needs, and their effect, much like peeling back layers of an onion: with the sting of the onion, each new layer may bring more unexpected tears, pain, and unintended consequences. However, each new layer provides greater depth, insight, and awareness into the unspeakable circumstances in the lives of the students we educate.

Consider poverty and hunger. While food is a basic human need, it is estimated that over 50 percent of students in public schools live in poverty (Southern Education Foundation, 2015). These are higher poverty rates than for most other developed countries (with the exception of Greece, Mexico, Israel, and Turkey). And, poverty has dire consequences for children. According to Feeding America (2017), impoverished children are more likely to experience hunger and food insecurity with lifelong effects like lower reading and mathematics scores, greater physical and mental health issues and chance of obesity, and more emotional and behavioral problems. Further, children from low income households between the ages of sixteen to twenty-four are seven times more likely to drop out of school than financially well-off peers (National Center for Education Statistics, 2016).

Extraordinary Stress

In addition to the pressure that goes along with the job and handling the stress that students and teachers experience, principals are tasked with the job of leading schools that are facing extraordinary challenges. Tragically, trauma and stress are exacerbated by what has become the new malignant normality: gun violence in the place that for so many has been the single bastion of safety. School shootings have occurred in school parking lots, college dormitories, hallways, cafeterias, and classrooms. In many cases, the shooter was between fifteen and nineteen years old (Ahmed & Walker, 2018).

Recently, we have also seen harsh refugee policies, escalating racism, continuing concerns over bullying and cyberbullying, ongoing violence for children in war-torn countries, horrific accounts of domestic violence, and alarming statistics in a new report on ACEs (Sacks & Murphey, 2018). A survey of young adults in eight eastern European countries finds that over half of the participants suffer at least one adverse childhood experience (Bellis et al., 2014). Forty-five percent of children in the United States have experienced one adverse experience, with higher rates for black and Latino children (Sacks & Murphey, 2018).

How Do We Teach and Practice Heart Centered Leadership?

We can teach and practice heart centered leadership the following ways: practice mindfulness, boost social intelligence, and build the other four Cs—(1) compassion, (2) confidence, (3) courage, and (4) community.

Practice Mindfulness

Heart centered leadership leads to change. It's important for leaders to remember that true transformation takes time and that they need to plan with intentionality and collaboration to make it effective and lasting. During this process, the ambiguity around success can cause leaders anxiety that threatens to derail their impact. Using mindfulness to quiet this particular anxiety is an effective method of healthily managing emotions.

The need for mindfulness is also heightened by societal violence. School leaders need to reflect on not only how heart centered practices such as mindfulness can enhance their own lives, but also how the practices can contribute to the overall good of the school, district, and community. To relieve their own stress, school leaders may find that the following mindfulness techniques are helpful.

- Find a quiet, peaceful space and meditate daily.
- Practice intentional breathing.
- Begin every meeting and each day with a two-minute grounding, positive "sit" to improve focus and clarity.
- Plan short breaks to practice mindfulness and break up the work day and stress.
- Encourage teachers and staff to take mini-mindful breaks at their desks between student transitions.
- Control multitasking and avoid just *doing* by practicing *being* in the moment, fully present, with all senses alive and active.
- Practice intentional responding and deliberate noticing.
- Make pausing and reflecting (without judgment on either successes or failures) a prerequisite to decision making, communication, or response (Williams, 2015).
- Engage in a physical activity such as running or yoga that allows you to reach a flow state.

To reduce the stress of teachers, staff, and students, school leaders can also lead the charge for incorporating mindfulness practices throughout the school day. We believe the quickest way to improve the school culture and reduce stress is for caring, competent administrators to strive to further compassionate schools—that these leaders are committed to finding and sharing the resources with teachers and staff.

One example of this kind of leader is Jillayne Flanders, a former K–3 elementary school principal and associate executive director of the Massachusetts Elementary School Principals Association. Flanders (2015) suggests the following.

- Be proactive.
- Develop relationships.
- Grow a whole-school attitude.
- Build a team.
- Find supportive resources.

Practicing Heart Centered Leadership: Kind Minds

Jillayne Flanders as a principal of an elementary school developed and implemented a Kind Mind program in a small school in South Hadley, Massachusetts. Through storytelling, music, and other expression, local singer and storyteller John Porcino reached out to students and, with their help, penned the "Kind Mind Song" (www.edimprovement.org/2015/03/giving-heart-kind-mind). The song came alive through illustrations of characters named Ruby, Tiger Cub, and Mouse, and symbols like the orange heart, which are tangible elements of kind acts to be celebrated. This was the beginning wave of weaving the tides of schoolwide change (Flanders, 2015). This is an example of leadership and seamlessly infusing heart centeredness into the whole community.

Principals are also in a position to further schoolwide mindfulness activities, including mindfulness moments. Mary Davenport, a teacher who is now teaching English in an international school in São Paulo, Brazil, writes about how she routinely uses mindfulness in her classes. Principals such as Kate Retzel at Lee Elementary School in Lee, Massachusetts, have adapted similar practices, even announcing times for mindfulness activities over the intercom. At Lee Elementary School, heart centered practice is naturally woven throughout the classrooms, hallways, lunchroom, and whole community to help alleviate the many stressors students come to school with and also face at school each day.

For example, lockdown drills have become standard practice at most schools in the United States, with a surge in gun violence riddling schools with tragedy. While these drills are necessary for student and school safety, they have also added a heightened level of anxiety, even for students who are normally well adjusted, and have compounded anxiety for those students already suffering. In response, school leaders like Kate Retzel have students and staff rotate through a series of mindfulness practice opportunities over the loudspeaker or in community meetings to the whole school community after lockdown drills.

Practicing Heart Centered Leadership: Lockdown Drill De-stress

On December 14, 2018, with the excitement and anticipation of the upcoming holiday break at Lee Elementary School in Lee, Massachusetts, the preK to grade 6 students participated in a lockdown drill. Just after the lockdown drill ended, the whole school community was led through and participated in calming breath work exercises and a song was shared to help alleviate students' anxiety and quiet their minds so they could peacefully return to their school day feeling loved and cared for (K. Retzel, personal communication, December 14, 2018).

Boost Social Intelligence

Effective, conscious leaders must have social intelligence. The following questions help determine one's own social intelligence (Goleman & Boyatzis, 2008).

- **Empathy:** Do you understand what motivates other people, even those from different backgrounds? Are you sensitive to others' needs?
- **Attunement:** Do you listen attentively and think about how others feel? Are you attuned to others' moods?
- **Organizational awareness:** Do you appreciate the culture and values of the group or organization? Do you understand social networks and know their unspoken norms?
- **Influence:** Do you persuade others by engaging them in discussion and appealing to their self-interests? Do you get support from key people?
- **Developing others:** Do you coach and mentor others with compassion and personally invest time and energy in mentoring? Do you provide feedback that people find helpful for their professional development?

- **Inspiration:** Do you articulate a compelling vision, build group pride, and foster a positive emotional tone? Do you lead by bringing out the best in people?
- **Teamwork:** Do you solicit input from everyone on the team? Do you support all team members and encourage cooperation?

Improving your mindfulness skills will help you hone your emotional intelligence. That skill helps you because, instead of responding reactively or emotionally, you acknowledge your thinking and needs, express yourself more clearly, and act more effectively.

HEART CENTERED LEADERSHIP EXERCISE: Press the Pause Button

Source: Adapted from Janice Marturano, n.d.

If you are feeling overwhelmed, with a neverending to-do list, your creativity may plummet. While we may yearn for a vacation and time away from our work, in reality, these vacations are short lived, and we return to work with a backlog that only increases our stress. Instead, try a mini-vacation or a series of small breaks, a purposeful pause. Here are a few ways to do this.

- **Start the day with a cup of coffee or tea:** Savor your cup of java, mindfully enjoying the flavor without distraction, without multitasking—no phones, videos, news—but rather just sitting and sipping for a few minutes.
- **Use the door:** In the morning, when you arrive at work, when your hand reaches for a door handle, take a few seconds to pause and be purposefully present. Feel your hand muscles as they tense in anticipation of pushing open the door, feel the smoothness of the door handle, feel the temperature in the room, and simply take in the experience as you transition from the morning preparation to your entry into the work environment.
- **Walk it off:** When you notice that your neck and shoulders are tightening up, or your heart is racing as you contemplate all that you should do, take a walk. It might be a walk to the breakroom, the bathroom, a classroom, or your next meeting. As you walk, just walk. Don't use this as a time to use your phone or to ruminate on what happened yesterday or what might happen today. When your mind starts to review these events, gently come back to the present, to your body's experience of walking.

Build the Other Four Cs

We know it is one thing to name a best practice and it is another to follow through with effective implementation. Inevitably, leaders will encounter barriers and obstacles as they attempt to turn schools around, advance best practices, or bring nontraditional approaches into schools. Yet for each barrier to heart centeredness, table 8.2 (page 166) has strategies that can address them.

Table 8.2: Overcoming Barriers to Heart Centered Leadership

Actions	Barriers	What Leaders Can Do
Actively listen.	It takes time to be patient and cultivate these skills.	Schedule time to listen. Ask questions. Practice.
Build trust.	It's not on your to-do list, or the school leader is entering a situation where trust has been broken.	Give someone a break. Be true to your word. Ask staff about their needs and respond with support—resources, encouragement, or something else.
Be conscious of student and teacher morale, stress, victories, community needs, and community stressors.	Some of these are not easy to address. You may feel powerless or that it is not part of your job.	Pay attention. Acknowledge needs. Restrict multitasking. Savor the good, the pleasant. Collaborate to come up with solutions.
Be compassionate.	In the middle of a crisis, it can be hard to think of others; you may feel a need to be firm in an effort to not show weakness.	Consider how all parties must feel, and what you can do to show caring, empathy, and kindness. Encourage everyone to think of others.
Be confident.	You may be uncertain.	Be positive, uplifting, and resourceful. Do some research, see a mentor, or talk to other school leaders.
Be courageous.	You may be going against a written or unwritten norm.	Start small. Savor successes. Collaborate.
Build community.	There might be various factions; it may be hard to find the time.	Consider the many communities within your school. Build communities from small teams to sharing with the larger whole. Find openings for success. Give others credit.

What Does Heart Centered Leadership Look Like Historically?

Heart centered leadership is seen in some of the most impactful world leaders throughout history. The historical examples of Mary Robinson and Ray Anderson show us that incorporating conscious intention, self-reflection, and compassion can be powerful ways to bring lasting, large-scale change.

Mary Robinson

Mary Robinson was born in 1944 and served as the first woman president of Ireland and then as United Nations (UN) High Commissioner for Human Rights (Marsh, n.d.). She embodied heart centered leadership through her commitment to elevating human rights issues to the world stage: in 1992, Robinson was the first head of state to visit Somalia after the country's civil war and famine, and in 1994 was the first to visit Rwanda after the genocide that occurred there. After leaving the UN, she founded and was involved with a number of initiatives to address human rights abuses in her home country and around the world, and focused on how climate change affects the poorest citizens. She was awarded the U.S. Presidential Medal of Freedom in 2009.

Ray Anderson

Ray Anderson was a U.S. businessman who was at the forefront of the movement for sustainable business practices in large corporations (Elkington, 2011). Born in 1934, Anderson founded Interface, Inc., one of the largest carpet manufacturers in the world. As chairman, he committed to his company's goal of eliminating negative impacts on the environment by 2020. Outside of his stewardship of climate work in manufacturing, he was committed to advancing climate justice on a national scale, co-chairing a climate action initiative, and creating a nonprofit foundation around the topic.

How Do We Measure Heart Centered Leadership?

The following tools measure heart centered leadership: *The Mindful Leader* by Michael Bunting (2016), the Barrett Values Centre, and S-CCATE.

The Mindful Leader

Understanding the importance of conscious (mindful and heartfelt) leadership means knowing your personal values system and how to best articulate what is most important in order to build trust. Without trust, says author Michael Bunting (2016), there is no leadership. In *The Mindful Leader: 7 Practices for Transforming Your Leadership, Your Organization and Your Life*, Bunting (2016) reminds us that as mindful leaders, living and leading from wholesome values truly transforms, frees, and authenticates us.

A heart centered leader is able to develop a depth of self-awareness, self-acceptance, and genuineness that fulfills and liberates from within. It is the desire to not just be a leader others can trust but a leader who is authentic and true to him- or herself.

Barrett Values Centre

Teachers and schools and district leaders can take a Personal Values Assessment (PVA) on the Barrett Values Centre website (BVC; www.valuescentre.com/tools-as-sessments/pva). In a short time, participants receive a personal analysis. In addition, BVC offers a fifteen- to twenty-minute course that helps you learn more about your values. BVC goes one step further during this journey to explore the world of values, why they are important, and how they influence your life and decision making. Their Seven Levels Model of Consciousness—(1) service, (2) making a difference, (3) internal cohesion, (4) transformation, (5) self-esteem, (6) relationship, and (7) survival (BVC, n.d.)—aligns with our Heart Centered Learning approach and what Bolman and Deal (1995) refer to as the heart of leadership living in the hearts of leaders. Heart centered leaders must look into their hearts first, to find the wisdom, importance, and significance of their leadership: "the force that sustains meaning and hope" (Bolman & Deal, 1995, p. 20).

S-CCATE

S-CCATE and the S-CCATE Supplement include several items related to heart centered, mindful, and compassionate school leadership. Table 8.3 has three factors that relate to conscious leadership.

Table 8.3: S-CCATE Conscious Leadership Components

Factor	In Action
Leadership and a compassionate school community	Teachers and administrators demonstrate fairness and equity.
Compassionate school policies	The principal's actions demonstrate that relationship building (with students, teachers, families, and community) is a priority.
Leadership and a compassionate school community	The principal effectively solves problems.

Reflection

To get the most out of this chapter, reflect on these questions after reading it.

- What are your strengths as a conscious leader?
- Do you intentionally incorporate activities into the school week and calendar to help relieve student and teacher stress? If not, might you consider including some?
- When you examine your school community, do you sense that justice, fairness, and equity permeate your activities, your teachers' interactions with students, and your plans for building stronger bonds with students and their families?
- Do you have your own stress relief or mindfulness practice?
- How compassionate are your school policies and practices? Where is there room for growth?

— Notes —

Taking Heart, Having Heart— Looking to Our Future

Wherever you go, go with all your heart.

—Confucius

key principle

Caring takes heart.

Take heart . . . have heart . . . follow your heart . . . listen to your heart. All are common actions we are urged to take. Where is education's heart? When you think of the students in your school, where are their hearts? What do they know of their hearts?

It is interesting that our hearts are in the center of our bodies—in contrast to our heads, which can hold such lofty thoughts and ideals. So, when we take a deep breath and consider heart centeredness . . . when we breathe into our hearts, we can immediately be more grounded, more available to be fully present in the moment, particularly if our hearts are strong and we are not wounded. However, thankfully, we have many strategies to help each other strengthen our hearts, overcome our wounds, and open up to hear and see more fully. Consider the vagus nerve and the interplay of heart and mind decision making discussed in chapter 2 (pages 32–33). Could *heart centered* possibly mean that we live and operate from a place of balance? Of centeredness? A place where we are not easily thrown off track? Not too easily swayed by the things that are less central to our lives, our purpose, our reasons for being and doing?

Expounding on Trust

To be engaged, as teachers and learners, to be passionate about teaching and learning, to seek the thrill of teaching and learning; with love and ethical caring—it is hard to imagine these things happening with our heads alone. In a similar vein, in her classic book, *In Schools We Trust*, Deborah Meier (2003) envisions schools as communities where students "could invent their own lives, but also a place deeply connected to the lives of adults" (p. 182). Meier (2003) talks about the realities of relationships between students and teachers in cultures of trust, listing criteria for trustworthy schools as "schools that work" (p. 20) and those who "do their best to make schooling engaging and fun" (p. 21). While other elements, such as competence and resources, are part of her criteria, she ends with "those seven [criteria,] plus that love which doesn't allow us to give up, is all there is to it" (p. 23). Hattie (2009) talks about learning as a "personal journey for the teacher and the student" (p. 23).

Engaging, fun, safe places of love. Perhaps these schools have heart? What visions come to mind as you read what Meier and Hattie have to say about education?

Becoming More Fully Aware

How might you describe our world? Peter Senge, C. Otter Scharmer, Joseph Jaworski, and Betty Sue Flowers (2004) suggest that we have become more a world of businesses than a human economy, our lives fragmented into discrete units of expertise, causing us to lose sight of our path and potential. Senge and his colleagues (2004) liken our dominant culture to a prison, to a separation from self, from one another, and from nature in a way that cages us in and restricts our ability to be all we could be. We can see the detrimental impact of ignoring the damage we have created and continue creating. With a sense of urgency, these authors ask us to simply stop the madness, pause in our busyness, let go of old ways, suspend our judgment, be more fully aware of our lives, rediscover our purpose, and to be one with each other and with nature.

A thread that connects the insights from Hattie (2009), Meier (2003), and Senge and colleagues (2004) into what might be sorely needed in the world is connected-ness—a sense of community and belonging.

Taking a Global Journey—Connection, Happiness, and Relationships

How do we strengthen opportunities to reduce alienation and enrich our lives and the lives of others? Consider the rich narrative of storytelling, attending to more than the facts, attending to more than academic achievement or personal accomplishments, and enjoying our journey. Stuart Grauer (2016) tells the story of his travels to schools around the world. As he uncovers unique gifts among schools and on trails, in deserts, and across streams in England, the United States, the Middle East, Cuba, Tanzania, and a few other remote areas, he shares both his quest and questions. Grauer begins with, "Can we restore story to a world obsessed with data?" In answer to that question, a teacher in Surrey, England, states, "Teachers start to feel as if their own stories don't matter"; many teachers feel marginalized or trapped (p. xvii).

Grauer (2016) also asks us to consider whether teaching should be about information or environment. The outcomes under these two possibilities could vary considerably. When summarizing some of his insights about his travels, Grauer (2016) provides an excerpt from a presentation he gave at a Starbucks in Washington state:

> Research says what we already knew, that people are not only the happiest, but also the most productive, when they are with people they care about. A great teacher understands that engagement . . . is about relationships that are forming in the class. Connection is the single most important thing of pedagogy. (p. 215)

Connection, happiness, and relationships can be related to tuning into and trusting our hearts, as well as letting go of the fear that drives us to think only with our heads (as if the solutions resided in our brains and as if we could use logic, information, analysis, and reasoning to create what our students need). It is as if we believed that, if we could instill sufficient knowledge, our students would be better informed. Thankfully, connectedness is valued, community is key, and mindful, heart centered communities are where educators and students feel supported, learn together, and thrive.

— Notes —

S-CCATE—A Visioning and Assessment Tool to Create Heart Centered Communities

One common desire that every human being has is to love and
be loved. At the end of our lives, it's how we measure our lives.

—Denise Di Novi

key principle

By measuring compassion within their schools, educators have a way to implement plans and monitor progress of Heart Centered Learning element development.

With Heart Centered Learning, we envisioned a process to help teachers determine what they want to learn as they implement the five Cs: (1) consciousness, (2) compassion, (3) confidence, (4) courage, and (5) community. The School Compassionate Culture Analytic Tool for Educators (S-CCATE) provides a systematic process for implementing Heart Centered Learning and key methods for identifying needs, planning for professional development and interventions, and reporting progress on non-academic factors. The S-CCATE takes between twelve and fifteen minutes to complete online.

S-CCATE was developed over a period of six years as we collaborated with a group of educational leaders, principals, neuroscientists, yoga and mindfulness practitioners, and teachers to identify how to measure factors that these leaders deemed most critical. The work began with a focus group at a meeting of the National Association of Elementary School Principals (Mason, Mullane, & Fitzpatrick, 2013). Over the course of six years, we reviewed related research (Berg, Osher, Moroney, & Yoder, 2017; Cohen, McCabe, Michelli, & Pickeral, 2009; CASEL, 2012; Duckworth & Yeager, 2015; Greenberg, Domitrovich, Weissberg, & Durlak, 2017; Heller & LaPierre, 2012;

Jones & Doolittle, 2017; McKown, 2015; Zelazo & Lyons, 2012) and continued to dialogue with educational leaders who provided input into the development of our measure of Heart Centered Learning. We conducted our first pilot studies in three sites in 2017.

In 2018, we completed a validation study with 814 educators, resulting in the final online version of S-CCATE that you can complete in twelve to fifteen minutes (Mason et al., 2018). The results of the validation study show high reliability and validity. Cronbach's alpha (CA) measures reliability, or consistency, between like items (Institute for Digital Research and Education, n.d.); The Spearman-Brown prophecy formula measures reliability "when the number of items in a questionnaire is changed" (de Vet, Mokkink, Mosmuller, & Terwee, 2017). The CA for the final forty items is 0.948; Spearman-Brown projects internal consistency reliability of 0.94 for the five factors. In that study, we also validated a companion measure: the S-CCATE Supplement (page 178).

In 2019, we collaborated with Yale University's Program for Recovery and Community Health and the New England Mental Health Technology Transfer Center, working with twenty-four fellows—school administrators, psychologists, social workers, and other leaders—to bring S-CCATE to the six New England states. To date, over 1,100 educators have used S-CCATE through this project.

Through a partnership with TeachLink (https://myteachlink.com), S-CCATE is now available nationally (https://s-ccate.org) and includes provisions for electronic reports and options to obtain both basic recommendations and action guides, which include customized recommendations for schools. Each action guide contains three major components.

1. Considerations for the whole community (students, educators, staff, and school leaders)
2. Suggested professional development
3. Suggested activities

With these provisions, S-CCATE is a valuable tool for monitoring a school's progress on the Every Student Succeeds Act (2015) and state assessments, and for obtaining funding for professional development to support school improvement.

S-CCATE measures teachers' and students' knowledge of trauma, equity, mindfulness, and neuroscience; the importance of ritual, consistency, and celebration; student understanding of emotions; the degree of effort to build confidence and courage; and applications of mindfulness to reduce stress. With S-CCATE, teachers rate their perception of their own knowledge and practices, as well as student and school-wide knowledge and practices. Using teacher perception to assess school climate has been demonstrated to be a valid and stable indicator of social-emotional adjustment (Brand, Felner, Seitsinger, Burns, & Bolton, 2008).

Core learning teams can use the S-CCATE educational teams to build schoolwide knowledge, consensus, and protocol to further compassion while also building a sense of community.

The S-CCATE Tool

As a result of the S-CCATE validation study, S-CCATE has five factors, each of which is described in this book; see table A.1.

Table A.1: S-CCATE Factors

Factor	Description	Chapter
Leadership and a compassionate school community	The principal's, environment's, culture's, and policies' ability to contribute to a compassionate school culture	4, 7, and 8
Conscious awareness of emotions and stress	Using neuroscience and neuroplasticity to explain how trauma, stress, and vulnerability interact, and how mindfulness can support positive outcomes in traumatized populations	3
Courage and resiliency	Demonstrating appropriate risk taking, gratitude, and constructive feedback	4 and 6
Confidence and positivity	Applying teachers' awareness of student stress and trauma to understand how to adjust instruction to provide more student support	4 and 5
Understanding of equity	Promoting student awareness of discrimination, poverty, and injustice	3 and 6

The reliability as demonstrated with CA and Spearman-Brown scores is displayed in table A.2.

Table A.2: S-CCATE Factor Reliability

Factor	Number of Items	Cronbach's Alpha	Spearman-Brown
Leadership and a compassionate school community	14	0.993	0.996
Conscious awareness of emotions and stress	7	0.861	0.967
Courage and resiliency	7	0.874	0.970
Confidence and positivity	8	0.797	0.940
Understanding of equity	4	0.826	0.977

At the end of chapters 3–8 are examples of items within S-CCATE that are used to measure the heart centered concept that is addressed in that chapter. With S-CCATE, teachers rate each item on a four-point scale: 1 = Needs Improvement, 2 = Emerging, 3 = Proficient, and 4 = Exemplary. Here is one item from the Leadership and Compassionate School Community Scale: "School culture reflects a spirit of happiness and joy." Teachers identify the level that most closely corresponds to the level of proficiency according to their individual opinion. These answers are then compiled electronically, and data are available in the form of means, medians, and ranges, as well as both descriptive and graphic representations.

The S-CCATE Supplement

The 2018 S-CCATE Supplement validation study was completed by 468 respondents, resulting in a scale of forty-nine items that can be completed in twelve to fifteen minutes, with high reliability and validity (CA of 0.952 and moderate Pearson correlations among factors ranging from 0.430 to 0.641, an indication of the independence of each factor). The S-CCATE Supplement measures eight factors.

1. Conscious communication
2. Compassion for self and others
3. Confidence and courage
4. Emotional self-regulation
5. Compassionate school policies
6. Human rights assurance and violence prevention
7. Culture and school community
8. Student protection and trauma support

Tables A.3 and A.4 present a description of each S-CCATE Supplement factor and the corresponding chapter in this book.

Table A.3: S-CCATE Supplement Factors

S-CCATE Supplement Factor	Description	Chapter
Conscious communication	By raising awareness of their own compassion, intentions, and actions, students and teachers can find ways to improve the understanding of each other's needs.	3
Compassion for self and others	All levels of the institution are assessed according to how their actions embody compassion, and awareness of others' needs.	4

Confidence and courage	Students' daily tasks, opportunities, and activities are assessed for positive development toward courage and confidence.	5 and 6
Emotional self-regulation	Mindfulness and self-regulation are instructed and there are opportunities for student reflection.	4
Compassionate school policies	Teachers, administrators, school personnel, and principals reflect on the structures and policies that enhance compassion.	8
Human rights assurance and violence prevention	Students and teachers express their understanding of violence juxtaposed with human needs.	4, 8, and 9
Culture and school community	School assemblies, calendar events, ceremonies, and other cultural structures within the school environment are assessed in terms of compassion and diversity.	7
Student protection and trauma support	The school provides supports to help meet the basic physical needs of the students.	8 and 9

Table A.4: Factor Reliability Estimates for the S-CCATE Supplement

Factor	# Items	CA	SB (49)
Conscious communication	8	0.881	0.978
Compassion for self and others	6	0.876	0.983
Confidence and courage	8	0.851	0.972
Emotional self-regulation	5	0.865	0.984
Compassionate school policies	6	0.849	0.979
Human rights assurance and violence prevention	4	0.771	0.976
Culture and school community	5	0.715	0.961
Student protection and trauma support	7	0.667	0.933

Factor subscales reliability adjusted via the Spearman-Brown to a full-scale length of forty-nine items.

Sample items from the S-CCATE Supplement are presented in figure A.1.

Instructions: Please select the category that is most representative of the status for the teacher, leader, or student.				
	1 = Needs Improvement	2 = Emerging	3 = Proficient	4 = Exemplary
Teachers and administrators consistently enforce antibullying policies.				
Students are given opportunities to think about their beliefs about violence.				
Academic and support staff are provided training and resources to carry out the school's approaches to consciousness and compassion.				

Figure A.1: Three items from the S-CCATE Supplement.

Figures A.2 and A.3 show how you can display S-CCATE and S-CCATE Supplement data graphically.

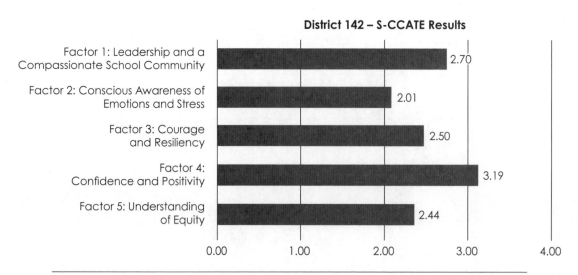

Figure A.2: Sample S-CCATE results.

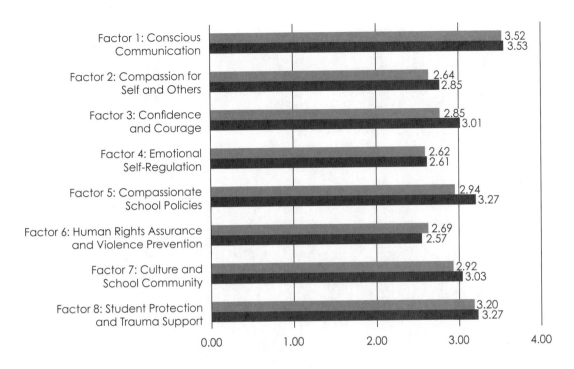

Figure A.3: Sample S-CCATE Supplement results.

The 2017 Heart Centered Learning pilot at Upper Providence Elementary School is a blueprint for informing and implementing protocol and procedures for schoolwide change. The approach begins with identifying a core learning team of between five and eight educators from across targeted grade levels and staff roles. This representation ensures teacher buy-in (Senge et al., 2012). The team-completed S-CCATE data are shared and, based on these data, teachers make professional development and intervention decisions. Like Lee Elementary implementation, the goal is building collaboration capacity during the compassionate school community development so that change is sustainable.

Figure A.4 (page 182) shows how the compiled data are displayed graphically.

S-CCATE Use

S-CCATE is used for planning, discussion, decision making, guidance, monitoring, and assessment of progress. It is the foundational tool for conducting a needs assessment and monitoring progress when implementing Heart Centered Learning. Educators begin with administering S-CCATE, followed by professional development to enhance teacher knowledge and skills and at least one intervention lasting three to five months. At the end of the three to five months, S-CCATE is readministered to measure progress. Schools have the option of also using the S-CCATE Supplement

I make an intentional effort to increase students' sense of comfort, trust, and security in my classes. — 6, 56, 283, 135

By my words and actions, I try to communicate to students that I care about them. — 7, 59, 203, 108

Visual displays in the school celebrate the cultural composition of the community surrounding the school. — 88, 203, 161, 27

I provide written, oral, and artistic opportunities for student self-expression. — 30, 173, 225, 47

Students are taught mindfulness practices (including meditation, deep breathing, or yoga) at school. — 130, 204, 113, 32

The principal's actions demonstrate that relationship building (with students, teachers, families, and community) is a priority. — 93, 147, 178, 62

My curriculum supports student understanding of diverse cultures. — 67, 220, 161, 62

Teachers have time within the school day to plan together. — 155, 154, 146, 24

Figure A.4: Graphical display of 5-SCATE data

for a more detailed follow-up. Once again, a core learning team reviews data from the assessments. Based on the data, members make additional professional development and intervention decisions.

S-CCATE and the S-CCATE Supplement are implemented at the school or district level with a secure electronic platform. Data are password protected and schools have access to comparison results from the national database. Individual teacher data remain confidential and anonymous.

With both instruments, teachers self-assess and rank perceptions of their knowledge, skills, and implementation of compassionate components in their classrooms, as well as their perception of student and schoolwide strengths and needs. You can administer S-CCATE and the S-CCATE Supplement multiple times. After the initial six to nine months of implementation, schools administer either or both of them (depending on focus areas) on an annual or semiannual basis.

Process of Change During Pilot Study

As principal Melissa Patschke indicates, the process of change takes strategy, leadership, time, teamwork, and certain fearlessness. Her school was one of the pilot sites for Heart Centered Learning using S-CCATE. Over the course of five months, the core learning team, led by teacher Brian Aikens, met five times with a Heart Centered Learning facilitator. Each teacher implemented his or her own mindfulness and Heart Centered Learning practices as recommended in Part II of this book. The core learning team practiced these exercises for a few minutes and a new exercise was introduced during each of their facilitated meetings. At each session, each teacher also shared from his or her personal practice and implementation in his or her classroom. Additional guidance and support throughout the five months were provided by the core learning team leader.

Using S-CCATE, teacher self-reports were recorded prior to implementation and at the end of the five-month pilot. The data showed that the greatest gains were made in increasing understanding of trauma and neuroscience, particularly the awareness of the relationship between bodily feelings and emotion. According to teacher self-reports on S-CCATE, teacher and student understanding of trauma increased from 1.9 (needs improvement) to 3.5 (proficient); teacher and student understanding of neuroscience, particularly in terms of their awareness of the impact on emotions, increased from 2.25 (emerging) to 2.85 (still emerging and closer to proficient). The highest final scores were in the areas of teacher awareness of how they express compassion in class (3.5) and student understanding of trauma (3.8—very close to exemplary).

Importance of Teamwork and Core Learning Teams

The need for teamwork is also echoed by education consultant and former principal Jill Flanders, who says:

It takes a team. At our early education school, the core learning team included a school psychologist, behavior therapist,
physical education teacher, a paraprofessional, two classroom
teachers, a parent, and a principal. Our goal was to create a
common language around mindfulness, kindness, and developmentally appropriate practices, and to deliver the message
through song and movement. (J. Flanders, personal communication, May 16, 2017)

With Heart Centered Learning, the core learning teams take on a different shape
and structure according to the visions and the needs of the individual school. For
example, at another pilot site, principal Kate Retzel wanted to ensure the core learning
team was representative of the staff at Lee Elementary. The teams at Lee, therefore,
included three teachers (with one specialty area teacher), three paraprofessionals (both
lower and upper elementary grades), the school principal, and the school adjustment
counselor (as pilot coordinator). The team at Lee was able to not only increase their
own awareness and compassion as they engaged in their heart centered practices, but
they also introduced students to mindfulness and naturally infused it in the classroom
and throughout the school. According to Kate:

Before Heart Centered Learning was introduced, teachers had
very little awareness of the extent of trauma, the neurobiology
behind children's responses to trauma, and how teachers can
use mindfulness to help children heal. I am thrilled by how fully
teachers are embracing this effort and also by the impact on
student self-regulation and positive changes in discipline at
Lee. (K. Retzel, personal communication, May 15, 2017).

Reflection

To get the most out of this appendix, reflect on these questions after reading it.

- Why might S-CCATE be a valuable tool to help your school implement
  Heart Centered Learning?
- What might your core learning team look like at your school?
- Why are needs assessment and monitoring systems important in seeking
  sustainable change?
- How do you see using S-CCATE most effectively in your school—as
  a visioning tool, a data tool, or as continuity and connection between
  professional development opportunities, for example?
- How can you use S-CCATE specifically for teacher team planning,
  discussion, decision making, guidance, monitoring, and progress
  assessment?

References and Resources

Abhakorn, M. L. J. (2014). Investigating the use of student portfolios to develop students' metacognition in English as a foreign language learning. *Journal of Language Teaching and Research, 5*(1), 46–55.

Ackerman, C. (2017). *9 self-compassion exercises and worksheets for increasing compassion.* Accessed at https://positivepsychologyprogram.com/self-compassion-exercises-worksheets/#exercises-self-compassion on July 5, 2019.

Adams, J. M. (n.d.). *Raising a compassionate child.* Accessed at www.parenting.com/article/raising-a -compassionate-child on July 10, 2019.

Adams, W. L. (2011). Angela Merkel, chancellor of Germany. *Time.* Accessed at http://content.time.com /time/specials/packages/article/0,28804,2005455_2005458_2005461,00.html on November 16, 2019.

Ahmed, S., & Walker, C. (2018). *There has been, on average, 1 school shooting every week this year.* Accessed at www.cnn.com/2018/03/02/us/school-shootings-2018-list-trnd/index.html on July 5, 2019.

Ahn, H. J., & Rodkin, P. C. (2014). Classroom-level predictors of the social status of aggression: Friendship centralization, friendship density, teacher-student attunement, and gender. *Journal of Educational Psychology, 106*(4), 1144–1155.

Ahn, H. J., Rodkin, P. C., & Gest, S. (2013). Teacher–student agreement on "bullies and kids they pick on" in elementary school classrooms: Gender and grade differences. *Theory Into Practice, 52*(4), 257–263.

Aknin, L. B., Hamlin, J. K., & Dunn, E. W. (2012). Giving leads to happiness in young children. *PLoS One, 7*(6), e39211.

Alaska Department of Education and Early Development. (2009). *Culturally responsive schools.* Accessed at www.ankn.uaf.edu/Publications/culturalstandards.pdf on December 10, 2019.

Alber, R. (2017). *Kindness: A lesson plan.* Accessed at www.edutopia.org/blog/kindness-lesson-plan -rebecca-alber on September 13, 2019.

Aldous, J. (2018). "Mindfulness" part of the curriculum at Grandview Heights school. *CBC News.* Accessed at www.cbc.ca/news/canada/edmonton/mindfulness-part-of-the-curriculum-at-grandview -heights-school-1.2804266 on November 15, 2019.

Allen, K. J. (2017). *The vagus nerve and why it matters.* Accessed at www.sonima.com/yoga/yoga-articles /vagus-nerve on August 5, 2019.

Allen, K., Kern, M. L., Vella-Brodrick, D., Hattie, J., & Waters, L. (2018). What schools need to know about fostering school belonging: A meta-analysis. *Educational Psychology Review, 30*(1), 1–34.

Alleva, R., Shannon, P., & Smith, M. (n.d.). *The effects of the Courage to Care program: Teaching empathy to rural New Hampshire seventh graders.* Accessed at www.academia.edu/26158303/The_Effects_of_ the_Courage_to_Care_Program_Teaching_Empathy_to_Rural_New_Hampshire_Seventh_Graders on August 12, 2019.

American Association of Suicidology. (2018). *Suicide reporting recommendations: Media as partners in prevention.* Accessed at www.suicidology.org/Resources/Recommendations-for-Reporting-on-Suicide on July 10, 2019.

American Foundation for Suicide Prevention, & Suicide Prevention Resource Center, Education Development Center. (2018). *After a suicide: A toolkit for schools* (2nd ed.). Waltham, MA: Education Development Center.

Anderson, D. L., & Graham, A. P. (2016). Improving student wellbeing: Having a say at school. *School Effectiveness and School Improvement, 27*(3), 348–366.

Anderson, L. H. (2011). *Speak.* New York: Square Fish.

Ang, R. P. (2005). Development and validation of the Teacher-Student Relationship Inventory using exploratory and confirmatory factor analysis. *Journal of Experimental Education, 74*(1), 55–73.

Arguelles, L., McCraty, R., & Rees, R. A. (2003). The heart in holistic education. *Encounter: Education for Meaning and Social Justice, 16*(3), 13–21.

Atkinson, J., & Chu, D. (2018). *ESSA's success (or failure) is up to all of us.* Accessed at www.edweek.org /ew/articles/2018/02/14/essas-success-or-failure-is-up-to.html on July 5, 2019.

Baer, D. (2017). *Knowing your actual, literal heart reduces anxiety and better decisions.* Accessed at www.thecut.com/2017/01/how-your-heart-talks-to-your-brain.html on August 5, 2018.

Baer, R. A., Smith, G. T., Hopkins, J., Krietemeyer, J., & Toney, L. (2006). Using self-report assessment methods to explore facets of mindfulness. *Assessment, 13*(1), 27–45.

Baker, J., Cobley, S., Schorer, J., & Wattie, N. (Eds.). (2017). *Routledge handbook of talent identification and development in sport.* New York: Routledge.

Bakosh, L. S., Snow, R. M., Tobias, J. M., Houlihan, J. L., & Barbosa-Leiker, C. (2016). Maximizing mindful learning: An innovative mindful awareness intervention improves elementary school students' quarterly grades. *Mindfulness, 7*(1), 59–67.

Baltimore City Schools. (2013). *Nation's Report Card reflects progress for Baltimore City students amid heightened expectations under new state standards.* Baltimore, MD. Accessed at www.baltimorecity schools.org/cms/lib/MD01001351/Centricity/domain/8049/2013_14_archive/20131218-TUDA.pdf on February 20, 2017.

Barnes, V. A., Pendergrast, R. A., Harshfield, G. A., & Treiber, F. A. (2008). Impact of breathing awareness meditation on ambulatory blood pressure and sodium handling in prehypertensive African American adolescents. *Ethnicity & Disease, 18*(1), 1–5.

Barnes, V. A., Treiber, F. A., & Davis, H. (2001). Impact of Transcendental Meditation on cardiovascular function at rest and during acute stress in adolescents with high normal blood pressure. *Journal of Psychosomatic Research, 51*(4), 597–605.

Barrett Values Centre. (n.d.). *The Barrett Model.* Accessed at www.valuescentre.com/barrett-model on August 8, 2019.

Baum, F. (1900). *The wonderful wizard of Oz.* Chicago: George M. Hill Collection.

Beecroft, G. D., Duffy, G. L., & Moran, J. W. (2003). *The executive guide to improvement and change.* Milwaukee: American Society for Quality.

Beesley, A. D., Clark, T. F., Barker, J., Germeroth, R. C., & Apthorp, H. S. (2010). *Expeditionary learning schools: Theory of action and literature review of motivation, character, and engagement.* Denver, CO: Mid-continent Research for Education and Learning.

Bellis, M. A., Hughes, K., Leckenby, N., Jones, L., Baban, A., Kachaeva, M., et al. (2014). Adverse childhood experiences and associations with health-harming behaviours in young adults: Surveys in eight eastern European countries. *Bulletin of the World Health Organization, 92*(9), 641–655.

Bemak, F., & Chung, R. C. Y. (2017). Refugee trauma: Culturally responsive counseling interventions. *Journal of Counseling & Development, 95*(3), 299–308.

Berg, J., Osher, D., Moroney, D., & Yoder, N. (2017). *The intersection of school climate and social and emotional development.* Washington, DC: American Institutes for Research.

Bergin, C., & Bergin, D. (2009). Attachment in the classroom. *Educational Psychology Review, 21*(2), 141–170.

Berkowitz, R., Moore, H., Astor, R. A., & Benbenishty, R. (2017). A research synthesis of the associations between socioeconomic background, inequality, school climate, and academic achievement. *Review of Educational Research, 87*(2), 425–469.

Bert, P. (2014). *Mindful compassion: How the science of compassion can help you understand your emotions, live in the present, and connect deeply with others.* Oakland, CA: New Harbinger.

Bethell, C. D., Davis, M. B., Gombojav, N., Stumbo, S., & Powers, K. (2017, October). *A national and across state profile on adverse childhood experiences among children and possibilities to heal and thrive.* Baltimore, MD: Johns Hopkins Bloomberg School of Public Health.

Biondi, A. (2018). Remembering Josephine Baker, trailblazing artist and activist. *Vogue.* Accessed at www.vogue.co.uk/gallery/josephine-baker-life-in-pictures on July 5, 2019.

Black, D. S., Milam, J., & Sussman, S. (2009). Sitting-meditation interventions among youth: A review of treatment efficacy. *Pediatrics, 124*(3), e532–e541.

Black, D. S., Sussman, S., Johnson, A., & Milam, J. (2009). Trait mindfulness helps shield decision-making from translating into health-risk behavior. *Journal of Adolescent Health, 51*(6), 588–592.

Blad, E. (2017). *No state will measure social-emotional learning under ESSA: Will that slow its momentum?* Accessed at www.edweek.org/ew/articles/2017/10/04/no-state-will-measure-social-emotional-learning-under.html on July 5, 2019.

Blaine, A. (2014). *Create safety by modeling vulnerability* [Blog post]. Accessed at www.tolerance.org/magazine/create-safety-by-modeling-vulnerability on July 10, 2019.

Blake, J. J., Kim, E. S., Lund, E. M., Zhou, Q., Kwok, O. M., & Benz, M. R. (2016). Predictors of bully victimization in students with disabilities: A longitudinal examination using a national data set. *Journal of Disability Policy Studies, 26*(4), 199–208.

Blankstein, A., Noguera, P., & Kelly, L. (2015). *Excellence through equity: Five principles of courageous leadership to guide achievement for every student.* Alexandria, VA: Association for Supervision and Curriculum Development.

Blaustein, M. E., & Kinniburgh, K. M. (2010). *Treating traumatic stress in children and adolescents: How to foster resilience through attachment, self-regulation, and competency.* New York: Guilford Press.

Block, J. (2016). *Teaching toward consciousness* [Blog post]. Accessed at www.edutopia.org/blog/teaching-toward-consciousness-joshua-block on December 1, 2017.

Block-Lerner, J., Adair, C., Plumb, J. C., Rhatigan, D. L., & Orsillo, S. M. (2007). The case for mindfulness-based approaches in the cultivation of empathy: Does nonjudgmental, present-moment awareness increase capacity for perspective-taking and empathic concern? *Journal of Marital and Family Therapy, 33*(4), 501–516.

Bloom, B. E. (2015). *Meeting the needs of women in California's county justice systems.* Accessed at www.frbsf.org/community-development/files/WomensToolkit.pdf on November 20, 2019.

Bloom, S. L., & Farragher, B. (2013). *Restoring sanctuary: A new operating system for trauma-informed systems of care.* Oxford: Oxford University Press.

Blumenfeld, S., Groves, B. M., Rice, K. F., & Weinreb, M. (2010). *Children and trauma: A curriculum for mental health clinicians.* Chicago: The Domestic Violence & Mental Health Policy Initiative.

Bolman, L. G., & Deal, T. E. (2011). *Leading with soul: An uncommon journey of spirit.* San Francisco: Jossey-Bass.

Bolman, L. G., & Deal, T. E. (2019). *Reframing the path to school leadership: A guide for teachers and principals* (3rd ed.). Thousand Oaks, CA: Corwin Press.

Bookbinder, L. J. (n.d.). *Empathy, listening skills & relationships.* Accessed at http://learning inaction.com/PDF/ELSR.pdf on November 15, 2018.

Border, G. (2017). *New York City students need comfort? In trots Petey the Shih Tzu.* Accessed at www.reuters.com/article/us-new-york-education/new-york-city-students-need-comfort-in-trots-petey-the-shih-tzu-idUSKBN1AR0V4 on November 1, 2019.

Borowsky, I. W., Taliaferro, L. A., & McMorris, B. J. (2013). Suicidal thinking and behavior among youth involved in verbal and social bullying: Risk and protective factors. *Journal of Adolescent Health, 53*(1), S4–S12.

Boyd, J. E., Lanius, R. A., & McKinnon, M. C. (2018). Mindfulness-based treatments for posttraumatic stress disorder: A review of the treatment literature and neurobiological evidence. *Journal of Psychiatry & Neuroscience, 43*(1), 7–25.

Bradford, B. (2005). *The book of ancient wisdom: Over 500 inspiring quotations from the Greeks and Romans.* Mineola, NY: Dover Publications.

Brand, S., Felner, R. D., Seitsinger, A., Burns, A., & Bolton, N. (2008). A large scale study of the assessment of the social environment of middle and secondary schools: The validity and utility of teachers' ratings of school climate, cultural pluralism, and safety problems for understanding school effects and school improvement. *Journal of School Psychology, 46*(5), 507–535.

Bremner, J. D. (2007). Neuroimaging in posttraumatic stress disorder and other stress-related disorders. *Neuroimaging Clinics of North America, 17*(4), 523–538, ix.

Brendtro, L. K., Brokenleg, M., & van Bockern, S. (2019). *Reclaiming youth at risk: Futures of promise* (3rd ed.). Bloomington, IN: Solution Tree Press.

Breslau, N., Peterson, E. L., Poisson, L. M., Schultz, L. R., & Lucia, V. C. (2004). Estimating posttraumatic stress disorder in the community: Lifetime perspective and the impact of typical traumatic events. *Psychological Medicine, 34*(5), 889–898.

Brooks, R. (2009). *Education and "charismatic" adults: To touch a student's heart and mind.* Accessed at www.drrobertbrooks.com/0009 on December 1, 2018.

Brooks, R., & Goldstein, S. (2011). *Raising resilient children: Fostering strength, hope, and optimism.* New York: McGraw Hill.

Brown, B. (2010). *The power of vulnerability* [Video file]. Accessed at www.ted.com/talks/brene_brown_on_vulnerability?language=en on November 16, 2019.

Brown, B. (2015). *Daring greatly: How the courage to be vulnerable transforms the way we live, love, parent, and lead.* New York: Penguin.

Brown, K. W., & Ryan, R. M. (2003). The benefits of being present: Mindfulness and its role in psychological well-being. *Journal of Personality and Social Psychology, 84*(4), 822–848.

Brown, K. W., & Ryan, R. M. (2004). Perils and promise in defining and measuring mindfulness: Observations from experience. *Clinical Psychology: Science and Practice, 11*(3), 242–248.

Brown, K. W., Ryan, R. M., & Creswell, J. D. (2007). Mindfulness: Theoretical foundations and evidence for its salutary effects. *Psychological Inquiry, 18*(4), 211–237.

Brown, P., Corrigan, M., & Higgins-D'Alessandra, A. (2012). *Handbook of prosocial education: Volume 1.* New York: Rowman & Littlefield.

Brown, S. L., & Brown, R. M. (2015). Connecting prosocial behavior to improved physical health: Contributions from the neurobiology of parenting. *Neuroscience & Biobehavioral Reviews, 55*, 1–17.

Bruns, E. J. (2015). Wraparound is worth doing well: An evidence-based statement. In E. J. Bruns & J. S. Walker (Eds.), *The resource guide to wraparound.* Portland, OR: National Wraparound Initiative.

Bruns, E. J., Rast, J., Peterson, C., Walker, J., & Bosworth, J. (2006). Spreadsheets, service providers, and the statehouse: Using data and the wraparound process to reform systems for children and families. *American Journal of Community Psychology, 38*(3–4), 201–212.

Bruns, E. J., & Suter, J. C. (2010). Summary of the wraparound evidence base. In E. J. Bruns & J. S. Walker (Eds.), *The resource guide to wraparound*. Portland, OR: National Wraparound Initiative.

Brunzell, T., Stokes, H., & Waters, L. (2016). Trauma-informed positive education: Using positive psychology to strengthen vulnerable students. *Contemporary School Psychology, 20*(1), 63–83.

Bunting, M. (2016). *The mindful leader: 7 practices for transforming your leadership, your organisation and your life*. Hoboken, NJ: Wiley.

Bunting, M. (2018). *How leaders can boost employee engagement through mindfulness*. Accessed at www.insidehr.com.au/leaders-employee-engagement-mindfulness on November 18, 2019.

Cameron, W. B. (1963). *Informal sociology: A casual introduction to sociological thinking*. New York: Random House.

Cannon, J. (2016). Education as the practice of freedom: A social justice proposal for mindfulness educators. In R. E. Purser, D. Forbes, & A. Burke (Eds.), *Handbook of mindfulness: Culture, context, and social engagement* (pp. 397–409). Switzerland: Springer.

Carrera, J. (2005). *Inside the yogic sutras: A comprehensive sourcebook for the study and practice of Pantanjali's yoga sutras*. Buckingham, VA: Integral Yoga Press.

Cassidy, S. (2016). *The Academic Resilience Scale (ARS-30): A new multidimensional construct measure*. Accessed at www.ncbi.nlm.nih.gov/pmc/articles/PMC5114237 on September 13, 2019.

Catapano, J. (n.d.). *How to build confidence into the self-conscious student*. Accessed at www.teachhub.com/how-build-confidence-self-conscious-student on July 10, 2019.

Catapano, J. (2009). *Technology in the classroom: A look at Google Classroom*. Accessed at www.teachhub.com/technology-classroom-look-google-classroom on October 18, 2019.

Center for American Progress. (2017). *NEW CAP report: Harnessing the power of social and emotional learning under ESSA*. Accessed at www.americanprogress.org/press/release/2017/06/28/434979/release-new-cap-report-harnessing-power-social-emotional-learning-essa on December 5, 2017.

Center for Educational Improvement. (n.d.). *Considering social emotional learning*. Accessed at www.edimprovement.org/heart-centered-education on July 5, 2019.

Centers for Disease Control and Prevention. (2014). *School connectedness: Strategies for increasing protective factors among youth*. Accessed at www.cdc.gov/healthyyouth/protective/connectedness.htm on December 5, 2017.

Centers for Disease Control and Prevention. (2016). *Understanding teen dating violence*. Accessed at https://stacks.cdc.gov/view/cdc/38280 on August 19, 2019.

Centers for Disease Control and Prevention. (2018). *Suicide rising across the US*. Accessed at www.cdc.gov/vitalsigns/suicide/index.html on August 12, 2019.

Chen, I. (2014). *How a bigger purpose can motivate students to learn*. Accessed at http://ww2.kqed.org/mindshift/2014/08/how-a-bigger-purpose-can-motivate-students-to-learn on November 18, 2019.

Chiesa, A., & Serretti, A. (2009). Mindfulness-based stress reduction for stress management in healthy people: A review and meta-analysis. *Journal of Alternative and Complementary Medicine, 15*(5), 593–600.

Chiesa, A., & Serretti, A. (2010). A systematic review of neurobiological and clinical features of mindfulness meditations. *Psychological Medicine: A Journal of Research in Psychiatry and Allied Sciences, 40*(8), 1239–1252.

Child Trends. (2014). *Children's exposure to violence: Indicators on child and youth well-being*. Accessed at www.childtrends.org/wp-content/uploads/2016/05/118_Exposure_to_Violence.pdf on July 5, 2019.

Childre, D., & Martin, H. (1999). *The HeartMath solution*. New York: HarperCollins.

Children International. (n.d.). *Child poverty in the U.S.* Accessed at www.children.org/global-poverty/global-poverty-facts/facts-about-poverty-in-usa on December 5, 2017.

Chirichello, M. (2018). *Leadership for the 21st century*. Accessed at www.edimprovement.org/2018/11/leadership-21st-century on July 5, 2019.

Chopra, D. (2010). *Journey into healing: Awakening the wisdom within you*. New York: Three Rivers Press.

Chopra, D., & Stern. E. (2017). *The healing breath–App with Deepak Chopra, MD & Eddie Stern* [Video file]. Accessed at www.youtube.com/watch?v=TA_KnwxZqR0 on August 5, 2019.

Clark, S. P., & Marinak, B. A. (2010). The attributes of kindness: Using narrative and expository texts to confront the "casualty of empathy." *International Journal of Learning, 17*(8), 295–305.

Cohen, G. L., Garcia, J., Apfel, N., & Master, A. (2006). Reducing the racial achievement gap: A social-psychological intervention. *Science, 313*(5791), 1307–1310.

Cohen, J., McCabe, L., Michelli, N. M., & Pickeral, T. (2009). School climate: Research, policy, practice, and teacher education. *Teachers College Record, 111*(1), 180–193.

Cole, S., O'Brien, J. G., & Gadd, M. G., Ristuccia, J., Wallace, D. L., & Gregory, M. (2005). *Helping traumatized children learn: A report and policy agenda*. Accessed at https://traumasensitiveschools.org/wp-content/uploads/2013/06/Helping-Traumatized-Children-Learn.pdf on July 5, 2019.

Collaborative for Academic, Social, and Emotional Learning. (2012). *Effective social and emotional learning programs: Preschool and elementary school edition*. Accessed at https://casel.org/wp-content/uploads/2016/01/2013-casel-guide-1.pdf on October 10, 2018.

Collaborative for Academic, Social, and Emotional Learning. (2018). *Our initiative*. Accessed at https://measuringsel.casel.org/our-initiative on October 1, 2018.

Connell, G. (2016, September 15). *10 ways to build relationships with students this year* [Blog post]. Accessed at www.scholastic.com/teachers/blog-posts/genia-connell/10-ways-build-relationships-students-year-1 on January 5, 2017.

Connolly, K. (2015). 10 reasons Angela Merkel is the most powerful woman in the world. *The Guardian*. Accessed at www.theguardian.com/world/2015/jan/07/ten-reasons-angela-merkel-germany-chancellor-world-most-powerful-woman on January 27, 2019.

Connor, K. M., & Davidson, J. R. T. (2003). Development of a new resilience scale: The Connor-Davidson Resilience Scale (CD-RISC). *Depression and Anxiety, 18*(2), 76–82.

Cook, A., Spinazzola, J., Ford, J., Lanktree, C., Blaustein, M., Cloitre, M., et al. (2017). Complex trauma in children and adolescents. *Psychiatric Annals, 35*(5), 390–398.

Cosley, B. J., McCoy, S. K., Saslow, L. R., & Epel, E. S. (2010). Is compassion for others stress buffering? Consequences of compassion and social support for physiological reactivity to stress. *Journal of Experimental Social Psychology, 46*(5), 816–823.

Costa, A. L., & Kallick, B. (2000). *Discovering and exploring habits of mind: A developmental series, Book 1*. Alexandria, VA: Association for Supervision and Curriculum Development.

Costello, E. J., Erkanli, A., Fairbank, J. A., & Angold, A. (2002). The prevalence of potentially traumatic events in childhood and adolescence. *Journal of Traumatic Stress, 15*(2), 99–112.

Coughlan, S. (2018). 2018 "worst year for US school shootings". *British Broadcasting Company*. Accessed at www.bbc.com/news/business-46507514 on September 9, 2019.

Courtois, C. A., & Ford, J. D. (2012). *Treatment of complex trauma: A sequenced, relationship-based approach*. New York: Guilford.

Cowie, H., & Oztug, O. (2008). Pupils' perceptions of safety at school. *Pastoral Care in Education: An International Journal of Personal, Social and Emotional Development, 26*(2), 59–67.

Cox, J. (n.d.). *Teaching strategies to build student confidence*. Accessed at www.teachhub.com/teaching-strategies-build-student-confidence on August 5, 2018.

Cozolino, L. (2013). *The social neuroscience of education: Optimizing attachment and learning in the classroom*. New York: Norton.

Crew, L. (1991). *Children of the river*. New York: Laurel-Leaf.

Crooks, C. V., Burleigh, D., Snowshoe, A., Lapp, A., Hughes, R., & Sisco, A. (2015). A case study of culturally relevant school-based programming for First Nations youth: Improved relationships, confidence and leadership, and school success. *Advances in School Mental Health Promotion, 8*(4), 216–230.

Crosnoe, R. (2005). Double disadvantage or signs of resilience? The elementary school contexts of children from Mexican immigrant families. *American Educational Research Journal, 42*(2), 269–303.

Csikszentmihalyi, M., Rathunde, K., & Whalen, S. (1993). *Talented teenagers: The roots of success and failure*. New York: Cambridge University Press.

Cuddy, A. (2014). *Amy Cuddy: 30 seconds on power poses* [Video file]. Accessed at www.youtube.com /watch?v=C4ACeoqEjeA on November 18, 2019.

Cupp, T. M. (2015). *Angela Merkel: First woman chancellor of Germany*. New York: Cavendish Square.

Currie, L. (2014). *Why teaching kindness in schools is essential to reduce bullying*. Accessed at www.edutopia .org/blog/teaching-kindness-essential-reduce-bullying-lisa-currie on November 11, 2019.

Dalai Lama. (2010). Our need for love [Blog post]. *Heal Your Life*. Accessed at www.healyourlife.com /our-need-for-love on September 9, 2019.

Darder, A., Baltodano, M., & Torres, R. D. (Eds.). (2003). *The critical pedagogy reader*. New York: Routledge.

Dasa, G. P. (2017). 5 traits of a mindful leader [Blog post]. *Workhuman*. Accessed at https://resources .globoforce.com/globoforce-blog/5-traits-of-a-mindful-leader on October 5, 2018.

Davenport, M. (2018). *Mindfulness in high school*. Accessed at www.edutopia.org/article/mindfulness -high-school on January 29, 2019.

Davidson, R. J., & Begley, S. (2013). *The emotional life of your brain: How to change the way you think, feel, and live—and how you can change them*. London: Penguin.

de Vet, H. C. W., Mokkink, L. B., Mosmuller, D. G., & Terwee, C. B. (2017). Spearman-Brown prophecy formula and Cronbach's alpha: Different faces of reliability and opportunities for new applications [Abstract]. *Journal of Clinical Epidemiology, 85*, 45–49. Accessed at www.ncbi.nlm.nih.gov /pubmed/28342902 on September 13, 2019.

Deci, E. L., Ryan, R. M., Schultz, P. P., & Niemiec, C. P. (2015). Being aware and functioning fully: Mindfulness and interest taking within self-determination theory. In K. W. Brown, J. D. Creswell, & R. M. Ryan (Eds.), *Handbook of mindfulness: Theory, research, and practice* (pp. 112–129).

Dee, T. S., & Jacobs, B. A. (2010.). *The impact of No Child Left Behind on students, teachers, and schools*. Washington, DC: Brookings Institution. Accessed at www.brookings.edu/wp-content/uploads/2010 /09/2010b_bpea_dee.pdf on January 5, 2018.

Demirtaş, A. S., Yildiz, M. A., & Baytemir, K. (2017). General belongingness and basic psychological needs as predictors of self-esteem in adolescents. *Journal of Educational Sciences & Psychology, 7*(2), 48–58.

Deresiewicz, W. (2014). *Excellent sheep: The miseducation of the American elite and the way to a meaningful life*. New York: Free Press.

Dewey, J. (2007). *Experience and education*. New York: Simon & Schuster. (Originally published 1938)

DeWitt, P. M. (2017). *School climate: Leading with collective efficacy*. Thousand Oaks, CA: Corwin.

Diamond, A., & Lee, K. (2011). Interventions shown to aid executive function development in children 4 to 12 years old. *Science, 333*(6045), 959–964.

DiCara, C., O'Halloran, S., Williams, L., & Brooks, C. (2009). *Maine youth suicide prevention program*. Augusta, ME: Maine Center for Disease and Prevention.

Diener, E., & Seligman, M. E. (2004). Beyond money: Toward an economy of well-being. *Psychological Science in the Public Interest, 5*(1), 1–31.

Duckworth, A. (2016). *Grit: The power of passion and perseverance.* New York: Simon & Schuster.

Duckworth, A. L., Peterson, C., Matthews, M. D., & Kelly, D. R. (2007). Grit: Perseverance and passion for long-term goals. *Journal of Personality and Social Psychology, 92*(6), 1087–1101.

Duckworth, A. L., & Yeager, D. S. (2015). Measurement matters: Assessing personal qualities other than cognitive ability for educational purposes. *Educational Researcher, 44*(4), 237–251.

Duncan, G. J., & Murnane, R. J. (2014). *Restoring opportunity: The crisis of inequality and the challenge for American education.* Cambridge, MA: Harvard Education Press.

Dunfield, K., Kuhlmeier, V. A., O'Connell, L., & Kelley, E. (2011). Examining the diversity of prosocial behavior: Helping, sharing, and comforting in infancy. *Infancy, 16*(3), 227–247.

Dunn, B. D., Evans, D., Makarova, D., White, J., & Clark, L. (2012). Gut feelings and the reaction to perceived inequity: The interplay between bodily responses, regulation, and perception shapes the rejection of unfair offers on the ultimatum game. *Cognitive, Affective, & Behavioral Neuroscience, 12*(3), 419–429.

Dunn, B. D., Galton, H. C., Morgan, R., Evans, D., Oliver, C., Meyer, M., et al. (2010). Listening to your heart: How interoception shapes emotion experience and intuitive decision making. *Psychological Science, 21*(12), 1835–1844.

Dunn, E. W., Akin, L. B., & Norton, M. I. (2008). Spending money on others promotes happiness. *Science, 319*(5870), 1687–1688.

Durlak, J. A., & DuPre, E. P. (2008). Implementation matters: A review of research on the influence of implementation on program outcomes and the factors affecting implementation. *American Journal of Community Psychology, 41*(3–4), 327–350.

Durlak, J. A., Weissberg, R. P., Dymnicki, A. B., Taylor, R. B., & Schellinger, K. B. (2011). Impact of enhancing students' social and emotional learning: A meta-analysis of school-based universal interventions. *Child Development, 82*(1), 405–432.

Dusenbury, L., & Yoder, N. (2017). *The collaborating states initiative (CSI) recommended process for developing state policies and guidelines to support social and emotional learning.* Accessed at https://files.eric.ed.gov/fulltext/ED581611.pdf on April 20, 2019.

Dweck, C. S. (2010). Even geniuses work hard. *Educational Leadership, 68*(1), 16–20.

Dweck, C. S. (2015). Growth mindset, revisited. *Education Week, 35*(5), 20–24.

Dweck, C. S. (2016). *Mindset: The new psychology of success.* New York: Ballantine. (Original work published 2006)

Dylan, B. (1985). [Liner notes]. In *Biograph* [Album]. New York: Columbia Records.

East, P., & Hokoda, A. (2015). Risk and protective factors for sexual and dating violence victimization: A longitudinal, prospective study of Latino and African American adolescents. *Journal of Youth and Adolescence, 44*(6), 1288–1300.

Eisenberg, M. E., Gower, A. L., McMorris, B. J., Rider, G. N., & Coleman, E. (2018). Emotional distress, bullying victimization, and protective factors among transgender and gender diverse adolescents in city, suburban, town, and rural locations. *The Journal of Rural Health, 35*(2), 270–281.

Elementary School Counseling. (2012). *School-wide programs.* Accessed at www.elementaryschool counseling.org/school-wide-programs.html on January 27, 2019.

Elias, M. J., Zins, J. E., Weissberg, R. P., Frey, K. S., Greenberg, M. T., Haynes N. M., et al. (1997). *Promoting social and emotional learning: Guidelines for educators.* Alexandria, VA: Association for Supervision and Curriculum Development.

Elkington, J. (2011). *Ray Anderson, sustainable business pioneer, dies aged 77.* Accessed at www.theguardian.com/sustainable-business/blog/ray-anderson-dies-interface-john-elkington-tribute on November 18, 2019.

Emerson, R. W. (n.d.). *BrainyQuote*. Accessed at www.brainyquote.com/quotes/ralph_waldo_emerson _104751 on February 3, 2020.

Erb, C. S., & Erb, P. (2018). Making amends: A restorative justice approach to classroom behavior. *Teacher Educators' Journal, 11*, 91–104.

Estrada, J. N., Jr., Gilreath, T. D., Sanchez, C. Y., & Astor, R. A. (2017). Associations between school violence, military connection, and gang membership in California secondary schools. *American Journal of Orthopsychiatry, 87*(4), 443–451.

Evans-Campbell, T. (2008). Historical trauma in American Indian/Native Alaska communities: A multilevel framework for exploring impacts on individuals, families, and communities. *Journal of Interpersonal Violence, 23*(3), 316–338.

Every Student Succeeds Act of 2015, Pub. L. No. 114-95 20 U.S.C. § 1177 (2015).

Farmer, T. W., Hall, C. M., Petrin, R., Hamm, J. V., & Dadisman, K. (2010). Evaluating the impact of a multicomponent intervention model on teachers' awareness of social networks at the beginning of middle school in rural communities. *School Psychology Quarterly, 25*(2), 94–106.

Farmer, T. W., Lines, M., & Hamm, J. V. (2011). Revealing the invisible hand: The role of teachers in children's peer experiences. *Journal of Applied Developmental Psychology, 32*(5), 247–256.

Federal Bureau of Investigation. (2018). *2018 hate crime statistics: Incidents and offenses*. Accessed at https://ucr.fbi.gov/hate-crime/2018/topic-pages/incidents-and-offenses on November 15, 2019.

Feeding America. (2017). *Child hunger fact sheet*. Accessed at www.feedingamerica.org/hunger-in-america /child-hunger-facts on November 2, 2019.

Felliti, V. J., Anda, R. F., Nordenberg, D., Williamson, D. F., Spitz, A. M., Edwards, V., et al. (1998). Relationship of childhood abuse and household dysfunction to many of the leading causes of death in adults: The adverse childhood experiences (ACE) study. *American Journal of Preventive Medicine, 14*(4), 245–258.

Feuerstein, R., Miller, R., Hoffman, M. B., Rand, Y., Mintzker, Y., & Jensen, M. R. (1981). Cognitive modifiability in adolescence: Cognitive structure and the effects of intervention. *The Journal of Special Education, 15*(2), 269–287.

Flanders, J. (2015, March). The KindMind project. *Wow!Ed*. Accessed at http://archive.constantcontact .com/fs126/1103736720061/archive/1120333810216.html on November 2, 2019.

Flook, L., Goldberg, S. B., Pinger, L., & Davidson, R. J. (2015). Promoting prosocial behavior and self-regulation skills in children through a mindfulness-based Kindness Curriculum. *Developmental Psychology, 51*(1), 44–51.

Flook, L., Smalley, S. L., Kitil, M. J., Galla, B. M., Kaiser-Greenland, S., Locke, J., et al. (2010). Effects of mindful awareness practices on executive functions in elementary school children. *Journal of Applied School Psychology, 26*(1), 70–95.

Foucault, M. (1991). *The Foucault effect: Studies in governmentality*. Chicago: University of Chicago Press.

Fowler, J. H., & Christakis, N. A. (2010). Cooperative behavior cascades in human social networks. *Proceedings of the National Academy of Sciences, 107*(12), 5334–5338.

Frank, J. L., Bose, B., & Schrobenhauser-Clonan, A. (2014). Effectiveness of a school-based yoga program on adolescent mental health, stress coping strategies, and attitudes toward violence: Findings from a high-risk sample. *Journal of Applied School Psychology, 30*(1), 29–49.

Frank, J. L., Kohler, K., Peal, A., & Bose, B. (2017). Effectiveness of a school-based yoga program on adolescent mental health and school performance: Findings from a randomized controlled trial. *Mindfulness, 8*(3), 544–553.

Frazier, S. N., & Vela, J. (2014). Dialectical behavior therapy for the treatment of anger and aggressive behavior: A review. *Aggression and Violent Behavior, 19*(2), 156–163.

Fredrickson, B. (2009). *Positivity: Top-notch research reveals the 3 to 1 ratio that will change your life*. New York: Three Rivers Press.

Fredrickson, B. L., Cohn, M. A., Coffey, K. A., Pek, J., & Finkel, S. M. (2008). Open hearts build lives: Positive emotions, induced through loving-kindness meditation, build consequential personal resources. *Journal of Personality and Social Psychology, 95*(5), 1045.

Fredrickson, B. L., Grewen, K. M., Coffey, K. A., Algoe, S. B., Firestine, A. M., Arevalo, J. M., et al. (2013). A functional genomic perspective on human well-being. *Proceedings of the National Academy of Sciences, 110*(33), 13684–13689.

Freire, P. (1970a). Cultural action and conscientization. *Harvard Educational Review, 40*(3), 452–477.

Freire, P. (1970b). *Pedagogy of the oppressed.* New York: Herder & Herder.

Freire, P. (1996). *Pedagogy of the oppressed* (Rev. ed.). New York: Continuum.

Gaither, C. (2014). Is it courage or something else? [Blog post]. *Clark Gaither.* Accessed at www.clark gaither.com/is-it-courage-or-something-else on August 12, 2019.

Galassi, J. (2017). *Strengths-based school counseling: Promoting student development and achievement.* New York: Routledge.

Garfinkel, S. N., Tiley, C., O'Keeffe, S., Harrison, N. A., Seth, A. K., & Critchley, H. D. (2016). Discrepancies between dimensions of interoception in autism: Implications for emotion and anxiety. *Biological Psychology, 114,* 117–126.

Gasson, S., & Donaldson, J. (2018). *Peer and vicarious framing, problematization, and situated learning in online professional masters course.* Accessed at https://scholarspace.manoa.hawaii.edu/bitstream/10125 /50132/1/paper0245.pdf on December 10, 2018.

Gazipura, A. (2009). *Meditation and self-compassion: A proposed relationship and mechanisms of influence.* Published dissertation, Pacific Graduate School of Psychology, Palo Alto, CA.

Geisler, F. C., Kubiak, T., Siewert, K., & Weber, H. (2013). Cardiac vagal tone is associated with social engagement and self-regulation. *Biological Psychology, 93*(2), 279–286.

Gemütlichkeit. (n.d.). *Wikipedia.* Accessed at https://en.wikipedia.org/wiki/Gem%C3%BCtlichkeit on December 15, 2018.

Geraci, J., Palmerini, M., Cirillo, P., & McDougald, V. (2017). *What teens want from their schools.* Washington DC: Thomas B. Fordham Institute.

Gest, S. D., Madill, R. A., Zadzora, K. M., Miller, A. M., & Rodkin, P. C. (2014). Teacher management of elementary classroom social dynamics: Associations with changes in student adjustment. *Journal of Emotional and Behavioral Disorders, 22*(2), 107–118.

Gilbert, P. (2009). Introducing compassion-focused therapy. *Advances in Psychiatric Treatment, 15*(3), 199–208.

Gilbert, P. (2010). *Training our minds in, with and for compassion: An introduction to concepts and compassion-focused exercises.* Accessed at www.getselfhelp.co.uk/docs/GILBERT-COMPASSION -HANDOUT.pdf on August 12, 2019.

Gilbert, P. (Ed.). (2017). *Compassion: Concepts, research, and applications.* New York: Routledge.

Gilbert, P., McEwan, K., Matos, M., & Rivis, A. (2011). Fears of compassion: Development of three self-report measures. *Psychology and Psychotherapy, 84*(3), 239–255.

Gladwell, M. (2008). *Outliers: The story of success.* New York: Little, Brown and Company.

Goetz, J. L., Keltner, D., & Simon-Thomas, E. (2010). Compassion: An evolutionary analysis and empirical review. *Psychological Bulletin, 136*(3), 351–374.

Goleman, D. (n.d.). *Social & emotional learning.* Accessed at www.danielgoleman.info/topics/social -emotional-learning on December 30, 2019.

Goleman, D. (2006). *Emotional intelligence: Why it can matter more than intelligence.* New York: Bantam Press.

Goleman, D., & Boyatzis, R. E. (2008). Social intelligence and the biology of leadership. *Harvard Business Review, 86*(9), 74–81.

Goleman, D., Boyatzis, R. E., & McKee, A. (2002). *The new leaders: Transforming the art of leadership into the science of results*. London: Little, Brown.

Golmohammdai, K., & Kuusilehto-Awale, L. (2013, December). International interconnected communities of caring, part I. *Wow!Ed*. Accessed at http://archive.constantcontact.com/fs126 /1103736720061/archive/1115877831363.html on October 20, 2019.

Golmohammdai, K., & Kuusilehto-Awale, L. (2014, January). International interconnected communities of caring, part II. *Wow!Ed*. Accessed at http://archive.constantcontact.com/fs193/1103192011285 /archive/1111826480457.html on October 20, 2019.

Goss, P., & Sonnemann, J. (2017). *Engaging students: Creating classrooms that improve learning*. Accessed at https://grattan.edu.au/wp-content/uploads/2017/02/Engaging-students-creating-classrooms-that -improve-learning.pdf on February 3, 2020.

Grant, M. (2018). *Teaching patience, kindness, and identity through Native American children's books*. Accessed at www.edimprovement.org/2018/04/teaching-patience-kindness-identity-native-american- childrens-books on August 12, 2019.

Grant, M., & Mason, C. (2017, September). Innovations in school counseling. *Wow!Ed*. Accessed at https://myemail.constantcontact.com/News-from-Center-for-Educational-Improvement .html?soid=1103736720061&aid=zetpSExtGQY on November 2, 2019.

Grauer, S. (2016). *Fearless teaching: Collected stories*. Roslyn Heights, NY: Alternative Education Resource Organization.

Gray, P. (2014). *Risky play: Why children love it and need it*. Accessed at www.psychologytoday.com/us /blog/freedom-learn/201404/risky-play-why-children-love-it-and-need-it on November 18, 2019.

Greater Good in Action. (n.d.). *Loving-kindness meditation*. Accessed at https://ggia.berkeley.edu/practice /loving_kindness_meditation on August 11, 2019.

Greenberg, M. (2012). *The six attributes of courage: Quotes and exercises to help you be your best and bravest self*. Accessed at www.psychologytoday.com/blog/the-mindful-self-express/201208/the-six-attributes -courage on August 8, 2018.

Greenberg, M. T., Domitrovich, C. E., Weissberg, R. P., & Durlak, J. A. (2017). Social and emotional learning as a public health approach to education. *The Future of Children, 27*(1), 13–32.

Greenberg, M. T., & Harris, A. R. (2011). Nurturing mindfulness in children and youth: Current state of research. *Child Development Perspectives, 6*(2), 161–166.

Greene, R. W. (2011). Collaborative problem solving can transform school discipline. *Phi Delta Kappan, 93*(2), 25–29.

Greenleaf, R. K. (2002). *Servant leadership: A journey into the nature of legitimate power and greatness* (25th anniversary ed.). New York: Paulist Press.

Grossmann, I., Sahdra, B. K., & Ciarrochi, J. (2016). *A heart and a mind: Self-distancing facilitates the association between heart rate variability, and wise reasoning*. Accessed at www.ncbi.nlm.nih.gov/pmc /articles/PMC4824766 on August 12, 2019.

Guillemets, T. (n.d.). Quotations about courage. *The Quote Garden*. Accessed at www.quotegarden.com /courage.html on November 17, 2019.

Haidt, J. (2005). *Wired to be inspired*. Accessed at https://greatergood.berkeley.edu/article/item/wired_to _be_inspired on December 3, 2018.

Hamilton, K., Mancuso, V., Mohammed, S., Tesler, R., & McNeese, M. (2017). Skilled and unaware: The interactive effects of team cognition, team metacognition, and task confidence on team performance. *Journal of Cognitive Engineering and Decision Making, 11*(4), 382–395.

Hanson, R. (2018). *Resilient: How to grow an unshakable core of calm, strength, and happiness*. New York: Harmony Books.

Happily (n.d.). *The science-based secrets to boosting your confidence*. Accessed at www.happify.com/hd/boost -your-self-confidence-infographic on April 10, 2019.

Hargreaves, A., Moore, S., Fink, D., Brayman, C., & White, R. (2003). *Succeeding leaders? A study of principal rotation and succession.* Toronto: Ontario Principals' Council.

Harvard University Center on the Developing Child. (n.d.a). *Resilience.* Accessed at https://developing child.harvard.edu/science/key-concepts/resilience on February 6, 2018.

Harvard University Center on the Developing Child. (n.d.b). *Toxic stress.* Accessed at https://developing child.harvard.edu/science/key-concepts/toxic-stress on July 5, 2019.

Hastürk, G., & Dogan, A. (2016). Effect of triadic teaching approach in some environmental subjects: Prospective science teachers practice. *International Journal of Environmental and Science Education, 11*(5), 893–905.

Hatalsky, L., & Johnson, S. (2015). *Did No Child Left Behind work?* Accessed at www.thirdway.org/memo /did-no-child-left-behind-work on March 5, 2017.

Hattie, J. (2009). *Visible learning: A synthesis of over 800 meta-analyses relating to achievement.* New York: Routledge.

Hattie, J. (2012). *Visible learning for teachers: Maximizing impact on learning.* New York: Routledge.

Hawkins, J. D., Catalano, R. F., Kosterman, R., Abbott, R., & Hill, K. G. (1999). Preventing adolescent health-risk behaviors by strengthening protection during childhood. *Archives of Pediatric Adolescent Medicine, 153*(3), 226–234.

HeartMath Institute. (n.d.). *Home.* Accessed at www.heartmath.org/resources/solutions-for-stress /overcoming-anxiety on July 5, 2019.

Heller, L., & LaPierre, A. (2012). *Healing developmental trauma: How early trauma affects self-regulation, self-image, and the capacity for relationship.* Berkeley, CA: North Atlantic Books.

Hendrickson, C. M., Neylan, T. C., Na, B., Regan, M., Zhang, Q., & Cohen, B. E. (2013). Lifetime trauma exposure and prospective cardiovascular events and all-cause mortality: findings from the heart and soul study. *Psychosomatic Medicine, 75*(9), 849–855.

Hepach, R., Vaish, A., & Tomasello, M. (2012). Young children are intrinsically motivated to see others helped. *Psychological Science, 23*(9), 967–972.

Hidi, S., & Renninger, K. A. (2006). The four-phase model of interest development. *Educational Psychologist, 41*(2), 111–127.

Hilliard, A. G. (1992). Behavioral style, culture, and teaching and learning. *The Journal of Negro Education, 61*(3), 370–377.

Holistic Life Foundation. (2016). *Mindful moment program.* Accessed at https://hlfinc.org/programs -services/mindful-moment-program on January 28, 2019.

Holt-Lunstad, J., Smith, T. B., & Layton, J. B. (2010). Social relationships and mortality risk: A meta-analytic review. *PLoS Medicine, 7*(7), e1000316.

Hornsveld, R. H., Kraaimaat, F. W., Muris, P., Zwets, A. J., & Kanters, T. (2015). Aggression Replacement Training for violent young men in a forensic psychiatric outpatient clinic. *Journal of Interpersonal Violence, 30*(18), 3174–3191.

Hoy, W. K., & Tarter, C. J. (2011). Positive psychology and educational administration: An optimistic research agenda. *Educational Administration Quarterly, 47*(3), 427–445.

Huang, K. Y., Calzada, E., Cheng, S., & Brotman, L. M. (2008, November). *Health disparities in children of immigrants and non-immigrants.* Symposium conducted at the On New Shores conference; Guelph, Canada.

Huang, K. Y., Cheng, S., & Theise, R. (2013). School contexts as social determinants of child health: Current practices and implications for future public health practice. *Public Health Report, 128*(Suppl. 3), 21–28.

Hutcherson, C. A., Seppala, E. M., & Gross, J. J. (2008). Loving-kindness meditation increases social connectedness. *Emotion, 8*(5), 720–724.

Inam, H. (2012). Breathe. Meditate. Lead. Ten ways mindfulness practice can make us better leaders [Blog post]. *Transformational Leadership.* Accessed at www.transformleaders.tv/breathe-meditate-lead -ten-ways-mindfulness-practice-can-make-us-better-leaders on September 13, 2019.

Ingraham, S. (2018). Teaching compassion to students and why it's important [Blog post]. *My Guru.* Accessed at www.myguruedge.com/our-thinking/myguru-blog/teaching-compassion-to-students on August 12, 2019.

Institute for Digital Research and Education. (n.d.). *What does Cronbach's alpha mean?* Accessed at https://stats.idre.ucla.edu/spss/faq/what-does-cronbachs-alpha-mean on September 13, 2019.

Jackson, Y. (2005). Unlocking the potential of African American students: Keys to reversing underachievement. *Theory Into Practice, 44*(3), 203–210.

Jackson, Y. (2011). *The pedagogy of confidence: Inspiring high intellectual performance in urban schools.* New York: Teachers College Press.

Jackson, Y., & McDermott, V. (2012). *Aim high, achieve more: How to transform urban schools through fearless leadership.* Alexandria, VA: Association for Supervision and Curriculum Development.

Jackson, Y., & McDermott, V. (2015). *Unlocking student potential: How do I identify and activate student strengths?* Alexandria, VA: Association for Supervision and Curriculum Development.

Jarden, A., Jose, P., Kashdan, T., Simpson, O., McLachlan, K., & Mackenzie, A. (2012). *International wellbeing study* [Unpublished raw data]. Accessed at www.wellbeingstudy.com on September 13, 2019.

Jazaieri, H., Jinpa, G., McGonigal, K., Rosenberg, E., Finkelstein, J., Simon-Thomas, E., et al. (2012). Enhancing compassion: A randomized controlled trial of a Compassion Cultivation Training program. *Journal of Happiness Studies, 14*(4), 1113–1126.

Jennings, P. A., Snowberg, K. E., Coccia, M. A., & Greenberg, M. T. (2011). Improving classroom learning environments by cultivating awareness and resilience in education (CARE): Results of two pilot studies. *The Journal of Classroom Interaction, 46*(1), 37–48.

Jiang, Y., Granja, M. R., & Koball, H. (2017). *Basic facts about low-income children.* Accessed at www.nccp.org/publications/pub_1170.html on January 31, 2018.

Jiang, Y., & Klietman, S. (2015). Metacognition and motivation: Links between confidence, self-protection and self-enhancement. *Learning and Individual Differences, 37*, 222–230.

Jones, S. M., & Doolittle, E. J. (2017). Social and emotional learning: Introducing the issue. *The Future of Children, 27*(1), 3–11.

Juvenile Justice Advisory Group. (n.d.). *Collaborative and proactive solutions.* Accessed at www.maine.gov /corrections/jjag/CPS.htm on June 10, 2019.

Kabat-Zinn, J. (2003). Mindfulness-based interventions in context: Past, present, and future. *Clinical Psychology: Science and Practice, 10*(2), 144–156.

Kang, D.-H., Jo, H. J., Jung, W. H., Kim, S. H., Jung, Y.-H., Choi, C.-H., et al. (2013). The effect of meditation on brain structure: cortical thickness mapping and diffusion tensor imaging. *Social Cognitive and Affective Neuroscience, 8*(1), 27–33.

Kanold, T. (2017). *Heart! Fully forming your professional life as a teacher and leader.* Bloomington, IN: Solution Tree Press.

Kasperski, R., Shany, M., & Katzir, T. (2016). The role of RAN and reading rate in predicting reading self-concept. *Reading and Writing: An Interdisciplinary Journal, 29*(1), 117–136.

Kaunhoven, R. J., & Dorjee, D. (2017). How does mindfulness modulate self-regulation in pre-adolescent children? An integrative neurocognitive review. *Neuroscience and Biobehavioral Reviews, 74*(A), 163–184.

Kay, K., & Shipman, C. (2014). *The confidence gap.* Accessed at www.theatlantic.com/magazine/archive /2014/05/the-confidence-gap/359815 on July 5, 2019.

Kay, K., & Shipman, C. (2018). *The confidence code for girls: Taking risks, messing up, and becoming your amazingly imperfect, totally powerful self.* New York: HarperCollins.

Kearney, W. S., Kelsey, C., & Herrington, D. (2013). Mindful leaders in highly effective schools: A mixed-method application of Hoy's M-scale. *Educational Management Administration and Leadership*, *41*(3), 316–335.

Kelder, S. H., Springer, A. S., Barroso, C. S., Smith, C. L., Sanchez, E., Ranjit, N., et al. (2009). Implementation of Texas Senate Bill 19 to increase physical activity in elementary schools. *Journal of Public Health Policy*, *30*(Suppl. 1), 221–247.

The Ken Blanchard Companies. (n.d.). *Home*. Accessed at www.kenblanchard.com on July 5, 2019.

Khalsa, S. (n.d.). *Yoga to balance the head and heart*. Accessed at www.3ho.org/articles/yoga-balance-head -and-heart on July 5, 2019.

Khalsa, S. B. S., & Gould, J. (2012). *Your brain on yoga*. New York: RosettaBooks.

Kidder, T. (1989). *Among schoolchildren*. Boston: Houghton Mifflin.

Kim, J. W., Kim, S. E., Kim, J. J., Jeong, B., Park, C. H., Son, A. R., et al. (2009). Compassionate attitude towards others' suffering activates the mesolimbic neural system. *Neuropsychologia*, *47*(10), 2073–2081.

Kinser, P. A., Goehler, L. E., & Taylor, A. G. (2012). How might yoga help depression? A neurobiological perspective. *Explore: The Journal of Science and Healing*, *8*(2), 118–126.

Kleitman, S., & Gibson, J. (2011). Metacognitive beliefs, self-confidence and primary learning environment of sixth grade students. *Learning and Individual Differences*, *21*(9), 728–735.

Koester, M. (2017, May 16). Heart rate variability: The amazing marker for understanding our body, health, and fitness [Blog post]. *Mark Koester*. Accessed at www.markwk.com/hrv-for-beginners.html on October 31, 2019.

Kohler-Evans, P., & Barnes, C. D. (2015). Compassion: How do you teach it? *Journal of Education and Practice*, *6*(11), 33–36.

Konrath, S. H., & Brown, S. (2013). The effects of giving on givers. In M. L. Newman & N. A. Roberts (Eds.). *Health and social relationships: The good, the bad, and the complicated* (pp. 39–64). Washington, DC: American Psychological Association.

Konrath, S., Fuhrel-Forbis, A., Lou, A., & Brown, S. (2012). Motives for volunteering are associated with mortality risk in older adults. *Health Psychology*, *31*(1), 87–96.

Koshal. (2011). Difference between courage and bravery [Blog post]. *Difference Between*. Accessed at www.differencebetween.com/difference-between-courage-and-vs-bravery on July 5, 2019.

Kouzes, J., & Posner, B. (2015). *Extraordinary leadership in Australia and New Zealand: The five practices that create great workplaces*. Melbourne, Australia: Wiley.

Kraftsow, G. (2002). *Yoga for transformation: Ancient practices for healing the body, mind and heart*. New York: Penguin Press.

Krull, E. (2018). Depression and letting go of negative thoughts [Blog post]. *PsychCentral*. Accessed at https://psychcentral.com/lib/depression-and-letting-go-of-negative-thoughts on November 18, 2019.

Kubzansky, L. D., Koenen, K. C., Spiro, A., Vokonas, P. S., & Sparrow, D. (2007). Prospective study of posttraumatic stress disorder symptoms and coronary heart disease in the Normative Aging Study. *Archives of General Psychiatry*, *64*(1), 109–116.

Lantieri, L., & Goleman, D. (2008). *Building emotional intelligence: Techniques to cultivate inner resilience in children*. Boulder, CO: Sounds True.

Lassiter, C. J. (2016). *The 4 types of everyday courage*. Accessed at http://corwin-connect.com/2017/01/4 -types-everyday-courage on August 5, 2018.

Lazar, S. W., Kerr, C. E., Wasserman, R. H., Gray, J. R., Greve, D. N., Treadway, M. T., et al. (2005). Meditation experience is associated with increased cortical thickness. *NeuroReport*, *16*(17), 1893–1897.

Learners Edge. (2016). *4 ways to create a classroom community* [Blog post]. Accessed at www.learnersedge .com/blog/4-ways-to-create-a-classroom-community on January 15, 2019.

Levine, P. A. (2008). *Healing trauma: A pioneering program for restoring the wisdom of the body*. Boulder, CO: Sounds True.

Lewis, K. R. (2015). *What if everything you knew about disciplining kids was wrong?* Accessed at www.motherjones.com/politics/2015/07/schools-behavior-discipline-collaborative-proactive-solutions-ross-greene on August 8, 2018.

Libbey, H. P. (2004). Measuring student relationships to school: Attachment, bonding, connectedness, and engagement. *Journal of School Health, 74*(7), 274–283.

Lindberg, S. (2018). *5 ways accepting your anxiety can make you more powerful*. Accessed at www.healthline.com/health/how-anxiety-can-make-you-more-powerful#1 on November 17, 2019.

Liu, C. H., & Robertson, P. J. (2012). Spirituality in the workplace: Theory and measurement. *Journal of Management Inquiry, 20*(1), 35–50.

Loizzo, J., Neale, M., & Wolf, E. J. (Eds.). (2017). *Advances in contemplative psychotherapy: Accelerating healing and transformation*. London: Taylor & Francis.

Lombardi, E. (2019). *20 most famous quotes from the Roman poet Ovid*. Accessed at www.thoughtco.com/quotes-from-the-roman-poet-ovid-740996 on November 16, 2019.

Loveless, T. (2015). *How well are American students learning?* Accessed at www.brookings.edu/wp-content/uploads/2016/06/2015-Brown-Center-Report_FINAL-3.pdf on January 25, 2019.

Luckner, A. E., & Pianta, R. C. (2011). Teacher-student interactions in fifth grade classrooms: Relations with children's peer behavior. *Journal of Applied Developmental Psychology, 32*(5), 257–266.

Lutz, A., Brefczynski-Lewis, J., Johnstone, T., & Davidson, R. J. (2008). Regulation of the neural circuitry of emotion by compassion meditation: Effects of meditative expertise. *PLoS ONE, 3*(3), e1897.

Lytle, S. L. (2008). *At last: Practitioner inquiry and the practice of teaching: Some thoughts on* Better. Accessed at http://repository.upenn.edu/gse_pubs/153 on December 10, 2018.

Maclellan, E. (2014). How might teachers enable learner self-confidence? A review study. *Educational Review, 66*(1), 59–74.

Magnuson, K., & Schindler, H. S. (2016). Parent programs in Pre-K through third grade. *The Future of Children, 26*(2), 207–221.

Mana, A., & Naveh, A. R. (2018). Facilitating a therapeutic environment: Creating a therapeutic community using a "wraparound" intervention program with at-risk families. *The Family Journal, 26*(3), 293–299.

Mandela, N. (2018). Mandela in his own words. *CNN*. Accessed at http://edition.cnn.com/2008/WORLD/africa/06/24/mandela.quotes on November 17, 2018.

Mankus, A. M., Aldao, A., Kerns, C., Mayville, E. W., & Mennin, D. S. (2013). Mindfulness and heart rate variability in individuals with high and low generalized anxiety symptoms. *Behaviour Research and Therapy, 51*(7), 386–391.

Manuello, J., Vercelli, U., Nani, A., Costa, T., & Cauda, F. (2016). Mindfulness meditation and consciousness: An integrative neuroscientific perspective. *Consciousness and Cognition, 40*, 67–78.

Marsh, M. (n.d.). *Mary Robinson: President of Ireland*. Accessed at www.britannica.com/biography/Mary-Robinson on November 17, 2019.

Marshall, D. S., Moutier, C., Rosenblum, L. B., Miara, C., & Posner, M. (2018). *After a suicide: A toolkit for schools* (2nd ed.). Waltham, MA: Education Development Center.

Marshbank, A. (2017). *Compassion as a classroom management tool*. Accessed at www.edutopia.org/article/compassion-classroom-management-tool on June 5, 2018.

Marshik, T, Ashton, P. T., & Algina, J. (2017). Teachers' and students' needs for autonomy, competence, and relatedness as predictors of students' achievement. *Social Psychology of Education, 20*(1), 39–67.

Martin, A. J. (2011). Courage in the classroom: Exploring a new framework predicting academic performance and engagement. *School Psychology Quarterly, 26*(2), 145–160.

Martin, G. R. R. (2016). *Game of thrones*. New York: Bantam.

Marturano, J. (n.d.). Research [Blog post]. *Institute for Mindful Leadership*. Accessed at https://instituteformindfulleadership.org/research on August 12, 2019.

Marturano, J. (2019, August). 3 ways to jump-start your day with mindful practice [Blog post]. *Institute for Mindful Leadership*. Accessed at https://instituteformindfulleadership.org/blog on October 18, 2019.

Marzano, J. A. (2017, December). Bringing grit into the classroom. *Wow!Ed*. Accessed at https://my email.constantcontact.com/News-from-Center-for-Educational-Improvement.html?soid=110373 6720061&aid=2TO7e1wPB2s on September 13, 2019.

Masia, B. (1964). *Taxonomy of educational objectives, book 2: Affective domain*. New York: Longman.

Maslow, A. H. (1943). A theory of human motivation. *Psychological Review, 50*(4), 370–396.

Maslow, A. H. (1971). *The farther reaches of human nature*. New York: Viking.

Mason, C. (2014). Adding compassion to the Common Core. *Wow!Ed*. Accessed at http://archive. constantcontact.com/fs126/1103736720061/archive/1117569797729.html on October 1, 2019.

Mason, C., & Banks, K. (2014). *Heart Beaming*. Alexandria, VA: Center for Educational Improvement.

Mason, C., Mullane, S., & Fitzpatrick, M. (2013). *Social emotional learning and compassion. Presentation and focus group*. Baltimore, MD: National Association of Elementary School Principals conference.

Mason, C., Rivers Murphy, M., Bergey, M., Mullane, S., Sawilowsky, S., & Asby, D. (2018). *Validation of the school compassionate culture analytic tool for educators (S-CCATE) supplement*. Vienna, VA: Center for Educational Improvement.

Mason, C., Rivers Murphy, M., & Jackson, Y. (2019). *Mindfulness practices: Cultivating heart centered communities where students focus and flourish*. Bloomington, IN: Solution Tree Press.

Mather, M., & Thayer, J. F. (2018). How heart rate variability affects emotion regulation brain networks. *Current Opinion in Behavioral Sciences, 19*, 98–104.

Mayo Clinic. (n.d.). *Core-strength exercises*. Accessed at www.mayoclinic.org/healthy-lifestyle/fitness/multi media/core-strength/sls-20076575?s=2 on July 5, 2019.

McClelland, M. M., & Cameron, C. E. (2011). Self-regulation and academic achievement in elementary school children. *New Directions for Child and Adolescent Development, 2011*(133), 29–44.

McCord, G. (n.d.). *Core curriculum*. Accessed at www.expandinglight.org/free/yoga-teacher/articles/gyandev /Engage-the-Core.pdf on July 5, 2019.

McCraty, R. (2003). *The energetic heart: Bioelectromagnetic interactions within and between people*. Boulder Creek, CA: HeartMath Institute.

McCraty, R. (2005). Enhancing emotional, social, and academic learning with heart rhythm coherence feedback. *Biofeedback, 33*(4), 130–134.

McCraty, R. (2015). The energetic heart: Biomagnetic communication within and between people. In P. J. Rosch (Ed.), *Bioelectromagnetic and subtle energy medicine* (2nd ed., pp. 125–140). New York: Taylor & Francis.

McCraty, R. (2018). *Coherence: The heart connection to personal, social and global health*. Accessed at www.thescienceofpsychotherapy.com/coherence-the-heart-connection-to-personal-social-and-global -health on July 30, 2019.

McCraty, R., & Royall, S. (2015). *Science of the heart: Exploring the role of the heart in human performance, volume 2*. Boulder Creek, CA: HeartMath Institute.

McCraty, R., & Schafer, S. B. (2016). Exploring dimensions of the media dream: Functional context in collective personae. In S. B. Schafer (Ed.), *Exploring the collective unconscious in the age of digital media* (pp. 1–39). Hershey, PA: Information Science Reference.

McCraty, R., & Zayas, M. A. (2014). *Cardiac coherence, self-regulation, autonomic stability, and psychosocial well-being*. Accessed at www.frontiersin.org/articles/10.3389/fpsyg.2014.01090/full on November 18, 2019.

McKown, C. (2015). Challenges and opportunities in the direct assessment of children's social and emotional comprehension. In J. A. Durlak, C. E. Domitrovich, R. P. Weissberg, & T. P. Gullotta (Eds.), *Handbook of social and emotional learning: Research and practice* (pp. 320–335). New York: Guilford Press.

McLeod, S. A. (2014). *Carl Rogers*. Accessed at www.simplypsychology.org/carl-rogers.html on March 30, 2018.

McMonigle, T. (2012). *Exploring parents' understanding and application of dialogic reading while teaching their preschoolers the social skills associated with courage, empathy, and love*. Accessed at http://purl.flvc .org/fsu/fd/FSU_migr_etd-5031 on April 15, 2018.

Mead, A. (1994). *Crossing the starlight bridge*. New York: Simon & Schuster.

Meeks, T. W., & Jeste, D. V. (2009). Neurobiology of wisdom: A literature overview. *Archives of General Psychology, 66*(4), 355–365.

Meier, D. (2003). *In schools we trust: Creating communities of learning in an era of testing and standardization*. Boston: Beacon Press.

Meiklejohn, J., Phillips, C., Freedman, M. L., Griffin, M. L., Biegel, G., Roach, A., et al. (2012). Integrating mindfulness training into K–12 education: Fostering the resilience of teachers and students. *Mindfulness, 3*(4), 291–307.

Mental Health Technology Transfer Center Network. (2019). *After a school tragedy . . . Readiness, response, recovery, & resources*. Accessed at https://mhttcnetwork.org/centers/mhttc-network-coordinating-office /after-school-tragedyreadiness-response-recovery-resources on April 10, 2019.

Michie, G. (2014). *On the importance of mirrors for students (and teachers)*. Accessed at www.huffington post.com/gregory-michie/on-the-importance-of-mirr_b_5604494.html on December 10, 2018.

Mikels, J. A., Maglio, S. J., Reed, A. E., & Kaplowitz, L. J. (2011). Should I go with my gut? Investigating the benefits of emotion-focused decision making. *Emotion, 11*(4), 743–753.

Miller, D. T. (1999). The norm of self-interest. *American Psychologist, 54*(12), 1053–1060.

Mindful Schools. (2016). *Our approach*. Accessed at www.mindfulschools.org/about-mindfulness/our -approach on January 20, 2018.

Mlodinow, L. (2018). *Elastic: Flexible thinking in a constantly changing world*. London: Penguin.

Mohammad, A. (2010). Relationship between self-esteem and academic achievement amongst pre-university students. *Journal of Applied Science, 10*(20), 2474–2477.

Mohseni, S. (2016). *Boss yourself—The way to victory through the power pose*. Accessed at www.gameplan-a .com/2016/08/boss-yourself-the-way-to-victory-through-the-power-pose on November 18, 2019.

Moll, J., Krueger, F., Zahn, R., Pardini, M., de Oliveira-Souza, R., & Grafman, J. (2006). Human fronto–mesolimbic networks guide decisions about charitable donation. *Proceedings of the National Academy of Sciences, 103*(42), 15623–15628.

Mongeua, L. (2016, May 18). Paper Tigers' documentary offers solutions to teaching traumatized kids [Blog post]. *Education Writers Association*. Accessed at www.ewa.org/blog-educated-reporter/paper-tigers -documentary-offers-solutions-teaching-traumatized-kids on September 30, 2017.

Moody, G., Cannings-John, R., Hood, K., Kemp, A., & Robling, M. (2018). *Establishing the international prevalence of self-reported child maltreatment: A systematic review by maltreatment type and gender*. Accessed at www.ncbi.nlm.nih.gov/pmc/articles/PMC6180456 on February 3, 2020.

Muhammad, A. (2009). *Transforming school culture: How to overcome staff division*. Bloomington, IN: Solution Tree Press.

Murdock, T. B., Anderman, L. H., & Hodge, S. A. (2000). Middle-grade predictors of students' motivation and behavior in high school. *Journal of Adolescent Research, 15*(3), 327–351.

Naimark, A. (n.d.). How to build self-confidence, strength, and resilience [Blog post]. *PsychCentral*. Accessed at https://psychcentral.com/blog/how-to-build-self-confidence-inner-strength-resilience on April 15, 2018.

National Center for Education Statistics. (2016). *The condition of education 2016*. Accessed at https://nces
.ed.gov/pubs2016/2016144.pdf on February 3, 2020.

National Center on Safe and Supportive Learning Environments. (n.d.). *School climate improvement*.
Accessed at https://safesupportivelearning.ed.gov/scirp/about on November 17, 2019.

National Scientific Council on the Developing Child. (2012). *Establishing a level foundation for life:
Mental health begins in early childhood*. Accessed at https://46y5eh11fhgw3ve3ytpwxt9r-wpengine
.netdna-ssl.com/wp-content/uploads/2008/05/Establishing-a-Level-Foundation-for-Life-Mental
-Health-Begins-in-Early-Childhood.pdf on September 13, 2019.

Nauret, R. (2018, August 8). Heart rate may influence decision-making [Blog post]. *PsychCentral*.
Accessed at https://psychcentral.com/news/2016/04/08/heart-rate-may-influence-decision-making
/101499.html on September 30, 2018.

Neff, K. D. (2003). The development and validation of a scale to measure self-compassion. *Self and
Identity*, 2, 223–250.

Neff, K. D., & Germer, C. K. (2013). A pilot study and randomized controlled trial of the mindful self-
compassion program. *Journal of Clinical Psychology*, 69(1), 28–44.

Niemiec, R. M. (2012). Mindful living: Character strengths interventions as pathways for the five
mindfulness trainings. *International Journal of Wellbeing*, 2(1), 22–33.

Niemiec, R. M., Rashid, T., & Spinella, M. (2012). Strong mindfulness: Integrating mindfulness and
character strengths. *Journal of Mental Health Counseling*, 34(3), 240–253.

Nishith, P., Mechanic, M. B., & Resick, P. A. (2000). Prior interpersonal trauma: The contribution to
current PTSD symptoms in female rape victims. *Journal of Abnormal Psychology*, 109(1), 20–25.

No Child Left Behind (NCLB) Act of 2001, Pub. L. No. 107-110, § 115, Stat. 1425 (2002).

Noddings, N. (2015). *The challenge to care in schools* (2nd ed.). New York: Teachers College Press.

Norton, B., Ferriegel, M., & Norton, C. (2011). Somatic expressions of trauma in experiential play
therapy. *International Journal of Play Therapy*, 20(3), 138–152.

Obomsawin, A. (1986). *Richard Cardinal: Cry from a diary of a Metis child* [Video file]. Montreal, Quebec:
National Film Board of Canada. Accessed at www.nfb.ca/film/richard_cardinal on February 2, 2019.

Olcoń, K., Kim, Y., & Gulbas, L. E. (2017). Sense of belonging and youth suicidal behaviors: What do
communities and schools have to do with it? *Social Work in Public Health*, 32(7), 432–442.

Olson, K., & Kemper, K. J. (2014). Factors associated with well-being and confidence in providing
compassionate care. *Journal of Evidence-Based Complementary and Alternative Medicine*, 19(4), 292–296.

Osher, D., Kidron, Y., Brackett, M., Dymnicki, A., Jones, S., & Weissberg, R. P. (2016). Advancing the
science and practice of social and emotional learning: Looking back and moving forward. *Review of
Research in Education*, 40(1), 644–681.

Osher, D., Kidron, Y., DeCandia, C. J., Kendziora, K., Weissberg, R. P., Wentzel, K. R., et al. (2016).
Interventions to promote safe and supportive school climate. In K. R. Wentzel & G. B. Ramani (Eds.),
Handbook of social influences in school contexts, emotional, motivation, and cognitive outcomes
(pp. 384–404). New York: Routledge.

Osterman, K. F. (2000). Students' need for belonging in the school community. *Review of Educational
Research*, 70(3), 323–367.

Owen, D., & Vista, A. (2017, November 15). Strategies for teaching metacognition in classrooms
[Blog post]. *Brookings*. Accessed at www.brookings.edu/blog/education-plus-development/2017/11/15
/strategies-for-teaching-metacognition-in-classrooms on December 1, 2018.

Palacio, R. J. (2012). *Wonder*. New York: Alfred A. Knopf.

Palmer, P. J. (2007). *The courage to teach: Exploring the inner landscape of a teacher's life* (10th anniversary
ed.). San Francisco: Jossey-Bass.

Palmer, P. J. (2014, July 10). Parker Palmer's thirteen ways of looking at community (. . . with a fourteenth thrown in for free) [Blog post]. *Center for Courage and Renewal*. Accessed at www .couragerenewal.org/13-ways-of-looking-at-community_parker-palmer on January 28, 2019.

Parker, A. E., & Kupersmidt, J. B. (2016). Two universal mindfulness education programs for elementary and middle-school students: Master mind and moment. In K. Schonert-Reichl & R. Roeser (Eds.), *Handbook of mindfulness in education: Integrating theory and research into practice* (pp. 335–354). New York: Springer.

Parkhill, M. R., & Pickett, S. M. (2016). Difficulties in emotion regulation as a mediator of the relationship between child sexual abuse victimization and sexual aggression perpetration in male college students. *Journal of Child Sexual Abuse, 25*(6), 674–685.

Pascoe, J. M., Wood, D. L., Duffee, J. H., & Kuo, A. (2016). Mediators and adverse effects of child poverty in the United States. *Pediatrics, 137*(4), e20160340.

Patel, C., & North, W. R. S. (1975). Randomised controlled trial of yoga and bio-feedback in management of hypertension. *The Lancet, 306*(7925), 93–95.

Paulson, S. (n.d.). *"I am because we are": The African philosophy of ubuntu.* Accessed at https://ttbook.org /interview/i-am-because-we-are-african-philosophy-ubuntu on January 31, 2020.

Paulson, S., Davidson, R., Jha, A., & Kabat-Zinn, J. (2013). Becoming conscious: The science of mindfulness. *Annals of the New York Academy of Sciences, 1303*(1), 87–104.

Pearson, G. (2009). Aristotle on the role of confidence in courage. *Ancient Philosophy, 29*(1), 123–137.

Pennsylvania Health Law Project. (2011). *Understanding "wraparound" services for children in health choices.* Accessed at www.phlp.org/wp-content/uploads/2011/11/Guide-to-Understanding-Wraparound-Services -Oct-20111.pdf on November 20, 2019.

Pennsylvania State University. (2010). *Researchers advocate kindness to combat bullying.* Accessed at https://medicalxpress.com/news/2010-04-advocate-kindness-combat-bullying.html on February 1, 2019.

Peterson, R. L., & Skiba, R. (2000). Creating school climates that prevent school violence. *Preventing School Failure: Alternative Education for Children and Youth, 44*(3), 122–129.

Piaget, J. (1950). *The psychology of intelligence.* New York: Routledge.

Pianta, R. C. (2001). *Student–teacher relationship scale* (professional manual). Lutz, FL: Psychological Assessment Resources.

Pianta, R. C., La Paro, K. M., Payne, C., Cox, M. J., & Bradley, R. (2002). The relation of kindergarten classroom environment to teacher, family, and school characteristics and child outcomes. *Elementary School Journal, 102*, 225–238.

Piers, E. V., Shemmassian, S. K., & Herzberg, D. S. (2016). *Piers-Harris Self-Concept Scale* (3rd ed.). Lutz, FL: Psychological Assessment Resources.

Pinger, L., & Flook, L. (2016). *What if schools taught kindness?* Accessed at https://greatergood.berkeley .edu/article/item/what_if_schools_taught_kindness on August 12, 2019.

Pinós-Pey, K. (2017). The social psychology of compassion and altruism. In J. Loizzo, M. Neale, & E. J. Wolf (Eds.). *Advances in contemplative psychotherapy: Accelerating healing and transformation* (pp. 89–101). London: Taylor & Francis.

Pollock, M. (2016). *What the polar explorers teach us about resiliency.* Accessed at www.weforum.org/agenda /2016/01/what-the-polar-explorers-teach-us-about-resilience on May 15, 2018.

Porter, J. F., & Critelli, J. W. (1992). Measurement of sexual aggression in college men: A methodological analysis. *Archives of Sexual Behavior, 21*(6), 525–542.

Poulin, M. J., Brown, S. L., Dillard, A. J., & Smith, D. M. (2013). Giving to others and the association between stress and mortality. *American Journal of Public Health, 103*(9), 1649–1655.

Presnell, D. (2018). Preventing and treating trauma, building resiliency: The movement toward compassionate schools in Watauga County, North Carolina. *North Carolina Medical Journal, 79*(2), 113–114.

Price-Mitchell, M. (2015). *Tomorrow's change makers: Reclaiming the power of citizenship for a new generation.* Bainbridge Island, WA: Eagle Harbor Publishing.

Prince-Embury, S. (2007). *Resiliency scales for children and adolescents: A profile of personal strength.* San Antonio, TX: Harcourt Assessment.

Raes, F., Pommier, E., Neff, K. D., & Van Gucht, D. (2011). Construction and factorial validation of a short form of the Self-Compassion Scale. *Clinical Psychology and Psychotherapy, 18*(3), 250–255.

Rainforth, M. V., Schneider, R. H., Nidich, S. I., Gaylord-King, C., Salerno, J. W., & Anderson, J. W. (2007). Stress reduction programs in patients with elevated blood pressure: A systematic review and meta-analysis. *Current Hypertension Reports, 9*(6), 520–528.

Rand, D. G., Greene, J. D., & Nowak, M. A. (2012). Spontaneous giving and calculated greed. *Nature, 489,* 427–430.

Rao, N., & Kemper, K. J. (2016). Online training in specific meditation practices improves gratitude, well-being, self-compassion, and confidence in providing compassionate care among health professionals. *Journal of Evidence-Based Complementary and Alternative Medicine, 22*(2), 237–241.

Rast, J., Bruns, E. J., Brown, E. C., Peterson, C. R., & Mears, S. L. (2007). *Impact of the wraparound process in a child welfare system: Results of a matched comparison study.* Unpublished program evaluation.

Rate, C. R., Clarke, J. A., Lindsay, D. R., & Sternberg, R. J. (2007). Implicit theories of courage. *Journal of Positive Psychology, 2*(2), 80–98.

Raub, J. (2004). Psychophysiologic effects of hatha yoga on musculoskeletal and cardiopulmonary function: A literature review. *Journal of Alternative and Complementary Medicine, 8*(6), 797–812.

Ravitch, D. (2016). *The death and life of the great American school system: How testing and choice are undermining education.* New York: Basic Books.

Reis, H. T., Sheldon, K. M., Gable, S. L., Roscoe, J., & Ryan, R. M. (2000). Daily well-being: The role of autonomy, competence, and relatedness. *Personality and Social Psychology Bulletin, 26*(4), 419–435.

Resnick, M. D., Bearman, P. S., Blum, R. W., Bauman, K. E., Harris, K. M., Jones, J., et al. (1997). Protecting adolescents from harm: Findings from the National Longitudinal Study on Adolescent Health. *Journal of the American Medical Association, 278*(10), 823–832.

Restorative Schools Vision Project. (2015). *Restorative justice (RJ)—social emotional learning (SEL)—narrative processes (NP).* Accessed at http://restorativeschoolsproject.org/wp-content/uploads/2015/10/Social-Emotional-Learning.pdf on November 17, 2019.

Reynard, A., Gevirtz, R., Berlow, R., Brown M., & Boutelle, K. (2011). Heart rate variability as a marker of self-regulation. *Applied Psychophysiology and Biofeedback, 36*(3), 209–215.

Rezek, C. A. (2012). A mind to manage. *International Journal of Leadership in Public Services, 8*(1), 33–38.

Rezek, C. A. (2013). *Mindfulness can improve leadership in times of instability.* Accessed at www.theguardian.com/public-leaders-network/2013/aug/14/mindfulness-develop-dynamic-leadership-instability on January 29, 2019.

Rich, S., & Cox, J. W. (2018). "What if someone was shooting?" *The Washington Post.* Accessed at www.washingtonpost.com/graphics/2018/local/school-lockdowns-in-america/on December 10, 2019.

Rimm-Kaufman, S., & Sandilos, L. (2011). *Improving students' relationships with teachers to provide essential supports for learning.* Accessed at www.apa.org/education/k12/relationships.aspx# on March 15, 2018.

Rivers Murphy, M. M. (2013). *A high quality service learning project: High school student learning experience.* Published doctoral dissertation, Northeastern University, Boston, MA.

Roberts, K. R. (n.d.). Awaken + rise up [Blog post]. *Kelly Rae Roberts.* Accessed at www.kellyraeroberts.com/awaken-rise-up on September 9, 2019.

Robertson-Kraft, C., & Duckworth, A. L. (2014). *True grit: Trait-level perseverance and passion for long-term goals predicts effectiveness and retention among novice teachers.* Accessed at www.ncbi.nlm.nih.gov /pmc/articles/PMC4211426 on August 12, 2019.

Robinson, M., Gould, S., & Lee, S. (2018). *There have been 154 mass shootings in the US so far in 2018— Here's the full list.* Accessed at www.businessinsider.com/how-many-mass-shootings-in-america-this -year-2018-2 on June 29, 2018.

Rodkin, P. C., & Gest, S. D. (2011). Teaching practices, classroom peer ecologies, and bullying behaviors among schoolchildren. In D. L. Espelage & S. Swearer (Eds.), *Bullying in North American schools* (2nd ed., pp. 75–90). New York: Routledge.

Rosenberg, M. (1965). *Society and the adolescent self-image.* Princeton, NJ: Princeton University Press.

Rossouw, P. J., & Rossouw, J. G. (2016). The Predictive 6-Factor Resilience Scale: Neurobiological fundamentals and organizational application. *International Journal of Neuropsychotherapy, 4*(1), 31–45.

Ryan, R. M., & Deci, E. L. (2000). Self-determination theory and the facilitation of intrinsic motivation, social development, and well-being. *American Psychologist, 55*(1), 68–78.

Ryan, T. (2012). *A mindful nation: How a simple practice can help us reduce stress, improve performance, and recapture the American spirit.* Carlsbad, CA: Hay House.

Ryan, T. G., & Ruddy, S. (2017). Restorative justice: A changing community response. *International Electronic Journal of Elementary Education, 7*(2), 253–262.

Rychly, L., & Graves. E. (2012). Teacher characteristics for culturally responsive pedagogy. *Multicultural Perspectives, 14*(1), 44–49.

Saakvitne, K. W., Gamble, S., Pearlman, L. A., & Lev, B. T. (2000). *Risking connection: A training curriculum for working with survivors of childhood abuse.* Baltimore, MD: Sidran Institute Press.

Sacks, V., & Murphey, D. (2018). *The prevalence of adverse childhood experiences, nationally, by state, and by race or ethnicity.* Accessed at www.childtrends.org/publications/prevalence-adverse-childhood-experiences -nationally-state-race-ethnicity on July 5, 2019.

Saltzman, A. (2014). *A still quiet place: A mindfulness program for teaching children and adolescents to ease stress and difficult emotions.* Oakland, CA: New Harbinger.

Schaafsma, M. (2017). *Learning kindness—through African American children's stories and experience.* Accessed at https://myemail.constantcontact.com/News-from-Center-for-Educational-Improvement .html?soid=1103736720061&aid=-aq8RpCUFwg on July 5, 2019.

Schaeffer, B. (2017). *What you should know about toxic stress.* Accessed at www.nami.org/Blogs/NAMI -Blog/August-2017/What-You-Should-Know-About-Toxic-Stress on October 1, 2018.

Schakohl, T. (2019). *Fact check: Did CS Lewis say, "Humility isn't thinking less of yourself–it's thinking of yourself less?"* Accessed at https://checkyourfact.com/2019/06/30/fact-check-cs-lewis-mere-christianity -humility-thinking-less-yourself/ on November 17, 2019.

Schaps, E. (2003). Creating a school community. *Educational Leadership, 60*(6), 31–33. Accessed at www.ascd.org/publications/educational-leadership/mar03/vol60/num06/Creating-a-School -Community.aspx on November 5, 2018.

Schmalzl, L., Powers, C., & Henje Blom, E. (2015). *Neurophysiological and neurocognitive mechanisms underlying the effects of yoga-based practices: Towards a comprehensive theoretical framework.* Accessed at www.frontiersin.org/articles/10.3389/fnhum.2015.00235/full on November 18, 2019.

Schneider, D. (2010). *Churchill leadership series: Behavior 7—A centered belief in himself and his abilities.* Accessed at www.scdigest.com/assets/Experts/Schneider_10-06-15.php on June 2, 2018.

Schonert-Reichl, K. A., Oberle, E., Lawlor, M. S., Abbott, D., Thomson, K., Oberlander, F., et al. (2015). Enhancing cognitive and social–emotional development through a simple-to-administer mindfulness-based school program for elementary school children: A randomized controlled trial. *Developmental Psychology, 51*(1), 52–66.

Schunk, D. H. (1989). Self-efficacy and cognitive achievement: Implications for students with learning problems. *Journal of Learning Disabilities, 22*(1), 14–22.

Sciberras, E., Lycett, K., Efron, D., Mensah, F., Gerner, B., & Hiscock, H. (2014). Anxiety in children with attention-deficit/hyperactivity disorder. *Pediatrics, 133*(5), 801–808.

Scott, J. (n.d.). Student ownership of education: Practicing democracy in schools. *Education Canada, 49*(2), 36–39. Accessed at www.edcan.ca/wp-content/uploads/EdCan-2009-v49-n2-Scott.pdf on June 5, 2018.

Search Inside Yourself Leadership Institute. (n.d.). *Developing self-confidence through meditation.* Accessed at https://siyli.org/resources/confidence-through-meditation on June 5, 2018.

Segerstrom, S. C., & Nes, L. S. (2007). Heart rate variability reflects self-regulatory strength, effort, and fatigue. *Psychological Science, 18*(3), 275–281.

Seligman, M. E. P., & Csikszentmihalyi, M. (2000). Positive psychology: An introduction. *American Psychologist, 55*(1), 5–14.

Semple, R. J., Droutman, V., & Reid, B. A. (2017). Mindfulness goes to school: Things learned (so far) from research and real-world experiences. *Psychology in the Schools, 54*(1), 29–52.

Senechal, J., Sober, T., Hope, S., Johnson, T., Burkhalter, F., Castelow, T., et al. (2016). *Understanding teacher morale.* Accessed at https://scholarscompass.vcu.edu/merc_pubs/56 on July 5, 2019.

Senge, P. (2006). *The fifth discipline: The art and practice of the learning organization.* New York: Doubleday.

Senge, P., Cambron-McCabe, N., Lucas, T., Smith, B., Dutton, J., & Kleiner, L. (2012). *Schools that learn: A fifth discipline fieldbook for educators, parents, and everyone who cares about education.* New York: Crown Business.

Senge, P. M., Scharmer, C. O., Jaworski, J., & Flowers, B. S. (2004). *Presence: Human purpose and the field of the future.* Cambridge, MA: The Society of Organizational Learning.

Seppala, E. (2013). *Science: The compassionate mind.* Accessed at www.psychologicalscience.org/observer/the-compassionate-mind on July 5, 2019.

Sergiovanni, T. J. (1999). *Building community in schools.* Hoboken, NJ: Wiley.

Seuffert, G. (2015). 4 ways to teach children to meet challenges with courage. *Seton Magazine.* Accessed at www.setonmagazine.com/homeschool/general-homeschooling/4-ways-teach-children-meet-challenges-courage on May 15, 2018.

Shapiro, D., & Shapiro, E. (2012, August 21). Meditate to boost your self-esteem [Blog post]. *HuffPost.* Accessed at www.huffpost.com/entry/meditation-self-esteem_b_1803862 on May 15, 2018.

Shapiro, S. L., Lyons, K. E., Miller, R. C., Butler, B., Vieten, C., & Zelazo, P. D. (2015). Contemplation in the classroom: A new direction for improving childhood education. *Educational Psychology Review, 27*(1), 1–30.

Sheinman, N. (2014). *Mindfulness with schools: Perspective and insights.* Presentation at Nan Tien Institute International Conference: Mindfulness, Education & Transformation; Berkley, Australia.

Sheinman, N., & Hadar, L. L. (2017). Mindfulness in education as a whole school approach: Principles, insights and outcomes. In T. Ditrich, R. Wiles, & B. Lovegrove (Eds.), *Mindfulness and education: Research and practice* (pp. 77–102). Newcastle, UK: Cambridge Scholars Publishing.

Shenk, J. W. (2005). *Lincoln's great depression.* Accessed at www.theatlantic.com/magazine/archive/2005/10/lincolns-great-depression/304247 on November 16, 2019.

Shonkoff, J. P. (2012). Leveraging the biology of adversity to address the roots of disparities in health and development. *Proceedings of the National Academy of Sciences, 109*(2), 17302–17307.

Shonkoff, J. P., Garner, A. S., Committee on Psychosocial Aspects of Child and Family Health, Committee on Early Childhood, Adoption, and Dependent Care, Siegel, B. S., Dobbins, M. I., et al. (2012). Early childhood adversity, toxic stress, and the role of the pediatrician: Translating developmental science into lifelong health. *Pediatrics, 129*(1), e224–e231.

Shonkoff, J. P., & Phillips, D. A. (2013). *From neurons to neighborhoods: the science of early childhood development.* Washington, DC: National Academy Press.

Siegel, C. G. (1995). *A handbook for school adjustment counselors/school social workers: A systemic perspective.* Pittsfield, MA: Author.

Silverthorne, S. (2010). *Mindful leadership: When east meets west.* Accessed at https://hbswk.hbs.edu/item/mindful-leadership-when-east-meets-west on July 5, 2019.

Singer, T., & Klimecki, O. M. (2014). Empathy and compassion. *Current Biology, 24*(18), R875–R878.

Sivanathan, N., Arnold, K. A., Turner, N., & Barling, J. (2004). Leading well: Transformational leadership and well-being. In P. A. Linley & S. Joseph (Eds.), *Positive psychology in practice* (pp. 241–255). Hoboken, NJ: Wiley.

Slawta, J., Bentley, J., Smith, J., Kelly, J., & Syman-Degler, L. (2008). Promoting healthy lifestyles in children: A pilot program of Be a Fit Kid. *Health Promotion Practice, 9*(3), 305–312.

Smith, J. (2016). *A psychologist says parents should do these 18 things to raise a more confident child.* Accessed at www.businessinsider.com/psychologist-explains-how-to-raise-a-more-confident-child-2016-11 on September 15, 2018.

Smith, J. (2018). Lee students join fight against hunger, stigma in their community. *Berkshire Eagle.* Accessed at www.berkshireeagle.com/stories/lee-students-join-fight-against-hunger-stigma-in-their-community,559603 on February 4, 2019.

Sodian, B., & Frith, U. (2008). Metacognition, theory of mind, and self-control: The relevance of high-level cognitive processes in development, neuroscience, and education. *Mind, Brain, and Education, 2*(3), 111–113.

Southern Education Foundation. (2015). *A new majority research bulletin: Low income students now a majority in our nation's public schools.* Accessed at www.southerneducation.org/publications/newmajority researchbulletin on August 19, 2019.

Sprecher, S., & Fehr, B. (2005). Compassionate love for close others and humanity. *Journal of Social and Personal Relationships, 22*(5), 629–651.

Steele, C. M., & Aronson, J. (1995). Stereotype threat and the intellectual test performance of African-Americans. *Journal of Personality and Social Psychology, 69,* 797–811.

Steele, C. M., & Aronson, J. (2004). *The stereotype threat.* Accessed at http://www.mtholyoke.edu/offices/comm/csj/092404/steele.shtml.

Steinem, G. (1993). *Revolution from within.* New York: Little, Brown.

Stevenson, S. (2012). There's magic in your smile: How smiling affects your brain [Blog post]. *Psychology Today.* Accessed at www.psychologytoday.com/us/blog/cutting-edge-leadership/201206/there-s-magic-in-your-smile on April 10, 2019.

Strauss, V. (2015). Revolt against high-stakes standardized testing growing—and so does its impact. *The Washington Post.* Accessed at www.washingtonpost.com on July 5, 2019.

Streeter, C. C., Gerbarg, P. L., Saper, R. B., Ciraulo, D. A., & Brown, R. P. (2012). Effects of yoga on the autonomic nervous system, gamma-aminobutyric-acid, and allostasis in epilepsy, depression, and post-traumatic stress disorder. *Medical Hypotheses, 78*(5), 571–579.

Substance Abuse and Mental Health Services Administration. (2012a). *Preventing suicide: A toolkit for high schools.* Rockville, MD: Author.

Substance Abuse and Mental Health Services Administration. (2012b). *Tips for talking with and helping children and youth cope after a disaster or traumatic event: A guide for parents, caregivers, and teachers.* Washington, DC: Author. Accessed at https://store.samsha.gov/product/tips-talking-helping-children-youth-cope-after-disaster-or-traumatic-event-guide-parents/sma12-4732 on October 18, 2019.

Sussman, S., Milam, J., Arpawong, T. E., Tsai, J., Black, D. S., & Wills, T. A. (2013). Spirituality in addictions treatment: Wisdom to know . . . what it is. *Substance Use & Misuse, 48*(12), 1203–1217.

Sze, J. A., Gyurak, A., Yuan, J. W., & Levenson, R. W. (2010). Coherence between emotional experience and physiology: Does body awareness training have an impact? *Emotion, 10*(6), 803–814.

Tatum, B. (1997). *Why are all the black kids sitting together in the cafeteria?* New York: Basic Books.

Taylor, R. D., Oberle, E., Durlak, J. A., & Weissberg, R. P. (2017). Promoting positive youth development through school-based social and emotional learning interventions: A meta-analysis of follow-up effects. *Child Development, 88*(4), 1156–1171.

Thompson, J. G. (2015, April 9). Thirty-three simple ways to be a more compassionate teacher [Blog post]. *Bam! Radio.* Accessed at www.bamradionetwork.com/edwords-blog/thirty-three-simple-ways-to-be-a-more-compassionate-teacher on March 18, 2018.

Thompson, J. G. (2018). *The first-year teacher's survival guide: Ready-to-use strategies, tools and activities for meeting the challenges of each school day* (4th ed.). San Francisco: Jossey-Bass.

Thompson, R. (2014). Stress and child development. *The Future of Children, 24*(1), 41–59.

Tigunait, P. R. (n.d.). *Yoga sutra 1.36-1.37.* Accessed at https://yogainternational.com/article/view/yoga-sutra-1-36-1-37-translation-and-commentary on November 13, 2019.

Time. (2003). The great survivor: Ernest Shackleton. Accessed at http://content.time.com/time/specials/packages/article/0,28804,1981290_1981354_1981610,00.html on October 18, 2019.

Tough, P. (2013). *How children succeed: Grit, curiosity, and the hidden power of character.* New York: Mariner Books.

Tough, P. (2016). *Helping children succeed: What works and why.* New York: Houghton Mifflin Harcourt.

Tremblay, M. S., Gray, C., Babcock, S., Barnes, J., Bradstreet, C. C., Darr, D., et al. (2015). Position statement on active outdoor play. *International Journal of Environmental Research and Public Health, 12*(6), 6475–6505.

Tung, R., Dalila Carlo, V. D., Colón, M., Del Razo, J. L., Diamond, J. B., Raynor, A. F., et al. (2015). *Promising practices and unfinished business: Fostering equity and excellence for black and Latino males.* Accessed at www.cce.org/files/PromisingPracticesUnfinishedBusiness_ES_FINAL.pdf on December 10, 2019.

TV Tropes. (n.d.). *Human-interest story.* Accessed at http://tvtropes.org/pmwiki/pmwiki.php/Main/HumanInterestStory on January 15, 2018.

Tye, J. (1998). *Never fear, never quit: A story of courage and perseverance.* New York: Dell.

U.S. Department of Health and Human Services. (2016). *Child maltreatment 2016.* Accessed at www.acf.hhs.gov/sites/default/files/cb/cm2016.pdf on July 5, 2019.

U.S. Department of Health and Human Services. (2019). *Child maltreatment 2017.* Washington, DC. Accessed at www.acf.hhs.gov/cb/research-data-technology/statistics-research/child-maltreatment on February 20, 2018.

Vagi, K. J., Olsen, E. O., Basile, K. C., & Vivolo-Kantor, A. M. (2015). Teen dating violence (physical and sexual) among US high school students: Findings from the 2013 National Youth Risk Behavior Survey. *JAMA Pediatrics, 169*(5), 474–482.

Vinay, A. V., Venkatesh, D., & Ambarish, V. (2016). Impact of short-term practice of yoga on heart rate variability. *International Journal of Yoga, 9*(1), 62–66.

Vollmann, W. T. (2010). *Poor people.* New York: HarperPerennial. (Original work published 2007)

Vygotsky, L. S. (1978). *Mind in society: The development of higher psychological processes.* Cambridge, MA: Harvard University Press.

Wade, R. Shea, J., Rubin, R., & Wood, J. (2014). Adverse childhood experiences of low-income urban youth. *Pediatrics, 134*(1), e13–e20.

Waldhelm, A. (2011). *Assessment of core stability: Developing practical models.* Unpublished doctoral dissertation, Louisiana State University, Baton Rouge. Accessed at https://digitalcommons.lsu.edu/gradschool_dissertations/1568 on November 15, 2018.

Wallace, N. E. (2006). *The kindness quilt.* New York: Marshall Cavendish.

Waller, W. (2014). *The sociology of teaching.* Eastford, CT: Martino Fine Books. (Original work published 1932)

Walter, U. M., & Petr, C. G. (2011). Best practices in wraparound: A multidimensional view of the evidence. *Social Work, 56*(1), 73–80.

Wang, M. T., & Holcombe, R. (2010). Adolescents' perceptions of school environment, engagement, and academic achievement in middle school. *American Educational Research Journal, 47*(3), 633–662.

Wanless, S. B., & Domitrovich, C. E. (2015). Readiness to implement school-based social-emotional learning interventions: Using research on factors related to implementation to maximize quality. *Prevention Science, 16*(8), 1037–1043.

Wartella, E., Lauricella, A. R., Cingel, D., & Connell, S. (2016). Children and adolescents: Television, computers, and media viewing. In H. Friedman (Ed.), *Encyclopedia of mental health* (pp. 272–278). Cambridge, MA: Academic Press.

Watkins, E. D., & Moulds, M. (2005). Distinct modes of ruminative self-focus: Impact of abstract versus concrete rumination on problem solving in depression. *Emotion, 5*(3), 319–328.

Washington State Office of Superintendent of Public Instruction. (2018). *Compassionate schools: The heart of learning and teaching.* Accessed at www.k12.wa.us/compassionateschools on June 1, 2019.

Waters, S., Lester, L., & Cross, D. (2014). How does support from peers compare with support from adults as students transition to secondary school? *Journal of Adolescent Health, 54*(5), 543–549.

Waxman, H. C., Gray, J. P., & Padron, Y. N. (2002). Resiliency among students at risk of academic failure. *Yearbook of the National Society for the Study of Education, 101*(2), 29–48.

Way, S. M. (2011). School discipline and disruptive classroom behavior: The moderating effects of student perceptions. *Sociological Quarterly, 52*(3), 346–375.

Weissberg, R. P., Durlak, J. A., Domitrovich, C. E., & Gullotta, T. P. (2015). Social and emotional learning: Past, present, and future. In J. A. Durlak, C. E. Domitrovich, R. P. Weissberg, & T. P. Gullotta (Eds.), *Handbook for social and emotional learning: Research and practice* (pp. 3–19). New York: Guilford Press.

Weng, H. Y., Fox, A. S., Shackman, A. J., Stodola, D. E., Caldwell, J. K., Olson, M. C., & Davidson, R. J. (2013). Compassion training alters altruism and neural responses to suffering. *Psychological Science, 24*(7), 1171–1180.

Welford, M. (2012). *The compassionate mind approach to building self-confidence.* London: Robinson.

Welford, M. (2013). *The power of self-compassion: Using compassion-focused therapy to end self-criticism and build confidence.* Oakland, CA: New Harbinger.

Wells, C. M. (2015). Conceptualizing mindful leadership in schools: How the practice of mindfulness informs the practice of leading. *Education Leadership Review of Doctoral Research, 2*(1), 1–23.

West Virginia Department of Education. (2014). *West Virginia Student Success Standards.* Accessed at https://wvde.state.wv.us/counselors/documents/WestVirginiaStudentSuccessStandards_FINAL2014.pdf on November 17, 2018.

Westera, W. (2011). On the changing nature of learning context: Anticipating the virtual extension of the world. *Educational Technology and Society, 14*(2), 201–212.

Wheeler, R. (2017). *Circling up for community building.* Accessed at www.edutopia.org/article/circling -community-building on August 12, 2019.

Williams, R. (2015). *Eye of the storm: How mindful leaders can transform chaotic workplaces.* Vancouver BC, Canada: Ray Williams Associates.

Wolpert, S. (2007). *Putting feelings into words produces therapeutic effects in the brain; UCLA neuroimaging effects study supports ancient Buddhist teachings.* Accessed at http://newsroom.ucla.edu/releases/Putting -Feelings-Into-Words-Produces-8047 on February 5, 2019.

Wolpow, R., Johnson, M., Hertel, R., & Kincaid, S. (2016). *The heart of learning and teaching: Compassion, resiliency, and academic success.* Olympia: Washington State Office of Public Instruction.

World Health Organization. (2010). *Socio-environmentally determined health inequities among children and adolescents*. Accessed at www.euro.who.int/__data/assets/pdf_file/0009/135891/e94866.pdf on July 5, 2019.

World Health Organization. (2012). *World health statistics: 2012*. Accessed at https://apps.who.int/iris /bitstream/handle/10665/44844/9789241564441_eng.pdf?sequence=1 on November 18, 2019.

Woodson, J. (2012). *Each kindness*. New York: Nancy Paulsen Books.

Wright, B. L., & Ford, D. Y. (2016). "This little light of mine": Creating early childhood education classroom experiences for African American boys PreK–3. *Journal of African American Males in Education, 7*(1), 5–19.

Wylson, A., & Chesley, J. A. (2016). *The benefits of mindfulness in leading transformational change*. Accessed at https://gbr.pepperdine.edu/2016/04/the-benefits-of-mindfulness-in-leading-transformational-change on January 5, 2018.

Young, K. (2016). *Hey Sigmund: How to build courage in kids*. Accessed at www.heysigmund.com/?s=how+ to+build+courage+in+kids on February 5, 2018.

Zardoya, I. (2017). What school leaders must learn about equity. *Education Week, 36*(1), 18.

Zelazo, P. D., & Lyons, K. E. (2012). The potential benefits of mindfulness training in early childhood: A developmental social cognitive neuroscience perspective. *Child Development Perspectives, 6*(2), 154–160.

Zenner, C., Herrnleben-Kurz, S., & Walach, H. (2014). *Mindfulness-based interventions in schools: A systematic review and meta-analysis*. Accessed at www.frontiersin.org/articles/10.3389/fpsyg.2014.00603 /full on November 18, 2019.

Zepeda, M., Varela, F., & Morales, A. (2004). *Promoting positive parenting practices through parenting education*. Accessed at https://files.eric.ed.gov/fulltext/ED496882.pdf on October 18, 2019.

Index

Mindfulness Practices
Christine Mason, Michele M. Rivers Murphy, and Yvette Jackson
Build compassionate school communities that prioritize high levels of learning and high levels of well-being. Based on the latest neuroscience research, *Mindfulness Practices* details how to use mindfulness to transform the way educators teach and students learn in preKindergarten through high school.
BKF833

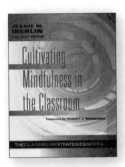

Cultivating Mindfulness in the Classroom
Jeanie M. Iberlin
Discover practical tools that align to the key categories of mindfulness benefits—stress reduction, attention, emotional control, positive self-concept, and positive interactions—and explore a step-by-step process for establishing a formal school or classroom mindfulness program.
BKL035

EMPOWER Your Students
Lauren Porosoff and Jonathan Weinstein
Discover how to use the elements of EMPOWER— exploration, motivation, participation, openness, willingness, empathy, and resilience—to make school a positive, meaningful experience in your students' lives. This highly practical resource offers engaging classroom activities and strategies for incorporating student values into curriculum.
BKF791

Two-for-One Teaching
Lauren Porosoff and Jonathan Weinstein
In *Two-for-One Teaching*, authors Lauren Porosoff and Jonathan Weinstein outline how to seamlessly incorporate social-emotional learning into academic classrooms. Empower students to discover what matters to them using research-based strategies that foster agency, community, self-reflection, and vitality in the classroom.
BKF923

"Tremendous, tremendous, tremendous!

The speaker made me do some very deep internal reflection about the **PLC process** and the personal responsibility I have in making the school improvement process work **for ALL kids.**"

—Marc Rodriguez, teacher effectiveness coach, Denver Public Schools, Colorado

PD Services

Our experts draw from decades of research and their own experiences to bring you practical strategies for building and sustaining a high-performing PLC. You can choose from a range of customizable services, from a one-day overview to a multiyear process.

Book your PLC PD today!
888.763.9045

Solution Tree